T0219867

Lecture Notes in Computer Science 10794

Commenced Publication in 1973
Founding and Former Series Editors:
Gerhard Goos, Juris Hartmanis, and Jan van Leeuwen

More information about this series at http://www.springer.com/series/7409

Giancarlo Fortino · A. B. M. Shawkat Ali
Mukaddim Pathan · Antonio Guerrieri
Giuseppe Di Fatta (Eds.)

Internet and Distributed Computing Systems

10th International Conference, IDCS 2017
Mana Island, Fiji, December 11–13, 2017
Proceedings

 Springer

Editors
Giancarlo Fortino
University of Calabria
Rende (CS)
Italy

A. B. M. Shawkat Ali
ilab Fiji
Lautoka
Fiji

Mukaddim Pathan
Telstra Corporation Limited
Melbourne, VIC
Australia

Antonio Guerrieri
ICAR-CNR
Rende (CS)
Italy

Giuseppe Di Fatta
University of Reading
Reading
UK

ISSN 0302-9743 ISSN 1611-3349 (electronic)
Lecture Notes in Computer Science
ISBN 978-3-319-97794-2 ISBN 978-3-319-97795-9 (eBook)
https://doi.org/10.1007/978-3-319-97795-9

Library of Congress Control Number: 2018950190

LNCS Sublibrary: SL3 – Information Systems and Applications, incl. Internet/Web, and HCI

This Springer imprint is published by the registered company Springer Nature Switzerland AG
The registered company address is: Gewerbestrasse 11, 6330 Cham, Switzerland

Preface

Following the previous nine successful editions of IDCS – IDCS 2008 in Khulna, Bangladesh, IDCS 2009 in Jeju Island, Korea, IDCS 2010 and IDCS 2011 in Melbourne, Australia, IDCS 2012 in Wu Yi Shan, China, IDCS 2013 in Hangzhou, China, IDCS 2014 in Calabria, Italy, IDCS 2015 in Windsor, UK, IDCS 2016 in Wuhan, China—IDCS 2017 was the tenth in the series to promote research in diverse fields related to the Internet and distributed computing systems.

"Health, Collaboration, Innovation, and Sustainability" are the main themes of our era. The Internet, including widespread use of mobile and wireless devices, has grown as a ubiquitous infrastructure to support the fast development of diversified services. The advents of the Internet of Things, cyber-physical systems, and big data are creating a new technology revolution, i.e., the next generation of the Internet or Industry 4.0. The integration of the digital world with the physical environment makes our world more intelligent and efficient. Large-scale networked intelligent systems require greater cooperation and interoperation of heterogeneous IoT platforms.

IDCS 2017 received papers on emerging models, paradigms, technologies, and novel applications related to Internet-based distributed systems, including Internet of Things, cyber-physical systems, wireless sensor networks, next-generation collaborative systems, extreme-scale networked systems, and cloud-based big data systems.

The audience included researchers and industry practitioners who were interested in different aspects of the Internet and distributed systems, with a particular focus on practical experiences with the design and implementation of related technologies as well as their theoretical perspectives.

IDCS 2017 received a large number of submissions from which 16 regular papers were accepted after a careful review and selection process. This year's conference also featured four invited talks: (1) "Experimental and CFD Studies to Optimize the Turbine System Applied to Wind, Hydro, and Marine Renewable Energy" by Professor Young-Ho Lee, Korea Maritime and Ocean University (KMOU), South Korea; (2) "Measurement-Oriented Machine Learning for Advanced Sensing Technologies" by Professor Takashi Washio, Osaka University, Japan; (3) "Distributed Generation Integration for Smart Grids" by Professor Hemanshu Pota, University of New South Wales, Australia; and (4) "Big Data — Big Application" by Professor Jinjun Chen, Swinburne University of Technology, Australia.

IDCS 2017 was held in the wonderful Mana Island Resort and Spa (Fiji Islands), in the heart of the Pacific Ocean. The conference organization was supported by the University of Fiji and Deakin University (Australia).

The successful organization of IDCS 2017 was possible thanks to the dedication and hard work of a number of individuals.

Specifically, we would like to thank Jashnil Kumar (Web Coordinator) for his commendable work with the conference organization. We also express our gratitude to the general chairs, Shawkat Ali, University of Fiji, Fiji, and Yang Xiang, Deakin University, Australia, and the conference chairs (Wenfeng Li, Rasib Khan, Giancarlo Fortino, Giuseppe Di Fatta, Mukaddim Pathan) for their support of the conference.

December 2017

Giancarlo Fortino
A. B. M. Shawkat Ali
Mukaddim Pathan
Antonio Guerrieri
Giuseppe Di Fatta

Organization

Honorary Conference Chairs

Rajkumar Buyya — University of Melbourne, Australia
Dimitrios Georgakopoulos — Swinburne University, Australia

General Chairs

A. B. M. Shawkat Ali — University of Fiji, Fiji
Yang Xiang — Deakin University, Australia

Conference Chairs

Wenfeng Li — Wuhan University of Technology, China
Rasib Khan — Northern Kentucky University, USA
Giancarlo Fortino — University of Calabria, Italy
Giuseppe Di Fatta — University of Reading, UK
Mukaddim Pathan — Telstra Corporation Limited, Australia

Technical Program Chairs

Christian Vecchiola — IBM Research, Australia
Xinyi Huang — Fujian Normal University, China
Domenico Rosaci — University of Reggio Calabria, Italy
Neeraj Sharma — The University of Fiji, Fiji

PhD Workshop Chair

Mengchu Zhou — New Jersey Institute of Technology, USA

Publicity and Industry Chairs

Surya Nepal — CSIRO, Australia
Yu Wang — Deakin University, Australia

Publications Chairs

Antonio Guerrieri — ICAR-CNR, Italy
M. G. M. Khan — The University of South Pacific, Fiji

Web Coordinator

Jashnil Kumar   The University of Fiji, Fiji

Steering Committee - IDCS Series

Jemal Abawajy   Deakin University, Australia
Rajkumar Buyya   University of Melbourne, Australia
Giancarlo Fortino   University of Calabria, Italy
Dimitrios Georgakopolous   RMIT University, Australia
Mukaddim Pathan   Telstra, Australia

Program Committee

Shawkat Ali   University of Fiji, Fiji
Gianluca Aloi   University of Calabria, Italy
Rajkumar Buyya   The University of Melbourne, Australia
Mert Bal   Miami University, USA
Jingjing Cao   Wuhan University of Technology, China
Xiaojiang Chen   Northwest University, China
Min Chen   Huazhong University of Science and Technology,
                            China
Massimo Cossentino   National Research Council of Italy
Zhicheng Dai   Huazhong Normal University, China
Marcos Dias De Assuncao   Inria Avalon, LIP, ENS de Lyon, France
Claudio De Farias   PPGI-IM/NCE-UFRJ
Jerker Delsing   Lulea University of Technology, Sweden
Giuseppe Di Fatta   University of Reading, UK
Sisi Duan   Oak Ridge National Laboratory, USA
Declan Delaney   University College Dublin, Ireland
Giancarlo Fortino   University of Calabria, Italy
Xiuwen Fu   Wuhan University of Technology, China
Joaquin Garcia-Alfaro   Telecom SudParis, France
Antonio Guerrieri   ICAR-CNR, Italy
Maria Ganzha   University of Gdańsk, Poland
Luca Geretti   University of Udine, Italy
Chryssis Georgiou   University of Cyprus, Cyprus
Raffaele Gravina   University of Calabria, Italy
John Gray   University of Manchester, UK
Bin Guo   Institut Telecom SudParis, France
Dimitrios Georgakopoulos   School of Computer Science and Information
                            Technology, Australia
Mohammad Mehedi Hassan   King Saud University, Saudi Arabia
Fazhi He   Wuhan University, China
Xiaoya Hu   Huazhong University of Science and Technology,
                            China

Youlun Xiong	Huazhong University of Science and Technology, China
Shengwu Xiong	Wuhan University of Technology, China
Xin-Qing Yan	North China University of Water Resources and Electric Power
Xiang Yang	Deakin University, VIC, Australia
Zhouping Yin	Huazhong University of Science and Technology, China
Norihiko Yoshida	Saitama University, Japan
Mengchu Zhou	New Jersey Institute of Technology, USA
Lanbo Zheng	Wuhan University of Technology, China

Contents

Issues and Concerns: Record Management in Cloud Service of Technology

Youngkon Lee[1(✉)] and Ukhyun Lee[2(✉)]

[1] e-Business Department, Korea Polytechnic University, Siheung, Korea
yklee777@kpu.ac.kr
[2] School of IT Convergence Engineering,
Shinhan University, Dongducheon, Korea
uhlee@shinhan.ac.kr

Abstract. Recently, a lot of companies are increasingly introducing cloud services for digital records management. The cloud services can dramatically lower the cost of archiving and managing digital records and provides a foundation for resilient management of digital records management, depending on the circumstances of the enterprise. However, due to the nature of service provided by third parties in the cloud, conflicting the nature of digital records and the intrinsic risks inherent in the cloud, many companies are reluctant to apply the cloud to their digital records management right away. In this paper, we analyze the risk factors of the digital records in the cloud services and discuss some alternative models to solve them.

Keywords: Cloud service · Record management · Risk management
SOA

1 Introduction

Cloud service refers to a service where users borrow as much as needed to pay the cost for amount you have used through the internet (network) on the IT resources such as computing, storage, software and network. Cloud services are emerging as the essential issue in the information technology due to location-independent resource sharing, availability via the Internet and mobile, on-demand services, and low cost.

Using cloud services, there are advantages of drastic cost reduction and preparation of new business foundation. Cost savings are made possible by economy of scale through cloud services, lowering initial investment costs for system implementation, dynamic scalability and usage-based billing. By introducing cloud services, enterprise agility could be dramatically improved by minimizing the time it takes to prepare computing resources and by convenience of use. In addition, the flexibility, resiliency, scalability and disaster prevention of cloud services greatly enhance the competitiveness of enterprises.

Currently, the explosive growth of digital contents including mobile, IoT and SNS is driving most businesses to quickly move their computing system to cloud services, and also is quickly moving e-documents and digital records to the cloud. In the near future, most digital records will be surely produced, preserved and utilized based on

G. Fortino et al. (Eds.): IDCS 2017, LNCS 10794, pp. 1–12, 2018.
https://doi.org/10.1007/978-3-319-97795-9_1

cloud services. A number of companies and government organizations have already shifted their on-premise business system to cloud services.

However, the reason why a lot of companies are still reluctant to adopt cloud in their record management is about safety and reliability problem of record management in cloud services, and risks due to lack of application examples. While the advantages of cloud services are well-known published, the disadvantages of cloud services, especially of the record management by cloud services, are not revealed clearly and most concern points that should be taken in using cloud services are buried.

The cloud service is essentially a type of service provided by a service provider, and all business rules and system operating rules are determined by the service provider. Therefore, if the business rules of the service provider or the system operation rule cannot meet the management criterion to satisfy the basic attribute requirement of the record, this means that the record management by the cloud service fails. Cloud data storages are more suited to flexible provisioning to meet dynamic enterprise needs than stability, and may be inherently unsuitable for long-term data retention. Problems with data privacy often occur while sharing data stores or applications between users. Also, due to the nature of the cloud service, the cloud service layer is becoming specialized, and the role of the service provider is being divided. In other words, as the cloud service is divided such as cloud providing only infrastructure, cloud service providing platform only, and cloud service providing only application, records management business becomes possible by the combination of these divided services. As a result, it is very difficult to ensure the consistency and quality of records management tasks.

The cloud service could also have social and legal issues such as personal information protection or law enforcement for data access. For example, because physical location of users and cloud service providers are ambiguous by virtualization of their hardware and network, it is ambiguous what country or area laws should be followed when government agencies want to access data stored in the cloud. Technological security issues are becoming serious because of the relatively easy leakage and loss of digital records due to unanticipated access by third parties other than the owner in the cloud service base. In addition, when personal information is leaked and disclosed among the digital records stored in the cloud, there could be legal risk factors such as personal information infringement.

In order to avoid or minimize these various issues and concerns, we need a governance system that governs holistically records management on the cloud service. To make governance, it is necessary to identify and analyze all the possible risks and issues that may arise from all concerned parties and systems in the record management life-cycle on the cloud service. In addition, by analyzing the pros and cons of various use cases that utilize cloud service for digital record management, it enables to prepare against risk factors in advance. Providing a reference architecture that can be referred to perform cloud record management will also help to reduce the risk of cloud record management.

This paper presents a cloud record management reference model that can be applied to records management based on representative cloud service architecture, as a preliminary step to create a cloud record management governance system. It also presents various records management use cases that utilize cloud services and also issues and concerns to be aware of when managing cloud records from a structural, systematic, user, social, and legal perspective.

2 Related Works and Research Model

Cloud record management has been conducted mainly in developed countries to provide practical guidelines under government initiative. The UK National Archives investigated cloud record management practices using digital cloud records and digital cloud records [1, 2]. In the United States, an digital record management guide that utilizes cloud computing has been developed and referenced in the course of performing cloud computing tasks [3]. Australia has developed guidelines for managing records management risks related to cloud computing and has developed cloud service certification requirements and guidelines for outsourcing digital data archiving [4]. These studies were developed as guidelines for storing national records in the cloud and did not provide systematic analysis of risk factors or issues.

This paper analyzes the roles and responsibilities of cloud stakeholders and the legal and social environmental factors of the cloud. Also, for public cloud architecture, we present use case analysis and reference architecture that can be used in public environment. Based on the analyzed results, the issues and concerns that may arise in using cloud digital records are presented (Fig. 1).

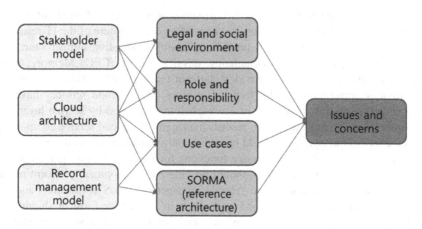

Fig. 1. Research model for cloud record management

3 Lifecycle Management and SORMA Architecture

3.1 Lifecycle Management for Cloud Digital Record

In addition to the requirements for records management in existing on-premise systems, there are more requirements for cloud management in order to manage records using cloud services. From the stage of creating the cloud digital record to the step of transmitting and storing the record to the cloud server and discarding the record kept in the cloud when the retention period is over, there are requirements necessary to manage the digital record securely and reliably at each step. Some cases may need to relocate digital records between cloud servers or use backup data to recover. In these processes, there are basically necessary requirements because it is cloud digital recording in each step as follows:

- Creation: In the cloud services, digital record should be created and managed in a way that ensures the authenticity and reliability of digital records.
- Distribution: Digital records create on the client side should be able to be transmitted to the cloud server securely, reliably and in a way of preserving integrity.
- Preservation: IaaS services should be provided to safely and reliably store digital records in the long term as third party repositories. Records stored redundantly in cloud storage should always be traceable.
- Migration: When records are migrated from one cloud storage to another, there should not be a change in the record due to the difference in the cloud architecture. After the migration, all records that were redundantly stored in the cloud storage should be completely disposed.
- Backup: Backup methods and plans for back up long-term archives in the cloud should be presented by cloud service providers.

3.2 SORMA Architecture for Reliable Digital Record Management

Cloud services are classified into IaaS (Infrastructure as a Service), PaaS (Platform as a Service), and SaaS (Software as a Service) depending on the nature of the IT resources they provide. IaaS is a service that provides a flexible computing infrastructure to a large number of customers by virtualizing physical server (CPU, Memory, O/S), storage, and network, and PaaS provides platform (such as OS or DB) as a service. SaaS provides applications in the form of services. These cloud services have the service components that are needed to accomplish their mission by service layer.

In order to apply cloud service to records management, special service components needed for record management should be additionally implemented. In the SaaS layer, the user needs to develop the necessary functions for the records management in the form of application. The PaaS layer should provide the development platform necessary for the implementation of the records management SaaS application and the functions for managing the developed application in the service form. It should also provide services for managing APIs and services (such as DB services) required for application development. IaaS should provide services to secure records for long term preservation. Services related to escalation or revocation of archived records should also be provided, and backup and recovery of archival storage should be provided in case of an emergency.

The cloud is strictly service-based and is based on Service Oriented Architecture (SOA). All computing resources, software, platforms, middleware and databases are provided in a form service. This technical report presents a Service Oriented Record Management Architecture (SORMA) reference architecture that combines SOA and RMS, and enables organizations or companies to refer to the development of cloud-based RMS.

- SORMA SaaS service is composed of services that constitute the digital record management application used by clients, and includes services such as acquisition, conversion, authentication and archiving.

- SORMA PaaS service is a service that provides all sorts of the necessary platforms to create and run a records management SaaS such as security, authentication, application development platform, application management and execution, and IaaS control and interface.
- SORMA IaaS service is a layer that provides services related to storage, archive, backup and disposal of digital records into the storage.

4 Stakeholder Model for Cloud Record Management

4.1 Client for Cloud Record Management

Enterprises and institutional digital record producers shall use cloud SaaS services to create digital records according to methods and systems that ensure the authenticity and reliability of digital records based on record management principles. Digital record producers shall be able to produce reliable digital records. Reliable records are the ones that can be trusted as complete and accurate representations of duties, activities and facts, etc. that the records are intended to demonstrate and can be relied upon to demonstrate their content in the course of subsequent work or activities.

Digital record production organizations shall establish and implement policies and procedures to manage production, receipt, transmission, maintenance and disposal of digital records in order to guarantee the authenticity of records. This shall authorize and confirm the production of digital records to ensure that digital records cannot be added, deleted, modified, used or concealed without permission.

Produced digital records shall be protected from unauthorized changes. In policies and procedures of recording, what to add or write to records once produced, under what conditions to permit additions or recordings, and to whom the access of adding or recording will be granted, shall be specified.

Contextual linkage information in records should include the information necessary to understand the action where records have been produced and used. Records shall be identifiable even in the context of broader categories of business activities and functions. It is desirable to maintain a linkage between records that have documented the activities performed in a sequential manner.

4.2 Cloud Service Providers

Cloud service providers shall be classified as IaaS providers, PaaS providers, and SaaS providers depending on the level of the cloud service layer, and they should be given roles and quality assurance to perform safe and reliable digital record management.

A SaaS provider may have its own SaaS software, or a SaaS delegate (agency) may act as a SaaS provider. The SaaS provider shall make an effort to enter into service level agreement (SLA) service quality management contract with the client and maintain the quality level accordingly. To make this possible, there shall be a mutual agreement on the SLA items to maintain the quality of service between the SaaS provider and the client.

The SaaS application shall have the function to take the digital records from the client in a form of information package, store it in IaaS in the form of archiving package, and manage the related metadata in a secure, fault-tolerant manner.

SaaS providers end up trying to fulfill their contractual arrangements with clients using these applications. The metadata items related to the items of the reliable information package under cloud environment also shall be established.

The role of the PaaS provider is to provide a platform to create and operate a record-keeping SaaS with stability and reliability [4]. It shall strive to maintain the functions and quality standards that the PaaS provider shall provide for digital records.

The role of the IaaS provider is to provide a trusted storage to keep the records [5]. With virtualization, it shall be able to stably store digital record metadata and digital records even if there is a change in record storage server or storage. IaaS providers shall be given roles and management items that shall be performed for secure and reliable digital records management in a distributed and virtualized storage area (Fig. 2).

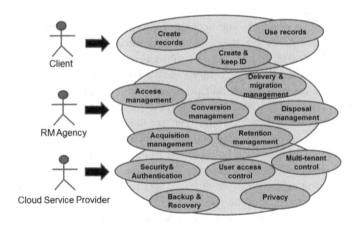

Fig. 2. Stakeholder model for cloud record management

5   Use Cases for Cloud Record Management

Various use cases analyses for cloud digital record management may occur depending on the stakeholder using cloud digital record and the type of cloud service used for digital record. This section will present advantages, disadvantages and risk factors according to the use cases.

5.1   SaaS Application Shared by Clients

This is the most common form of performing digital recording duties using cloud service [6]. A client performs digital record management duties using SaaS style RM application. RM Application is provided as a form of online software and has partially modified or changed user interface on the software configuration by the request of client (Fig. 3).

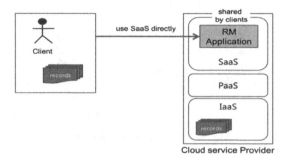

Fig. 3. SaaS application shared by clients

5.2 SaaS Application Shared by Clients

This use case is an instance where a client uses RM application by developing directly based on PaaS [7]. A client develops RM application as a form he or she desires and uses as a form of on premise by mounting on a PaaS. This usually has the purpose of developing and operating an RM software as a form for companies or institutions with certain scale or greater to satisfy their own requirements (Fig. 4).

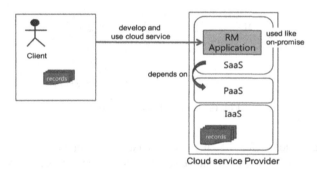

Fig. 4. SaaS application developed by a client

5.3 IaaS Just Used by a Client

This is a use case where client uses only IaaS on digital record management [8]. Since IaaS is the most inexpensive method to utilize computer hardware resources, it is a form of storing enormous amount of digital record into IaaS and performing most of other digital recording duties at the client side (Fig. 5).

Such method has advantage in that client is able to eliminate computer rooms, computer servers and server workers, etc. requiring a lot of maintenance costs within an institution through the cloud while maintaining unique digital recording duties and software as they are for the most part. This method could be considered as having advantage of being able to minimize various risk factors that cloud has while minimizing the shock followed by the introduction of cloud in digital recording duties.

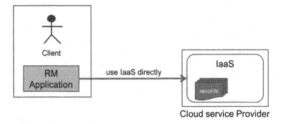

Fig. 5. IaaS just used by a client

However, the interface between existing RM application and IaaS shall continue to be managed while delicate control and monitoring on of IaaS storage medium by RM application may be very difficult. Also, if the digital record storing policy between the client and the IaaS service provider are in conflict with each other, it may be difficult to find a clue to the solution (Fig. 6).

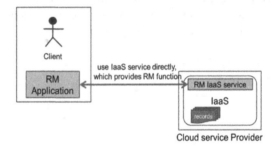

Fig. 6. IaaS with RM functions

Some special clouds for digital record management implements a basic function related to RM inside the cloud to enable cloud to utilize cloud more easily through this function. This basic function provides an interface to handle duties such as search, storage, transfer and destruction, etc. of digital record to enable clients to interwork with IaaS more easily.

6   Risk Factors in Cloud Record

6.1   Cloud Service Risk Factors

The cloud basically has a configuration based on a service-oriented architecture (SOA). Therefore, the cloud digital record management has almost the same risks as SOA. The risk factors followed by inherence of SOA in the cloud are as follows:

- Internal logic, management, and activity cannot be seen from being hidden inside the service
- Difficult to know the best method to use the service

- Difficult to identify the root cause of the problem
- Service provider-centered structure. Therefore, it can only be dependent on the service provider
- There shall be clear conditions for e-Discovery
- Difficult to know how to manage internal services
  Functions essential for digital record management may not be provided

Cloud service technology is very fast changing, and there are many standards, products, and related committees. There is always the possibility that business continuity will be violated due to changes in cloud technology, changes in cloud service providers, or changes in standards. In other words, there is always the possibility of changing cloud service. Provisioning which quickly provisions computing resources according to the clients' demand in the cloud service is one of the most important advantages of the cloud. However, provisioning may act as a risk for stable and long-term digital record keeping, and may act as a factor to hinder reliability of digital records in gear with data ownership issues and the characteristics of cloud data that gets stored by regional distribution.

6.2   Cloud Service Providers

Cloud is a type of service where multiple multi-tenants share a pool of computing resources. Therefore, the risk of disclosure of important information or personal information, or the privacy problem of the individual institutional record management system, may occur.

Client authentication is a starting point for secure and reliable cloud record management, and strict management of access rights to applications, usage levels, and digital record ownership is essential.

There is always a need for client authentication methods to maintain the reliability of cloud digital records, access rights management based on authentication, use level management, ownership management, and preparation against privacy breach and security threats.

6.3   Cloud System Risk Factors

In a cloud environment, there is a need for measures to cope with virtualization, which can affect server virtualization, storage virtualization, and network virtualization. Server virtualization and provisioning affect the performance, availability management, and backup recovery management of digital records management.

Storage location of digital records due to storage virtualization, risk due to distributed processing, and risk of loss of metadata due to changes in configuration management. There are also security threats due to security and access risks due to network virtualization, and digital record multi-tenancy (IaaS, PaaS, and SaaS) environment. Multi-Tenancy is a technology that allows multiple tenants to share an application, while at the same time configuring an individual usage environment. It is an essential technology for client customized application configuration, while retaining performance in the nature of cloud services. However, the core information of the application needs to be shared, and the customized script is easily exposed, making it relatively vulnerable to security. Therefore, it is necessary to diagnose the risk due to multi-tenancy for each layer, and to define the management items necessary for maintaining secure and reliable digital records.

The digital record metadata includes both the business context and the descriptive data of the digital record. Metadata takes up a very important position in search and utilization of digital records. Because of the nature of cloud services, there is no guarantee that metadata and digital records will always be stored in the same storage as the server, and one may suffer from various problems such as link loss, consistency issues due to distributed processing, and incorrect link information. Therefore, a linkage system between metadata writing and digital recording appropriate for cloud service type is absolutely necessary.

The safe and fault-tolerant metadata and digital record storage and utilization plan according to the configuration change of cloud service server or storage configuration is needed.

Cloud uses a method of distributing a single file across multiple servers or storage in terms of resource availability. In other words, cloud is based on storing files in a multiple distribution style. Ensuring consistency and integrity of multiple stored files, completeness of disposition and disposal, and retrieval and utilization of legitimate data can be a difficult problem. In such cases, the master copy shall be determined for multiple copies and shall serve as a copy of the original. If the content of one of the copies is unintentionally changed, delete this and make a copy using the master copy again. Authenticity and integrity of digital records are very difficult to maintain in a typical cloud environment, and there is also a need to require fundamental structural changes in cloud services.

When digital records are distributed across cloud services, there is a need to define the administrative and functional requirements that shall be followed to ensure authenticity and integrity of the document. Cloud is a system in which a large number of users share computing resources. Therefore, computing resources are easily exposed and have a structure that cannot emphasize only security in terms of performance and convenience. Therefore, systems and regulations are required for the following security items:

- Security policy,
- Security organization/operation,
- Personnel security in institutions,
- Assets and controls,
- Accident management procedures,
- Service continuity,
- Security compliance,
- Malware response,
- Access control,
- Service security,
- User access management,
- Management of access rights,
- Encryption of personal information,

- Prevention of forgery and falsification,
- User authentication.

Cloud services consist of relatively rapidly changing technological elements and service providers are also trying to introduce improved technologies sooner. If a cloud-based digital record system cannot keep up with the development pace of the cloud, it can quickly become old-fashioned within the cloud. If the adopted cloud takes the rate of change slowly, the digital recording system may lock-in to the cloud. As the digital record system becomes dependent on cloud services, it will be structured to accommodate the changes in policy and technology of cloud service providers. There needs to be a way to identify these risk factors and to avoid the cloud lock - in phenomenon while keeping pace with the current technology in the digital records system in the cloud.

In digital document transfer using cloud shared storage, it shall be able to transfer by maintaining structure and contextual relationship of the digital records and corresponding metadata. There is a risk of loss of metadata link and corruption of contextual relationship due to virtualization. In the case of the acquisition of digital records consisting of several components, it is necessary to maintain the relationship between the components so that they can be managed as a single record.

7 Conclusion

In this paper, we analyzed the risk factors of digital records in the cloud. The risk factors come from the fact that the cloud is essentially a service type, problems caused by the cloud system and service providers, and legal/social problems that the cloud has intrinsically. These problems can potentially cause major problems in cloud digital records management, and are becoming a major source of corporate reluctance to apply the cloud to digital records. In order to solve these problems, quality control of cloud digital record service based on SLA should be preceded, and overall governance system should be established for cloud service provider, organization and business.

References

1. Na, J.: Qualitative study on service features for cloud computing. J. Digit. Contents Soc. **12** (3), 319–327 (2011)
2. Qiu, M.M., Zhou, Y., Wang, C.: Systematic analysis of public cloud service level agreements and related business values. In: Proceedings of International Conference on Services Computing, pp. 729–736, June 2013
3. Wu, C., Zhu, Y., Pan, S.: The SLA evaluation model for cloud computing. In: Proceedings of International Conference on Computer, Networks and Communication Engineering, pp. 331–334, May 2013
4. Badidi, E.: A cloud service broker for SLA-based SaaS provisioning. In: Proceedings of International Conference on Information Society, pp. 61–66, June 2013

5. Venticinque, S., Aversa, R., Di Martino, B., Rak, M., Petcu, D.: A cloud agency for SLA negotiation and management. In: Guarracino, M.R., et al. (eds.) Euro-Par 2010. LNCS, vol. 6586, pp. 587–594. Springer, Heidelberg (2011). https://doi.org/10.1007/978-3-642-21878-1_72

6. Wang, Z., Tang, X., Luo, X.: Policy-based SLA-aware cloud service provision framework. In: Proceedings of International Conference on Semantics Knowledge and Grid, pp. 114–121, October 2011

7. He, H., Ma, Z., Chen, H., Shao, W.: Towards an SLA-driven cache adjustment approach for applications on PaaS. In: Proceedings of the Asia-Pacific Symposium on Internetware, pp. 11–20, October 2013

8. Ayadi, I., Simoni, N., Aubonnet, T.: SLA approach for "Cloud as a Service". In: Proceedings of International Conference on Cloud Computing, pp. 966–967. IEEE Computer Society, June 2013

9. Alhamad, M., Dillon, T., Chang, E.: Conceptual SLA framework for cloud computing. In: Proceedings of International Conference on Digital Ecosystems and Technologies, pp. 606–610, April 2010

Dynamic Service Migration via Approximate Markov Decision Process in Mobile Edge-Clouds

Zhuoling Chen[1], Hong Yao[1], Lin Gu[2(✉)], Deze Zeng[1], and Kun Zheng[1]

[1] School of Computer Science,
China University of Geosciences, Wuhan, Hubei, China
[2] School of Computer Science and Technology,
Huazhong University of Science and Technology, Wuhan, China
lingu@hust.edu.cn

Abstract. By hosting cloud-based services at the network edge, mobile edge cloud has shown great advantage in reducing network overhead and latency of cloud services. In large scale mobile edge cloud, service migration is inevitable with the users movements, to guarantee service quality and reduce service cost. Due to the uncertainty of the users movements, it is very challenging to find the optimal migration strategy. In this paper, we study the problem of dynamic service migration in the mobile edge cloud for cost minimization. We formulate the problem as a Markov Decision Process (MDP) problem, which captures general cost models and provides a mathematical framework to design optimal service migration policies. However, solving the MDP problem suffers from the curse of dimensionality. To deal with this problem, we further exploit the special structure of the problem and propose an approximate MDP-based dynamic service migration method, which reduces the dimension of state space from a multi-dimensional mobility pattern to a two-dimensional mobility pattern. The extensive simulation and numerical results show that the approximate MDP method significantly reduces the cost of migration and transmission.

1 Introduction

Mobile applications offer a fast and convenient way for information access and has become a primary way in globe communication. It is reported that there will be 4.4 billion mobile application users in 2017, representing about 58.7% of the global population. These mobile applications are typically comprised of a front-end component running on the mobile device and a back-end component performing data processing and computation on the cloud. However, with the growing popularity of mobile applications, the huge-volume data traffic between the front-end and the back-end has not only caused a heavy burden of communication bandwidth, but also led to intolerable transmission delays and degraded service to end users [1]. In addition to real-time interaction and low latency,

© Springer Nature Switzerland AG 2018
G. Fortino et al. (Eds.): IDCS 2017, LNCS 10794, pp. 13–24, 2018.
https://doi.org/10.1007/978-3-319-97795-9_2

supporting for mobility and geographic distribution is critical as mobile users and traffic become today's mainstream [2]. To address these challenges, a new emerging concept, known as mobile edge computing (MEC), has been delivered and become a promising technology. By utilizing the network edge MEC can host data processing on edge infrastructure distributed across the network [3].

Nowadays, MEC is widely regarded as a promising platform to facilitate the following services: (i) services requiring very low latency, e.g., online gaming, video conferencing, vehicular applications, e-health applications; (ii) geographically distributed services, e.g., Internet-of-Things (IoT) services; and (iii) large-scale distributed control systems, e.g., intelligent transportation systems, smart grid [4]. The great potential of MEC has raised much attention in both academia and industry. Many well-known related terms or concepts therefore have been proposed, such as Fog Computing [4], Cloudlets [5], and Follow Me Cloud [6].

One of the key issue in MEC is service management, such as service placement, service migration and task scheduling. In this paper, we focus on the issue of service migration that how to adapt the service location according to the user location change during user movement at runtime. Specially, we consider the scenario that a service is shared by a group of geo-distributed users, who can access the service with different transmission cost mainly determined by the distances between the service and the users. This raises the trade-off between the service migration cost and the transmission cost. Due to uncertainty in user mobility as well as possible non-linearity of the migration and transmission costs, it is challenging to find the optimal decision of the migration towards total cost minimization.

To address this problem, we use the Markov Decision Process (MDP) framework to study the dynamic service migration problem in the MECs. We notice that the first-order transition probability of the user location is quasi-static for long period and non-uniformly distributed. With respect to such fact, Markov chain model has been regarded as an effective tool to capture the temporal correlations of the locations. Consequently, we adopt the Markov chain model to study the dynamic service migration problem. In particular, we jointly investigate the service migration cost and transmission cost during user movement. The main contributions of this paper are summarized as follows:

- We formulate the dynamic service migration problem as an MDP problem to design optimal service migration policy objective to minimizing the long-term total cost.
- As using the traditional MDP method to solve our problem will produce a state space dimension that is too large to solve, we further propose an approximate MDP-based dynamic service migration to avoid the curse of dimensionality, and reduce the dimension of state space from multi-dimensional mobility pattern to two-dimensional mobility pattern.
- We conduct extensive simulations to validate the performance of our proposed method and compare the proposed method with other strategies that including never-migrate, myopic [7], and always-migrate policies.

The rest of this paper is organized as follows. Section 2 presents the related work in mobile edge-cloud dynamic service migration. We describe the system model and formulate the dynamic service migration problem in Sect. 3. In Sect. 4, we propose optimal and approximate algorithms for the problem. Simulations are conducted in Sect. 5 with numerical results, and we draw concluding remarks in Sect. 6.

2   Related Work

The general problem of service migration in cloud computing systems has been considered in several recent works. Specifically, Goswami et al. [8] focus on service migration due to the dynamic nature of the clouds. Tao et al. [9] find a way to reduce the cost of cloud computing platform by migrating the VM. Han et al. [10] study a dynamic VM migration model because of dynamic resource demands from VMs in data centers, where the average power consumption and the resource shortage over a long period are considered. Later, Wang et al. [11] considers virtual machine (VM) migration planning in data center network, where the problem of how to schedule multiple VMs migration and how to distribute the network bandwidth is researched.

However, the above works only study migration problem on traditional cloud systems and not consideri user mobility which has become a key factor in MECs. Mach et al. [12] investigate the performance of MECs, where the works focusing on mobility management and particularly on the VM migration consider mostly a scenario when only the users share a single computing node. Ksentini et al. [13] focus on deciding on the policy by considing a tradeoff between migration cost and user perceived quality based on Markov Decision Process of one-dimensional (1-D) mobility pattern. Later on, Bokani et al. [14] further develop an MDP method in vehicular environment, where the optimal control strategy of HTTP-based adaptive streaming is needed due to network bandwidth variation. However, these studies mainly consider one-dimensional (1-D) mobility pattern with a specifically defined cost function. Therefore, Wang et al. [7] further consider a two-dimensional (2-D) mobility pattern, where the MDP problem of two-dimensional (2-D) mobility model is approximatively solved by the distance-based MDP of one-dimensional (1-D) mobility pattern. However, it only considers a single user situation and multiple users' multi-dimensional mobility pattern is not studied. In this paper, instead of considering one-user-one-service, we consider the scenario that a service is shared by multiple mobile users.

3   Problem Formulation

3.1   System Model

We consider an MEC where multiple mobile users share a cloud service. As shown in Fig. 1, we assume there are N users and let $L = \{m_1, m_2, m_3, ..., m_{|L|}\}$

denotes the set of possible locations, where each location $m \in L$ is associated with an MEC that can host the service. We adopt a slotted scheduling framework where time is divided into a sequence of time-slots. During a time-slot, the location of user l is fixed. Only at the beginning of next time-slot, the location of user l may change. In a time-slot, the service can be placed on any MEC. We denote $u_l(t)$ and $s(t)$ as locations of the user l and service at the time-slot t, respectively, where $s(t), u_l(t) \in L$. We use $\boldsymbol{U}(t) = [u_1(t), u_2(t), ..., u_N(t)] \in \Phi$ as the aggregation of all users' locations at time-slot t, where Φ is the set of all possible $\boldsymbol{U}(t)$. Let $\Phi = \{\eta_1, \ldots, \eta_{|\Phi|}\}$. We have $\boldsymbol{\eta}_i = [\eta_{i,1}, \ldots, \eta_{i,N}]$ as a vector of the all user locations and $\boldsymbol{\eta}_i \in \Phi$, where $\eta_{i,l}$ is the user l's location at state η_i.

At the beginning of time-slot t, because all users will be connected to the currently service instance that is hosted in location $s(t)$, and certain transmission costs between users and service will be incurred. In order to decrease the transmission costs from all users, we can migrate the service to a suitable location $s'(t)$ at the beginning of time-slot t. When the service is migrated from one location $s(t)$ to another location $s'(t) \in L$, certain migration cost $c_m(x)$ will be incurred, where we assume that migration can be completed in a time-slot. Base on [7], we can calculate the migration cost as

$$C^m(x) = \begin{cases} 0, & \text{if } x = 0, \\ b + d\alpha^x, & \text{if } x > 0, \end{cases} \tag{1}$$

where x is the distance between $s(t)$ and $s'(t)$, i.e., $x = \|s(t) - s'(t)\|$. Not that when the service is not migrated, i.e. $s(t) = s'(t)$ and $x = 0$, the migration cost is $C^m(0) = 0$. When the migration is completed, all users are connected to the service in location $s'(t)$ to transmit data. Because of different sizes of data to be transmitted for different users, the transmission cost of the user l is denoted as

$$C_l^d(y_l) = \begin{cases} 0, & \text{if } y_l = 0, \\ f_l + h_l \beta^{y_l}, & \text{if } y_l > 0, \end{cases} \tag{2}$$

where y_l is the distance between user l in location $u_l(t)$ and service in location $s'(t)$, i.e., $y_l = \|u_l(t) - s'(t)\|$. Specially, we define $C_l^d(0) = 0$ when the service is in the same location as user l, i.e., $u_l(t) = s'(t)$.

3.2   Markov Decision Process Problem Formulation

A MDP can be denoted as a tuple $(S, A, P_{sa}, R_{sa}, \gamma)$, where S is a set of system states, A denotes a set of possible actions, P_{sa} and R_{sa} denote the transition probability and the immediate reward when action a is taken in state s, and γ denotes a discounting factor for future reward. And solution given by the MDP presents how to make the decision considering the immediate and future discounted reword in each state s.

In this paper, the system state in time-slot t can be specified by

$$\boldsymbol{S}(t) = [\boldsymbol{U}(t), h(t)] \in \Omega. \tag{3}$$

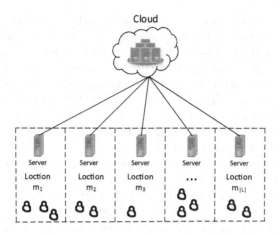

Fig. 1. Application scenario of MECs

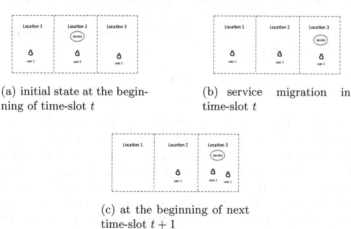

(a) initial state at the beginning of time-slot t

(b) service migration in time-slot t

(c) at the beginning of next time-slot $t+1$

Fig. 2. The transformation of the system state from current time-slot t to next time-slot $t+1$

where $\Theta = \Omega \times L$ denotes the space of the system states. We use $\pi = \{m_1, m_2, \ldots, m_{|L|}\}$ as a set of actions. Our goal is to design a control policy that minimizes the total cost including the service migration cost and the transmission costs in long-term T. It is denoted as

$$\min_{a \in \pi} \lim_{T \to +\infty} \sum_{t=0}^{T} C_{a(t)}(\boldsymbol{S}(t)), \tag{4}$$

where $C_{a(t)}(S(t)) = C^m(||s(t) - a(t)||) + \sum_{l=1}^{N} C_l^d(||u_l(t) - a(t)||)$ denotes the cost in time-slot t.

Note that the system state may change due to the service migration and the user mobility. As is show in Fig. 2(a), we can see that the system initial state is $S(t) = [1, 3, 2, 2]$ at the beginning of the time-slot t. When the migration action $a(t) \in \pi$ is given in the system state $S(t)$, the intermediate state $S'(t)$ is fixed. In Fig. 2(b), when the control action $a(t) = 3$ is completed, the system state change to the intermediate state $S'(t) = [1, 3, 2, 3]$. In Fig. 2(c) when from current time-slot t to next time-slot $t + 1$, all users may move and the system state changes to state $S(t + 1) = [2, 3, 3, 3]$. We can see that location of the service is $a(t)$ at the beginning of the time-slot $t + 1$.

Based on the above example, when service is migrated by the action $a(t)$ in the time-slot t, the location of service becomes $s(t + 1) = a(t)$ at the beginning of the next time-slot $t + 1$. The action $a(t)$ in current state $S(t)$ may have an impact on the cost in the time-slot $t + 1$. Thus, we should consider that the immediate cost and the future discounted cost caused by the action a in the current time-slot t.

By transforming the long-term total cost minimization into minimizing the immediate cost and future discount cost in each time-slot, our dynamic service migration problem can be formulated as an MDP problem. The optimal solution is given by Bellman's equation:

$$V(S_i) = \min_{a \in \pi} \{C_a(S_i) + \gamma \sum_{S_j \in \Omega} P[S_j \mid S_i, a] V(S_j)\}, \tag{5}$$

where $C_a(S_i)$ is the immediate cost and $\gamma \sum_{S_j \in \Omega} P[S_j \mid S_i, a] V(S_j)$ denotes a future discounted cost caused by the current action a in state S_i.

$P[S_j \mid S_i, a]$ denotes transition probability from state S'_i to S_j. When S_i and control action a are given in the state S_i, the intermediate state S'_i is fixed and location of service is a at the beginning of the next time-slot. So we only consider the transition probability from S'_i to the next state S_j in (5). We assume that the locations of different users are independent. When the control action a is given in the state S_i, the transition probability of the system state S_i at the time-slot t can be denoted as

$$
\begin{aligned}
P[S(t+1) \mid S(t), a] &= P[U(t+1), s(t+1) \mid U(t), s(t), a] \\
&= P[U(t+1) \mid U(t)] P[s(t+1) \mid s(t), a] \\
&= P[U(t+1) = \eta_j \mid U(t) = \eta_i] \\
&= \prod_{l=1}^{N} P_l[\eta_{j,l} \mid \eta_{i,l}] \\
&= \varphi_{i,j}
\end{aligned}
\tag{6}
$$

For a control action a applied in the state S_i, the location of the service shall be determined. Therefore, we have $P[s(t+1) \mid s(t), a] = 1$. We assume that the transition of the user location is independent. For each user l, we can capture the temporal correlation of location by the available transition probability distribution P_l of user l. Therefore, $\varphi_{i,j}$ can be obtained.

In order to simplify the problem, we restrict the transition probability distribution $\boldsymbol{P}_l$ of user l according to the parameters r_l^0, q_l^0, r_l and q_l. From current time-slot t to the next time-slot $t + 1$, each user l may moves one step to the left with probability q_l or the right with probability r_l and stays in the same location with probability $1 - q_l - r_l$. Especially, when $u_l(t) = m_1$, user l may move one step to the right with probability r_l^0 or stays in the same location with probability $1 - r_l^0$. When $u_l(t) = m_{|L|}$, user l may moves one step to the left with probability q_l^0 or stays in the same location with probability $1 - q_l^0$.

4   Approximate MDP Algorithm

4.1   Markov Decision Process

Our goal is to minimize the immediate cost and the future discounted cost in each time-slot. We can get the optimal solution by solving the equivalent Bellman's equation (5). When the estimated transition probability distribution $\boldsymbol{P}_l$ from each user l is given, we can obtain the transition probability $\varphi_{i,j}$. The Bellman's equation can be solved via value iteration or policy iteration [15, 16].

Algorithm 1. Value Iteration algorithm

Require:
  The estimated transition probability distribution $\boldsymbol{P}_l, \forall l$
Ensure:
  The optimal cost function V^* and the optimal action a^*
1: Initialize: $t \leftarrow 0, V^0(\boldsymbol{S}_i) \leftarrow 0, \forall \boldsymbol{S}_i \in \Omega$;
2: **while** not converge **do**
3:    $t = t + 1$
4:    **for** $\boldsymbol{S}_i \in \Omega$ **do**
5:      $V^t(\boldsymbol{S}_i) = \min_{a \in \pi}\{C_a(\boldsymbol{S}_i) + \gamma \sum_{\boldsymbol{S}_j \in \Omega} P[\boldsymbol{S}_j \mid \boldsymbol{S}_i, a]V^{t-1}(\boldsymbol{S}_j)\}$;
6:    **end for**
7: **end while**
8: **for** $\boldsymbol{S}_i \in \Omega$ **do**
9:    $a^*(\boldsymbol{S}_i) = \arg \min_{a \in \pi}\{C_a(\boldsymbol{S}_i) + \gamma \sum_{\boldsymbol{S}_j \in \Omega} P[\boldsymbol{S}_j \mid \boldsymbol{S}_i, a]V^*(\boldsymbol{S}_j)\}$
10: **end for**

As is show in Algorithm 1, line 5 update the cost function to V^t based on the previous function V^{t-1} iteratively, and finally find the optimal cost function V^*. After obtaining the cost function V^*, we can find the optimal control policy a^* in line 8–9 accordingly. Based on Algorithm 1, we can see that all the states Θ need to be traversed, requiring exponential time and space cost. To address this problem, a heuristic algorithm is proposed to solve this problem.

4.2   Approximate Markov-Decision-Process

In this section, a method for reducing the state space needed to be traversed is proposed.

First, we define ρ_l as expected probability distributions at each location for the user l. Therefore, the expected location $e_l(t)$ of user l at the time-slot t is denoted as

$$e_l(t) = \lceil \sum_{i=1}^{|L|} m_i \cdot \rho_l \rceil, \tag{7}$$

where $\rho_l = \lim_{n \to \infty} \omega_l (\boldsymbol{P}_l)^n$, and $(P_l)^n$ denotes the N-Step transition probability distribution from user l. ω_l is a row vector. If $u_l(t) = m_i$, we have $\omega_l(i) = 1$, otherwise $\omega_l(i) = 0$. For example, when we assume $u_l(t) = m_2$ and $|L| = 3$, we have $\omega_l = [0, 1, 0]$.

Second, at each time-slot t, the special state of user l for the state $\boldsymbol{S}(t) \in \Omega$ is denoted as

$$\boldsymbol{k}^l_{S(t)} = [e_1(t), e_2(t), \cdots, u_l(t), \cdots, e_N(t), s(t)] \tag{8}$$

We choose some key states K_l according to the expected state $e_l(t)$ at the time-slot t as

$$K_l = \{\boldsymbol{k}_{l,m_1}(t), \boldsymbol{k}_{l,m_2}(t), \cdots, \boldsymbol{k}_{l,m_{|L|}}(t)\}, \tag{9}$$

with $\boldsymbol{k}_{l,m_i}(t) = [u_1 = e_1(t), u_2 = e_2(t), \cdots, u_l = m_i, \cdots, u_N = e_N(t)), s(t)]$, $i = 1, 2, \cdots, |L|$ and $K = \cup_{l=1}^{N} K_l$ represents a set of key states to replace the space of the system states Ω.

We denote $\widehat{V}_l(\boldsymbol{k}^l_{S(t)})$ as the per-user l's cost function at each time-slot t. We have

$$\widehat{V}_l(\boldsymbol{S}_i) = \min_{a \in \pi} \{C_a(\boldsymbol{S}_i) + \gamma \sum_{\boldsymbol{S}_j \in K_l} P[\boldsymbol{S}_j \mid \boldsymbol{S}_i, a]\widehat{V}_l(\boldsymbol{S}_j)\} \tag{10}$$

According to the above discussion, the proposed approximate MDP algorithm is summarized in Algorithm 2.

As shown in Algorithm 2, we firstly calculate the expected state e_l, the special state of user l for the state $\boldsymbol{S} \in \Omega$ and a set of key states K_l for each user l in lines 2–3. Then, lines 5–10 intend to find the per-user l's optimal cost function $\widetilde{V}_l^*$ in state $\boldsymbol{S}$. Note that the state space K_l and cost function $\widehat{V}(\cdot)$ (lines 9–10) in Algorithm 2 are different with the state space Ω and cost function $V(\cdot)$ of lines 4–5 in Algorithm 1. In Algorithm 2, the state space K_l from user l can be approximatively regarded as the two-dimensional state space, where we only need to consider the mobility of the user l. But in Algorithm 1, the state space Ω is the $N + 1$-dimensional state space. According to the value of per-user l's optimal cost function $\widehat{V}_l^*$, we can get the smallest value of $\widehat{V}^*$ and determine the optimal control action a^*.

Algorithm 2. Approximate MDP algorithm

Require:
>   The estimated transition probability distribution $\boldsymbol{P}_l, \forall l$

Ensure:
>   The optimal cost function $\widehat{V}^*$ and the optimal action a^*

1: $\forall \boldsymbol{S} \in \Omega$;
2: **for** $l = 1...N$ **do**
3:     solve e_l, $\boldsymbol{k}_S^l$ and K_l from (7), (8) and (9) in state S;
4: **end for**
5: **for** $l = 1...N$ **do**
6:     Initialize: $t \leftarrow 0, \widehat{V}_l^0(\boldsymbol{S}_i) \leftarrow 0, \forall \boldsymbol{S}_i \in K_l$;
7:     **while** not converge **do**
8:         $t = t + 1$;
9:         **for** $\boldsymbol{S}_i \in K_l$ **do**
10:             $\widehat{V}_l^t(\boldsymbol{S}_i) = \min_{a \in \pi} \{C_a(\boldsymbol{S}_i) + \gamma \sum_{\boldsymbol{S}_j \in K_l} P[\boldsymbol{S}_j \mid \boldsymbol{S}_i, a] \widehat{V}_l^{t-1}(\boldsymbol{S}_j)\}$;
11:         **end for**
12:     **end while**
13:     Get the $\widehat{V}_l^*$ of the user l in state $\boldsymbol{S}$;
14: **end for**
15: For all users, select the smallest $\widehat{V}^*$ and get the corresponding a^* in state $\boldsymbol{S}$;

As discussed above, we can see that in Algorithm 2 only local states and feature states are used to update the per-user cost function. As a result, the state space is $\Theta(N \cdot |L|)$ in Algorithm 2, indicating that the complexity is reduced significantly from exponential to polynomial.

5   Performance Evaluation

In this section, we compare the performance of approximate MDP and Never migrate, Myopic migrate and Always migrate. The simulations are performed in MATLAB on a computer with Intel Core i5-6500 CPU, 8 GB memory, and 64-bit Windows 7. Based on approximate MDP based dynamic service, we study the long-term expected discounted total cost (Fig. 3).

We randomly chosen parameter r_l^0, q_l^0, r_l and q_l for each user l and obtain parameter P_l, the matrix of the user l's transition probability. Based on [7], we set $\beta = 0.8$ as the transmission cost function parameters. We have $h_l < 0$ and $f_l + h_l = 0$ for different user l, where they are empirically estimated. Regarding service migration cost, we set $\alpha = 0.8$ and fix $b + d = 1$ as a constant. In the simulation, different values of the parameter $d < 0$ express different sizes of data to be migrated. The average total cost from the proposed approach is compared with the costs from three optional policies, including the never-migrate policy, the myopic policy that chooses actions to minimize the one time-slot cost, and the always-migrate policy which chooses actions to minimize the one time-slot transmission cost. The simulations are run with 100 continuous states.

Firstly, we investigates the effect of different numbers of MECs varying from 5 to 15. Since the migration costs of service and transmission costs of users are

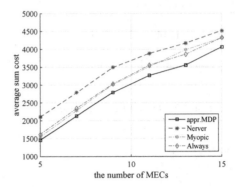

Fig. 3. The average total cost under different number of MECs

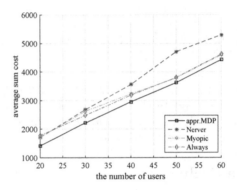

Fig. 4. The average total cost under different number of users

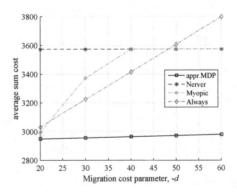

Fig. 5. The average total cost under different $-d$

related to the location of users and service, the total cost increases when the number of the MECs increases.

Then, we study how the four algorithms perform under different number of users. As shown in Fig. 4, based on $|L| = 10$, as the number of users increases, the transmission costs of users also increase. We can see that the average total cost of the approximate MDP method is slowly close to the average total cost of always-migrate policy and the average total cost of myopic policy because of increase of the transmission costs that is caused by increase of the number of users. And as the number of users increases, the transmission costs of all users will gradually increase, but the migration cost will not increase. Therefore we can observe that the average total cost of myopic policy will gradually coincide with the average total cost of always-migrate policy.

In Fig. 5, we investigate how parameter $-d$ affect the total cost. As value of parameter $-d$ increases, the migration cost also increases under the same conditions, we can see that the average total cost of the approximate MDP method is not big variation because the approximate MDP method not only takes into account the current state but also the impact of future. When the migration cost is lager enough, the action determined by myopic policy is that service is not migrated, hence the average total cost of the myopic policy will gradually coincide with the average total cost of the always-migrate policy. And the average total cost of the always-migrate policy increases rapidly due to the increase of the migration cost.

Nevertheless, we can always observe that the average total cost of the approximate MDP method is smaller than the rest of policies.

6   Conclusions

In this paper, we study the cost-minimization dynamic migration of a service shared by multiple users in MECs. We first describe the problem as an MDP problem. In order to make the problem tractable, we simplify it by considering only the locations of the users and the service as system status of MDP problem. To solve the problem, we first design an value iteration algorithm, which suffers the curse of high dimensionality. Therefore, we further invent a computation-efficient approximate MDP to reduce the dimension of state space from multi-dimensional mobility pattern to two-dimensional mobility pattern. Extensive simulation based performance evaluation results show that average total cost obtained by our proposed approach is smaller than some competitors such as never-migrate policy, myopic policy and always-migrate policy.

Acknowledgment. This research was supported by the NSF of China (Grant No. 61673354, 61602199, 61672474, 61402425, 61501412) and the Provincial NSF of Hubei (Grant No. 2016CFB107, 2015CFB400). This paper has been subjected to Hubei Key Laboratory of Intelligent Geo-Information Processing, China University of Geosciences, Wuhan 430074, China.

References

1. Deng, R., Lu, R., Lai, C., Luan, T.H.: Towards power consumption-delay tradeoff by workload allocation in cloud-fog computing. In: IEEE IC, pp. 3909–3914 (2015)
2. Dinh, H.T., Lee, C., Niyato, D., Wang, P.: A survey of mobile cloud computing: architecture, applications, and approaches. In: WCMC, pp. 1587–1611 (2013)
3. Roman, R., Lopez, J., Mambo, M.: Mobile edge computing, Fog et al.: a survey and analysis of security threats and challenges. FGCS **78**, 680–698 (2016)
4. Bonomi, F., Milito, R., Natarajan, P., Zhu, J.: Fog computing: a platform for Internet of Things and analytics. In: Bessis, N., Dobre, C. (eds.) Big Data and Internet of Things: A Roadmap for Smart Environments. SCI, vol. 546, pp. 169–186. Springer, Cham (2014). https://doi.org/10.1007/978-3-319-05029-4_7
5. Satyanarayanan, M., Chen, Z., Ha, K., Hu, W., Richter, W., Pillai, P.: Cloudlets: at the leading edge of mobile-cloud convergence. In: ICMC, pp. 1–9 (2014)
6. Taleb, T., Ksentini, A., Frangoudis, P.: Follow-me cloud: when cloud services follow mobile users. IEEE TCC, 1 (2016)
7. Wang, S., Urgaonkar, R., Zafer, M., He, T., Chan, K., Leung, K.K.: Dynamic service migration in mobile edge-clouds. In: IFIP Networking, pp. 1–9 (2015)
8. Goswami, A., Patel, R.P.: Service migration in cluster based cloud computing environment. In: ICIP, pp. 468–471 (2015)
9. Tao, F., Li, C., Liao, T., Laili, Y.: BGM-BLA: a new algorithm for dynamic migration of virtual machines in cloud computing. IEEE TSC **9**(6), 910–925 (2016)
10. Han, Z., Tan, H., Chen, G., Wang, R., Chen, Y., Lau, F.C.: Dynamic virtual machine management via approximate markov decision process. In: INFOCOM, pp. 1–9 (2016)
11. Wang, H., Li, Y., Zhang, Y., Jin, D.: Virtual machine migration planning in software-defined networks. In: IEEE TCC (2017)
12. Mach, P., Becvar, Z.: Mobile edge computing: a survey on architecture and computation offloading. IEEE Commun. Surv. Tutor. 1 (2017)
13. Ksentini, A., Taleb, T., Chen, M.: A Markov decision process-based service migration procedure for follow me cloud. In: ICC, pp. 1350–1354 (2014)
14. Bokani, A., Hassan, M., Kanhere, S., Zhu, X.: Optimizing http-based adaptive streaming in vehicular environment using Markov decision process. IEEE ToM **17**(12), 2297–2309 (2015)
15. Bellman, R., Kalaba, R.E.: Dynamic programming and modern control theory, vol. 81 (1965)
16. Bertsekas, D.P.: Dynamic programming and optimal control, vol. 1, no. 2, Athena Scientific Belmont, MA (1995)

Architecture-Independent Cloud Computation for Sensor Environment and Its Applications

Jingtao Sun[1(✉)], Kento Aida[1,2], and Tomoya Tanjo[1]

[1] National Institute of Informatics, 2-1-2, Hitotsubashi, Chiyoda-ku 101-8430, Japan
{sun,aida,tanjo}@nii.ac.jp
[2] Department of Informatics, The Graduate University for Advanced Studies,
Hayama, Japan

Abstract. Recently, due to the low cost of electronic devices and the spread of networks, researches on self-adaptive systems has become a boom by utilizing advanced Internet of Things (IoT) technology. However, many researches designed and built their systems on the basis of specific targets or specific applications using a fixed architecture. With the operation of such systems, various usage situations always change. This paper proposes a novel approach to dynamically changing the system architectures when its environments are changed. The key idea behind the proposed approach is to introduce a relocation of software components between various sensors as a basic mechanism for geographically inter-cloud systems. It is constructed as a middleware system, based on Docker for Java-based general-purposed self-adaptive sensor applications. This paper describes the design of our approach with several scenarios, e.g., dynamically adaptive the vehicle tracking system architecture among Peer-to-Peer, Client/Server and Ad-Hoc.

Keywords: Architecture-independent
Relocation of software components · Middleware
Inter-cloud · Docker · Internet of Things

1 Introduction

Recently, due to the low cost of electronic devices and the spread of networks, researches on self-adaptive systems has become a boom by utilizing advanced Internet of Things (IoT) technology. However, many researches designed and built their systems on the basis of specific targets or applications using a fixed architecture [4–6]. However, with the geographical environment is changed, remote control become very difficult, and with the processing computation on cloud system, both of them are difficult to provide the best computing resources for developing IoT-sensor networks and its applications.

Several researchers have attempted to introduce adaptations into cloud computing systems [1,3,9]. However, most of the researches provide the adaptability in the development of their target sensor applications and their systems.

© Springer Nature Switzerland AG 2018
G. Fortino et al. (Eds.): IDCS 2017, LNCS 10794, pp. 25–36, 2018.
https://doi.org/10.1007/978-3-319-97795-9_3

They present adaptation to dynamic adapt the changes by using several methods, such as migrating the virtual machine (VM) or container for adaptation, and designed multi-agents systems for adaptive the computation resources for cloud computing, and service-oriented software architecture for adaptive sensor networks on their specified applications. However, those researches focuses on adapting network traffic, or adapting specific IoT-sensor applications by using specified architectures. With the operation of such sensor systems, various usage situations always change, such as network input and output at geographically spaces, routing switching, remote information retrieval and flexible sensor distribution.

For solving this problem, we consider an independent sensor architecture that could elastically change the structure of their systems, and for providing this platform to the general sensor applications. We design and implement our system as a self-adaptive middleware, and which is also embed on a Docker Container [13] in advance. This is because it could avoid cumbersome system settings and software updates, users can efficiently and quickly distributed their sensor networks and their applications. Then through our designed user-defined policy for the software components which could be relocated between different various sensors for adaptive the changes. In addition, we present three policy formats to execute user-defined policies which consist of three parts: condition, action, relation to control the location of software component's execution at *Runtime*.

On the other hand, the contribution of this paper can be summarized as follows:

- We present a docker-based self-adaptive middleware to adapt to various changes for IoT-sensor applications and their systems through elastically change their fixed architectures.
- We design three policy formats for users to define their requirements for adaptations, and we also design a dynamically methods invocation mechanism for communicating the migrated software components with the destination's components.
- By using the proposed middleware, we describes three scenarios which build on a geographically IoT-sensor based vehicle tracking application to show the strength of our approach.

The remainder of this paper is organized as follows. Section 2 introduces the related works. Section 3 describes five requirements and our proposal. We elaborate our design and implementation in Sect. 4. In Sect. 5, we describe three scenarios, such as dynamically adaptive the range of geographically retrieve in a resiliently structure for vehicle tracking system. Conclusion and future work are summarized in Sect. 5.

2 Related Works

The architecture-independent studies are attracting attention in the area of intercloud [1–4] and IoT-sensor based system [5–8]. There have been several attempts to develop cloud computation for sensor system and its application. Most of them have aimed at managing network traffic or specific targets using fixed architectures.

The most typical approaches focus on service-oriented or model-driven adaptation for cloud-based sensor systems. Kecskemeti [2] proposed an approach to autonomously operate cloud federations by controlling their behaviors by using knowledge management systems. Through the user-defined rules, the instances of cloud can be dynamically invoked by the *Cloud Broker* for adaptation. However, due to the design is based on specific *Cloud-Broker* that handles the queue, it can not by changing their specific architecture to improve the ability of adaptation in high load balancing among different processors. ActivFORMS [4] and PLASMA [6] are proposed that is a model/goal-driven approaches for self-adaptation in small-scale mobile robotic through various sensors. However, both of them are need to modify or re-plan their requirements when the changes occurred. In addition, these approaches only support some simple changes in the conditions, when the conditions of change is relatively complex, modify/re-plan the active model is not only complicated task, but also the solution to *Conflict problem* is also not be shown.

There have been several attempts [5, 7, 8] to support service-oriented software architecture for adaptation in the literature on adaptive sensor systems. Manna [5] is a management architecture that take into account specific characteristic networks. However it aimed at managing network traffic through reconfiguration and adaptation instead of an elastic architecture with the requirements of sensor application changes. [7] proposed an adaptive middleware that can self-organized sensor networks, and it can optimized efficiently to build higher-level service structures. In addition, Kovatsch proposed a thin server architecture that within an application domain and force devices into knowing these profiles to relieves embedded servers from the burden of application logic for adaptation [8]. However, those approaches do not separate the functionality of software components and its adaptability. The separation of concerns can not only improve the maintenance of adaptation, but also it enables to reuse in the separate development of an applications functional behavior and its adaptive behavior involving crosscutting concerns.

On the other hand, there are several researchers proposed migration of virtual machine (VM) or multi-agents [1, 3]. Nagin proposed an approach that migrate the VM through inter-cloud for adaptation [1]. It enables to achieve cross-cloud services, including mobility of workloads between clouds. However, compared to migrate VMs, migration of containers[1] are more efficient, light and easily for management. Compared to migrate VM or container, mobile agents is also a typical approach. [3] proposed an approach to achieve an intelligent services based on cloud computing and multi-agents. The key point is that the mobile agents themselves do not provide adaptability. On the other hand, it is difficult to describe the adaptation conditions for realizing adaptability.

---

[1] In our research, we use the Docker [13] for implement our system.

3   Approach

As the requirements of IoT-sensor based applications and their systems may often change, such as network input and output at geographically spaces, routing switching, remote information retrieval and flexible sensor distribution, our self-adaptive middleware system need adapt to such changes. Our approach introduces the relocation of software components between sensors which embedded on a Docker Container for adaptation.

3.1   Requirements

In general, IoT-sensor based applications and their systems are often constructed on fixed architectures. However, with the usage situations, many cases are difficult to adaptive the users or system environment changes on their systems. In this paper, we forces on solving this problem by developing an elastic system which can dynamically adaptive different kinds of changes according to the following five requirements.

- **Architecture-Independent:** When developing application programs, developers often select specific system structures to built their systems on the cloud depending on their using cases, but as the demand or geographical location changes, the fixed structures often require repetitive modifications to complex adaptation conditions. So we need an elastic structure that can adapt to the changes of their systems dynamically, even in different geographical locations.
- **Separation of concerns:** The computational and adaptive behavior should be provided separately to the developer, thus avoiding cumbersome code analysis and maintenance for the program developer when the functional module is designed. Separation of concerns can also be more convenient for developers to easily define the adaptation conditions and behaviors.
- **General-sensor-applications:** Many researches try to provide different platforms on target applications or built a on clouds, however, in order to reduce the cost of structural on different platforms and satisfy the requirements of more general-sensor-applications. Our approach should implemented as a practical middleware to support general-purpose applications.
- **Self-adaptability:** With the operation of the fixed architecture of IoT-sensor systems, various usage situations always change. We need to make sure that the requests are rightly response to users at the same time, our adaptive middleware could have an ability of self-adaptability to dynamically adapt the changes of sensor applications and their systems.
- **Limited resources:** IoT-sensor may very small and have limited resources, e.g., processing, storage resources, and networks. Our approach should be available with such limited resources, and resiliently use the resources to satisfy the user's requirements on inter-cloud systems.

3.2   Inter-cloud Based Adaptation

The traditional sensor network architecture is deploying the information which collected by the different types of sensors via gateway sensor to variety of cloud platform such as Amazon EC2, Google Cloud Platform, Azure for processing. However, our approach (Fig. 1) firstly deploy Docker environment for developers based on their needs. Each Docker image contains the self-adaptive middleware that we proposed. Secondly, when our middleware dynamically capture the changes of their developed sensor applications, then through the relocation of software components between sensors to flexibly change their architecture for adaptation. In addition, each software component have their own policies for adaptation.

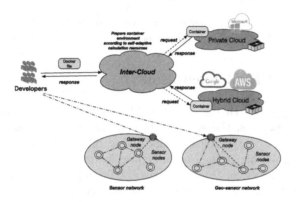

Fig. 1. Container-based adaptation for sensor network

Deployable Software Component. Each sensor application usually implemented by one or more software components for processing their data. So in this approach, we through duplication and/or migration of such software components between different types of sensors for re-organizing their fixed architectures for adaptive various changes from sensor applications and or user requirements.

Each software component is general-purpose and a programmable entity. We defined them as a collection of Java objects which like JavaBeans component. Through the user-defined policies, it can be deployed at destination sensor node, while it have started to run. For easily management and control those software components, we designed an *Active* interface on our middleware system. It follows a life-cycle, and is primarily responsible for serializing software components and deep copying for objects. Each software component need to implemented it for develop their applications. Moreover, the *Active* interface has four common methods, such as *creation, migration, duplication and destroy*.

User-Definable Policy. Each software component have one or more policies, where each policy is basically defined as condition, action, relation for deification, and the policy developers can add to/delete from their policies or update the policies on the Policy Management database. Our policy definition follows Scheme [14] language, we provide the condition statements, such as *if, cond* expression, and the loop statement, such as *let* expression to define their complex requirements. However, our policy definition follows the three concepts:

- When the specified policy instructs the its software component, the specified software components must response their instructs. The destination side refers to another software component instead of the sensor itself.
- We separated the policy from the software component, so in our approach, when more than one dimension must be considered for adaptation, we choose improve the *Priority* to carry out the policy adaptation.
- Each policy can be explicitly configure for one time within the specified sensor.

We designed three policy formats for users to easily defined the changes for adaptation. The details is described in Sect. 4.3.

4   Design and Implementation

The proposed approach that is based on Docker execution environment, with the user-defined policies, the software components which running on various cloud platforms can be dynamically relocated at different implementation environments to flexible change their architectures for IoT-sensor applications.

Our middleware system (Fig. 2) consists of three parts: an adaptation manager, a runtime system and two database, where each of the middleware systems are implemented on a same docker environment, they could coordinated with one another through a network. The first part is responsible for managing user-defined policies for relocation of software components, and real-time monitoring the changes between inside and outside of their systems. In addition, we private a sensor actuator API for developers to control their IoT-sensors. The second part is responsible for configuring the docker environment, executing and relocating software components between different cloud platforms, not only that it also responsible for communicating the relocated software components with software components on destination instance, through dynamic methods invocation mechanism. The third part is responsible for saving the user-defined policies and the state of relocated software components.

4.1   Runtime System

In order to implement the user-defined policy, such as relocation of software components or duplication of software components or destroy the specified software components, we designed an *Runtime System*. It consists of four parts as follows:

- *Container Manager* is responsible for pushing and pulling the Docker Container, which is implemented by us. Each Docker Container not only embedded our middleware, but also we defined the network between instances

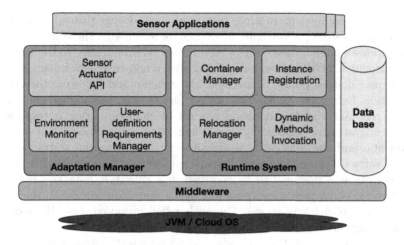

Fig. 2. Self-adaptive middleware for relocation of software components

directly to ensure that the sensor applications can quickly allocate reasonable computational resources through the cloud services[2].

- *Instance Registration* is responsible for automatically registering the instance information and the destination information for relocation of software components, which were saved in our database (The details are distributed in Sect. 4.2).
- *Relocation Manager* is responsible for migrating the software components which is implemented as several object sets. According to the invoked objects, Relocation Manager compress the objects with the corresponding class file, then deploy the sets to the destination sensor. In addition, it also responsible for duplicating the invoked object sets, which is implemented by serialization and clone interface[3].
- *Dynamic Methods invocation* is responsible for invoking methods of the relocated software components through package name, class name, object id, object name, object state, method name, which is implemented by an interface called, *Invocation*.

4.2   Adaptation Manager

Sensor application developers can firstly initial layout of their distribution environment on a Docker according to their own requirements by using our designed *Sensor Actuator API*, then our environment monitor could catch the changes between inside and outside of their systems and applications, if the change is occurred, the user-defined policy will be executed and deploy the target software component to the destination sensors, where each adaptation manager is

---

[2] Developers only need to configure the Docker file according to their own requirements.

[3] In our implementation, we adopted deep clone, not shallow clone.

running with a component runtime system on each docker through a network. Each runtime system periodically advertises its address to the others through UDP multicasting, and these sensors then return their addresses to the Runtime system through a TCP channel for building with a non-centralized management.

Each user-defined policy is specified like Scheme and following the Action Specification Language (ASL) [10] style. The syntax periodic=(condition(), action(), relation()) where condition is a set of changes, action is responsible for single migrating or duplicating then it migrating or destroying their software components, and the relation is responsible for recording the states between migrated software component with destination software component. The design of our policies was intended to be specified in a rule-style notation. However, more of the existing general-purpose languages were focus on define their conditions instead of defining action. The author had proposed a condition-action based language [9], however it has drawbacks in description of the relationship between migrated and destination side, and automatically identify, and balance the cloud resources for sensor networks, in order to further improve the ability of cross-platform for IoT-sensor systems, we enhanced our policy management.

In this paper, the heart of how to control the software components action need several techniques. For this reason, based on our ASL style, we designed three built-in policies for adaptation on IoT-sensor systems.

- **Relocation Policy.** When a software component has a *relocation policy*, if the user-defined condition specified in the policy is satisfied, it instructs the software component to migrate from the current to defined instance of destination, in which they may run at different sensors.
- **Publication Policy.** When a software component follows this policy, and even if the condition specified is satisfied, the policy will instructs the software components to make a number of clone, which can be defined by developers, and then instructs the clone to migrate from the current instance to multiple destinations.
- **Self-extermination Policy.** When a software component has a *self-extermination policy*, if the condition specified in the policy is satisfied, it will automatically terminate itself.

4.3   Database

There are a various of user-defined policies and the history record of software component relocation which running on each runtime. Therefore, for managing them, we created two essential database in Google Cloud Platform by using PostgreSQL. The two databases are shown as follows:

- **Policy Management** is responsible for storing the user-defined policies, and it supports to manage these policies, such as query, add, update, delete.
- **History Record Management** is responsible for storing the destination information, the number of copies and invoked methods when software component migrated to their destinations. It also supports the record retrieval, and other basic functions.

5   Geo-Sensor Based Vehicle Tracking Application

Based on above discussion, in this section we briefly introduce how our docker-based self-adaptive middleware system cloud adapt to such changes of IoT-sensor-based vehicle tracking applications by architecture-independent approach. We show two scenarios to describe the proposal.

5.1   Dynamically Adaptive the Range of Geographically Retrieve

This application is for adaptive the range of geographically retrieve on vehicle tracking system. Generally, with the requirements of developing, many researches build such targets on Peer-to-Peer, and/or Ad-hoc, and/or Client-Server architectures [11,12]. In this scenario, we mainly introduce how our approach could change the fixed system architecture for adaptive the changes in both of application and user requirements.

We can assume that an IoT-sensor group is built on a Peer-to-Peer architecture, and there are two software components running on them in *Area A* which shown in Fig. 3. The former is *Position Estimation* software component, which is responsible for monitoring the tracking targets, and sharing the information in their sensor group at Area A. The latter is *Capture Target* software component, which is responsible for capturing the vehicle targets, and sent the captured target information with alarm to cloud center for management.

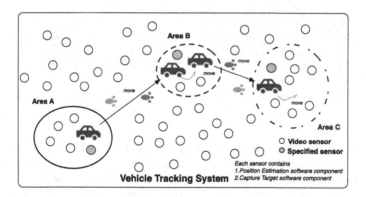

Fig. 3. Adaptive the range of geographically retrieve on vehicle tracking system

Changing Architecture from Peer-to-Peer to Client/Server. When the sensor group in area A detects and finds the pursuit target, and the specified sensor captured the position information of target. However, once the tracking target entry to the next area, the peer-to-peer architecture itself can not issue fast and efficient instructions for monitoring nodes in the next network. In this case, if the vehicle tracking application issues an instruction of reduce the tracking range for precise pursuing the location of the target, and its surrounding situation, we can let the sensor group of area B fast re-organize their architecture from peer-to-peer to client/server through relocation of *Position Estimation* software components, and specialized *Capture Target software component* between area A and B (Fig. 4). This is because it cloud allows a small range of geographically sensors to quickly collect and process the captured features, such as by using super resolution to increase the pixel for the moving target through the high speed of deployment on Client/Server architecture. Moreover, we also can change the Client/Server back to Peer-to-Peer architecture through our approach. We using the *Relocation Policy* for defining their adaptive programs as follows:

(define relationship (component_id state priority))
(define relocation (component_id ip_address class_name
method_name relationship))
(cond
(and (range_of_sensors) (network_latency)) relocation)

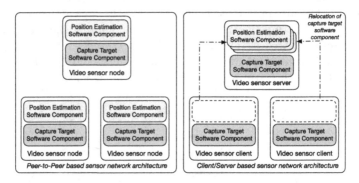

Fig. 4. Dynamically change the sensor architecture from Peer-to-Peer to Client/Server

Changing Architecture from Client/Server to Ad-Hoc. Similar to the above case, we also can assume if the vehicle tracking application issues an instruction of improve the tracking range with the target moving from Area B into Area C, and collect its surrounding situations. We can let the sensor group of Area C fast re-organize their architecture from client/server to Ad-Hoc network through duplication of *Position Estimation* software components under the target moving situation, and then relocation them to other sensors in Area C. In this case, the client/server can be adaptively changed to ad-hoc network through the characteristics of Ad-Hoc network (Fig. 5). It does not use a dedicated base station and is temporarily interconnected by using the relay function of the terminal itself. With this feature, when the tracking target entry into new areas like Area C, we can issue warnings and assistance requests in a timely manner after the tracking target was captured. We using the *Publication Policy* for defining their adaptive programs as follows:

```
(define ip_address_list (filed1 filed2 ....filedn))
(define relationship (component_id state priority))
(define publications (component_id ip_address_list class_name
method_name relationship))
(cond
(range_of_sensors) publications)
```

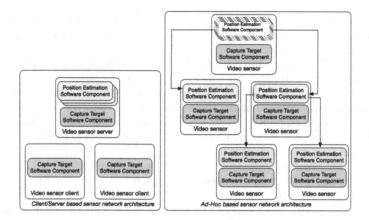

Fig. 5. Dynamically change the sensor architecture from Client/Server to Ad-Hoc

5.2 Current State

In this section, we introduced several scenarios to self-adaptive their system architecture for IoT-sensor applications on a vehicle tracking system. While, there are several issues still work in process. For now, our middleware system is implemented. However, (1) next we first do is verify the performance of our middleware on a vehicle tracking system in our future work; (2) incorrect user-defined policies may cause conflicts between relocation of software components. We plan to improve the implementation of the policy priority and conflict avoid automatic certification to improve our research.

6 Conclusion

In this paper, we presented an architecture-independent inter-cloud based self-adaptive middleware for sensor environment and its application. It introduced a rapid construction deployment in Docker environment, and then through reloca-tion of software components between sensors as a basic adaptation mechanism to dynamically self-originated system architecture. In addition, we also introduced three policy formats which based on Scheme language for users to easily define their adaptive conditions, actions, and relationships, and the two scenarios were described for show how to achieve our proposal.

In the future, we planed to improve the implementation of the policy priority and conflict avoid automatic certification to improve our research, and we also plan to develop more applications to verify our middleware system. In the last, we calculate the sensor application to provide dynamic allocation of cloud resources to achieve more efficient and more economical solution.

References

1. Nagin, K., Hadas, D., Dubitzky, Z., et al.: Inter-cloud mobility of virtual machines. In: Proceedings of the 4th Annual International Conference on Systems and Storage, pp. 1–12. ACM (2011)
2. Kecskemeti, G., Maurer, M., Brandic, I., et al.: Facilitating self-adaptable Inter-Cloud management. In: 20th Euromicro International Conference on Parallel, Distributed and Network-Based Processing (PDP), pp. 575–582. IEEE (2012)
3. Talia, D.: Towards internet intelligent services based on cloud computing and multi-agents. In: Gaglio, S., Lo Re, G. (eds.) Advances onto the Internet of Things. AISC, vol. 260, pp. 271–283. Springer, Cham (2014). https://doi.org/10.1007/978-3-319-03992-3_19
4. Iftikhar, M.U., Weyns., D.: ActivFORMS: active formal models for self-adaptation. In: Proceedings of the 9th International Symposium on Software Engineering for Adaptive and Self-Managing Systems, pp. 125–134. ACM
5. Ruiz, L.B., Nogueira, J.M., Loureiro, A.A.F.: MANNA: a management architecture for wireless sensor networks. IEEE Commun. Mag. **41**(2), 116–125 (2003)
6. Tajalli, H., Garcia, J., Edwards, G., et al.: PLASMA: a plan-based layered architecture for software model-driven adaptation. In: Proceedings of the IEEE/ACM international conference on Automated Software Engineering, pp. 467–476. ACM (2010)
7. Golatowski, F., Blumenthal, J., Hand, M., et al.: Service-oriented software architecture for sensor networks. In: International Workshop on Mobile Computing (IMC), pp. 93–98, 2003
8. Kovatsch, M., Mayer, S., Ostermaier, B.: Moving application logic from the firmware to the cloud: towards the thin server architecture for the Internet of Things. In: 2012 Sixth International Conference on Innovative Mobile and Internet Services in Ubiquitous Computing (IMIS), pp. 751–756. IEEE (2012)
9. Sun, J., Satoh, I.: Theory and implementation of an adaptive middleware for ubiquitous computing systems. J. Inf. Process. **20**(4), 1–9 (2016)
10. Mellor, S.J., Tockey, S., Arthaud, R., LeBlanc, P.: Software-platform-independent, precise action specifications for UML. The Unified Modeling Language, UML, pp. 281–286 (1999)
11. Hsieh, J.-W., Yu, S.-H., et al.: Automatic traffic surveillance system for vehicle tracking and classification. IEEE Trans. Intell. Transp. Syst. **7**(2), 175–187 (2006)
12. Sharp, C., Schaffert, S., et al.: Design and implementation of a sensor network system for vehicle tracking and autonomous interception. In: EWSN, pp. 93–107 (2005)
13. Docker. https://www.docker.com/
14. Eisenberg, M.B., Abelson, H.: Programming in SCHEME. Course Technology Press, Boston (1993)

A Proposed Adaptive Rate Algorithm to Administrate the Video Buffer Occupancy for Smooth Video Streaming

Saba Qasim Jabbar[1,2(✉)], Dheyaa Jasim Kadhim[3], and Yu Li[1]

[1] Wuhan National Laboratory for Optoelectronics, Division of Communication
and Intelligent Networks, School of Electronics and Information,
Huazhong University of Science and Technology,
Wuhan 430074, Hubei, People's Republic of China
shura2007515@yahoo.com
[2] Computer Engineering Department, University of Baghdad, Baghdad, Iraq
[3] Electrical Engineering Department, University of Baghdad, Baghdad, Iraq

Abstract. Video streaming has become an irreplaceable technology in modern smart devices especially with the appearance of dynamic streaming over HTTP (DASH). However, the fluctuating and instability of wireless networks is still one of the greatest challenges to video streaming process. Video quality deteriorates by the amount of time that video streaming process has stopped playing because of the buffer starvation state. In this work, an adaptive rate algorithm is proposed for getting smooth video playback continuity by monitoring the available bandwidth and administrating the video buffer occupancy. Most of the conventional algorithms try to fill the video buffer quickly with available video segments which it may degrade the quality of experience (QoE) since these video segments may have low bitrate versions. So our proposed algorithm administrates the video buffer occupancy and maintains its filling with segments of high quality versions by estimating the available throughput and measuring the video buffer level. The estimation of the available throughput for the next segments is done based on the previously observed throughput of the last downloaded segment that keeps the buffer at accepted level. Through the simulation results, we checked effectiveness and robustness of our proposed algorithm under three different network bandwidth conditions namely: step-down, long term fluctuation and sudden-drop conditions. Simulation results show that the proposed algorithm has fast reaction to these cases through adapting the video bitrate accordingly and maintain the video buffer away from the risk of underflow. Also we compared the proposed algorithm with other conventional algorithms in terms of average video bitrates, number of video bitrate switches and number of playback interruptions. We found that our proposed algorithm outperforms these algorithms in achieving high video bitrates, low number of video bitrate switches and minimum number of playback interruptions.

Keywords: Video streaming · Video buffer · Quality of experience (QoE)
Adaptive rate algorithm

© Springer Nature Switzerland AG 2018
G. Fortino et al. (Eds.): IDCS 2017, LNCS 10794, pp. 37–49, 2018.
https://doi.org/10.1007/978-3-319-97795-9_4

1 Introduction

High speed broadband networks with enhancements in display technology of different devices (e.g., smart phone, laptop and personal media player) have enabled video streaming to achieve the most popular services in mobile applications. Video streaming controls Internet traffic over all network types in the world [1]. Recently, a new type of video transfer techniques have been presented to transfer video via different channels such as wireless network which is called adaptive streaming [2]. This technique is used widely for multimedia streaming service, adopted by Microsoft smooth streaming, adobe dynamic streaming, Netflix and Apple HTTP Live Streaming, etc. Also, 3GPP and MPEG encouraged standardization of adaptive streaming named dynamic adaptive streaming over HTTP (DASH) [3]. In DASH system media content is split into a series of small segments, each segment is encoded in several versions with different bit rates and qualities then streamed to user's device according to its requests. For each media streaming, the server generates media presentation description file (MPD). Before playing the video, DASH user will fetch the MPD file from the server to have the information about the media types, resolution, encoded alternatives of the media content, segment sizes, etc. At user side, a network condition will be monitored by DASH user and dynamically a suitable version for coming segment to download will be selected through the rate adaptation algorithm. Under good network conditions, the DASH user will ask the server to present a good quality version and when the network condition is bad; user's device will detect the network change and request a low quality version. At DASH server side, each segment is offered with a different bit rates and each video rate is linked with a group of encoding factors such as frame rate, resolution.

The adaptation rate algorithm is major in DASH service, since unsuitable bit-rate may result in bad video quality or playout interruption, further degrade the QoE. The target of adaptation rate algorithm is to rise the video quality through meeting conflicting objectives in a way enhancing the user's viewing experience, such as choosing a group of video bit rates which are the highest feasible, a voiding unnecessary bitrate switches and keeping the buffer content to avoid interruption of playback [4, 5]. To improve the user experience, the adaptive algorithms mainly determine the video rates based on existing bandwidth and the state of the playback buffer, one approach to pick a video rate relied on estimated throughput as in [6–8]. The adaptation rate algorithms of two other business solutions, namely Microsoft's seamless streaming and Netflix with OSMF are assessed in [9], and the experimental outputs decided that none of them gives smoother quality adaptation with the fixed playback buffer. However, in a very changing environment, accurate estimation of throughput becomes a challenge.

Many adaptation algorithms consider the video buffer and estimated throughput to identify the video rates as in [10, 11]. Rahman [12] proposed an algorithm to determine video bitrates based on estimated throughput and buffer occupancy where buffer levels are dynamically determined relied on the sizes of upcoming segments. In [13, 14], models have been suggested to study the video temporal quality, however they do not include change of bitrate during streaming cycle. In [15], the authors have studied the impact of the bitrate variation on QoE, presented good notes about how the alteration of frequency and amplitude will effect on user experience. In [16], an adaptation algorithm for video streaming over HTTP is proposed. This algorithm consists from two phases: fast phase for increasing the buffer level to predefined threshold value and steady phase for controlling the buffer level from going back to underflow state, so the algorithm could limit the number of video quality switches. Several studies have been performed to understand the impact of QoE on users' participation. The video playing time and user retention have been found based on QoE. Improving video quality depends on the number of bitrate switches and interrupting events. In this paper, we try to enhance the quality of experience through maintaining the interruption and switching rate at low level. An adaptive rate algorithm is suggested which determines the video bitrates based on both the estimated throughput and the content of the buffer. The proposed algorithm administrates the buffer occupancy to maintain the buffer fill with high quality segments without the situation of an empty buffer.

The work of this paper is organized as follows: Sect. 2 describes the main principles of our system design including two main units: throughput measurement unit and video buffer measurement unit. Section 3 gives a detailed description of our proposed adaptive rate algorithm, while Sect. 4 shows the simulation results that will be drawn from our experiments to describe our proposed algorithm as compared to other algorithms. Finally, Sect. 5 will give the main conclusions are gained with this work.

2   System Design

The HTTP user downloads a video streams and splits them into multiple segments. All the segments have an equivalent length of τ sec. Then, the video segments are saved in multiple separate representations at the HTTP server. The set of representations available for the video streaming is denoted by V_r where $V_r = \{V_{r1}, V_{r2}, \ldots\ldots, V_{rm}\}$. The user dynamically picks a video quality from the set V_r for the upcoming segment. V_{rmin} and V_{rmax} are the representations with the lowest and highest video rates in the set V_r. The video rates which they are higher and lower than the current video rate are denoted by $V_r\uparrow$ and $V_r\downarrow$ respectively. The proposed video streaming structure of the HTTP adaptation system is described in Fig. 1.

In this system, server content is represented by a media presentation description (MPD) file with group of video segments of m various representation qualities. The user asks the MPD from the server, and the received MPD file is interpreted by a parser in the user. The mentioned file is used for requesting video segments from the streaming server. The suggested system for the HTTP dynamic adaptive at user aspect consists of two units namely: throughput measurement (TM) unit and video buffer

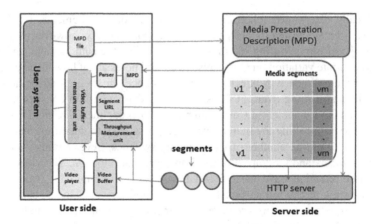

Fig. 1. Dynamic adaptive video streaming system

measurement unit (VBM). Video segments are requested by the HTTP user relied on the decision of the video buffer measurement unit (VBM). This unit dynamically selects video rate for each segment. The HTTP user sends HTTP GET requests to the HTTP server to download the segments. The HTTP server transmits the video to the user through the bottleneck link. The downloaded segments are saved in the video buffer, then sending them to the video player. The throughput measurement unit (TM) estimates the throughput for next segment, and then feeds the measuring throughput to video buffer measurement unit (VBM) for selecting the next video rate before downloading the segment.

In this work, the segments are downloaded using the serial segment fetch method. The data of τ seconds is added to the buffer once the current segment is fully downloaded and the user starts playing the video. The purpose behind the proposed algorithm is to maintain the video buffer filled with high quality versions, and to control the video buffer level when there is a throughput fluctuation. The algorithm is applied immediately after downloading $(n-1)^{th}$ segment in order to select the suitable bitrate for next segment. Before bring the upcoming segment from the streaming server, the current network condition is estimated by throughput measurement unit (TM) which it will be discussed in details with video buffer measurement unit (VBM) in the following subsections.

A. **Throughput Measurement Unit (TM)**

Estimating available bandwidth considers a significant role in choosing video rate. The user is able to estimate the upcoming segments throughput based on the previous throughput notifications. So choosing the video rate for the upcoming segment is relied on the throughput T_{n-1} of the last downloaded segment that keeps the buffer stability even some oscillates in the video rate curve. As the bandwidth of the network fluctuates over time, the estimated throughput $\hat{T}_{n-1}$ is smoothed by a weighted transferring average scheme as:

$$\hat{T}_n = \rho T_{n-1} + (1 - \rho)\hat{T}_{n-1} \tag{1}$$

where ρ is a weighing factor to explain the changing in network conditions. $\hat{T}_n$ is the estimated throughput and T_n is the available throughput. A large value of ρ means the network conditions has changed abruptly and so the upcoming bandwidth is calculated by giving more weight to the last available throughput. Contrarily, bandwidth is calculated by giving more weight to the last estimated throughput. The value of ρ is updated dynamically relating to the available wireless link conditions and the throughput is estimated accordingly. Before requesting the next segment, the video buffer measurement unit will select the suitable bitrate for download the segment according to the current buffer status and the estimated throughput value which is fed from the throughput measurement unit.

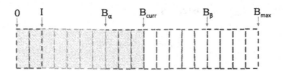

Fig. 2. Video buffer

B. Video Buffer Measurement Unit (VBM)

This unit is responsible for checking the status of video buffer and then adjusting the downloaded throughput for the upcoming segment to keep the level of the buffer close to the targeted level. Initially we define three threshold values in the level of the buffer I, B_α and B_β as shown in Fig. 2 below, which they are measured in seconds with $0 < I < B_\alpha < B_\beta < B_{max}$ where B_{max} is the maximum buffer level.

Here, B_α and B_β are the operating thresholds for the video buffer while B_{targ} is regarded as the mid-point between the running thresholds, which it is given by:

$$B_{targ} = \frac{B_\beta + B_\alpha}{2} \tag{2}$$

If the current buffer level B_{curr} is equal to target level B_{targ} and $(B_{curr}\text{-}B_{last})$ near zero then $\hat{T}_n$ is not adjusted, B_{last} is the last buffer level. Otherwise, an adjusting factor λ_n based on buffer occupancy is considered to put B_{curr} near B_{targ} and $(B_{curr} - B_{last})$ near zero as it is cleared below:

$$\lambda_n = (1 + \lambda_1)(1 + \lambda_2) \tag{3}$$

where λ_1 is deals with the space between buffer current state and the target state i.e.: how close the buffer current state B_{curr} to the target state B_{targ} and it is calculated as shown below:

$$\lambda_1 = \frac{B_{curr} - B_{targ}}{B_{targ}} \tag{4}$$

While λ_2 is calculated as follows:

$$\lambda_2 = \frac{B_{curr} - B_{last}}{B_{max}} \tag{5}$$

After estimating λ_n, $\hat{T}_n$ is adjusted as:

$$\tilde{T}_n = \lambda_n \cdot \hat{T}_n \tag{6}$$

3 Proposed Adaptive Rate Algorithm

In this section, we will give a detailed description of our proposed adaptive rate algorithm. This proposed algorithm is used for: (1) maintaining the video buffer filled with high-quality segments; (2) decreasing the interruption duration especially when there is a noted degradation in system throughput and (3) protecting the buffer from return to underflow level. The proposed algorithm is applied immediately after downloading the $(n - 1)^{th}$ segment. Then the algorithm specifies the video rate to download the next segment. The video streaming session is divided into two stages of the process: the initiation stage and normal stage. The purpose of the initiation stage is to prevent the user from giving away the video session since it starts before the buffer being empty. During the initiation stage, the user loads a little information that may be utilized to determine the video rate. Therefore, the conservative approach is initially considered, and since the content of the buffer gradually rises, the risk is taken in the selection of video rate. The algorithm sets the minimum available video bitrate V_{rmin} for the first downloaded segment. The reason behind fixing the minimum video rate for the first segment is to reduce the delay after the user demand video and before operating the video. Additionally, the user does not have any notification about the case of the network at the starting of the video streaming session.

For $B_{curr} < I$ where I is a threshold value equals to 2τ, the user changes to high video rate if $V_{r\uparrow} < \delta_1 \times T_{n-1}$. Otherwise the user changes to a higher video rate if $V_{r\uparrow} < \delta_2 \times T_{n-1}$ where δ_1 and δ_2 are two threshold margins and $(\delta_1 < \delta_2)$. The proposed algorithm continues to employ the initiate stage until a reduction in the level of the buffer is monitored. When the user monitors a reduction in the buffer level, it switches to a normal stage, four cases are considered through this stage:

1. The user chooses V_{rmin} as the next bitrate.
2. The user chooses the bitrate of the next segment to be less than the current segment bitrate.
3. The user chooses the bitrate of the next segment to be more than the current segment bitrate.
4. The user chooses the bitrate of the next segment to be the same as the current segment bitrate.

To choose the bitrate of next segment from the V_r set, the following conditions must be met:

a. If $B_{curr} < B_\alpha$ Then $V_{r^{next}} = V_{rmin}$
b. If $(B_n - B_{curr}) \geq 0$ Then $V_{r^{next}} = V_r(y)$

If the buffer content falls under B_α, V_{rmin} is always chosen. The reason is that it is essential matter to avoid the interruption of operation. When the buffer content lower than B_α, there is a significant risk of buffer underflow in the existence of throughput volatility. If the buffer content is above B_α, the user selects the highest video rate less than the adjusted throughput. After that, when an increasing in the network throughput is noticed, the bitrate of next segment increases as a response. So two conditions should be met:

a. $V_{r\uparrow} < \tilde{T}_n$
b. $(B_n - B_{curr}) \geq 0$

The first condition ensures that the chosen video bitrate is low than the adjusted throughput to avoid draining the buffer. A reduction in the content of the buffer when $V_{r\uparrow} < \tilde{T}_n$ suggests that the throughput was overestimated. The reason beyond the second condition is that it reduces the frequency of the video rate switching by not increasing the video rate when the user monitors a drop in the buffer content, to prevent the risk of a likely step down in the near future. If a drop in the adjusted throughput below the selected bitrate then the video rate is reduced until the following condition is satisfied $V_{r\uparrow} < \tilde{T}_n$.

The following steps show the procedure of implementing proposed algorithm:

Definitions :

$$V_r(y) = \{V_{r1}, V_{r2}, \ldots, V_{rm}\}$$

$I, B_\alpha, B_\beta, B_{max}$: Buffer threshold values

V_{rnext} : video rate chosen for next segment

V_{rcurr} : current video rate of recent download segment

$V_{r\uparrow}$: next higher video rate

B_{curr} : current buffer status at last downloaded segment

B_n : buffer status during the download of $(n)^{th}$ segment

$\tilde{T}_n$: adjusted Throughput of $\hat{T}_n$

δ_1, δ_2 : threshold values $(\delta_1 < \delta_2)$

— —

Input : $T_{n-1}, \tilde{T}_n, B_{curr}$

Output : V_{rnext}

If the initiate stage == true then

    If $B_{curr} < I$ then

        If $V_{r\uparrow} < \delta_1 \times T_{n-1}$ then $V_{rnext} = V_{r\uparrow}$

    Else

        If $V_{r\uparrow} < \delta_2 \times T_{n-1}$ then $V_{rnext} = V_{r\uparrow}$

    End If

Else If the normal stage == true then

    If $B_{curr} < B_\alpha$ then

        $V_{rnext} = V_{rmin}$

        Else if $V_{r\uparrow} < \tilde{T}_n$ then

        For $y = 0$ to length of $V_r(y)$

            If $V_r(y) > \tilde{T}_n$ then

            Break

            End If

            $y++$

        End for

    If $(B_n - B_{curr}) \geq 0$ then

        $V_{rnext} = V_r(y)$

    Else

        $V_{rnext} = V_{rcurr}$

    End If

Else If $\quad V_{r^{curr}} > \tilde{T}_n$ then

$$V_{r^{next}} = \max \left\{ V_r(y) : V_r(y) < \tilde{T}_n \right\}$$

Else

$$V_{r^{next}} = V_{r^{curr}}$$

End If

End If

_____

4 Simulation Results

In this section, we evaluate the performance of our proposed algorithm and compare its performance with other related works such as QDASH [10] and AAA [16]. Through our simulation, we consider ten representation levels which it is provided by HTTP server for adapting video bitrates as: (300, 500, 700, 1000, 1200, 1400, 1600, 1800, 2000, and 2500) kbps. The video buffer length is 60 s and the segment length is 4 s while the two margins δ_1 and δ_2 are set to 0.5 and 0.75 respectively. I, B_α, ρ and B_β are set to 2τ, 5, 0.9 and 12 respectively. In this simulation, we consider three types of bandwidth conditions: (1) step-down condition; (2) fluctuation condition and (3) sudden-drop in the available bandwidth condition.

Figure 3 shows the behavior of our proposed algorithm under the first condition of stepping down, so we consider the throughput is gradually decreasing and we can show below how our proposed algorithm is responding to this case in term of video bitrate and video buffer level respectively. In this figure, the proposed algorithm drops the video bitrate gradually at time 28 s when the throughput decreases. Video buffer level is below B_α so the algorithm decreases the video bitrate to V_{rmin} for avoiding any playback interruption. This feature of the proposed algorithm can offer sustainable QoE in video streaming applications. Figure 4 shows the behavior of our proposed algorithm under the network bandwidth large fluctuation condition, and this figure shows

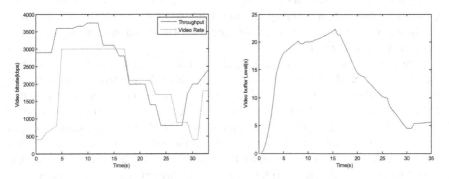

Fig. 3. System throughput and video buffer under step-down condition

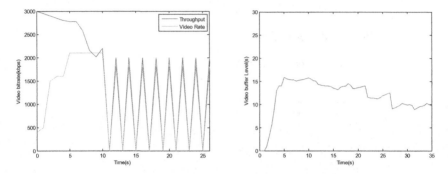

Fig. 4. System throughput and video buffer under fluctuation condition

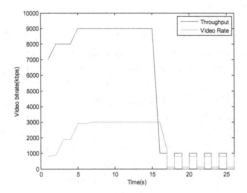

Fig. 5. System throughput vs. video rate under sudden-drop condition

how our proposed algorithm is quickly responded to the bandwidth fluctuation which is one of the main features of the adaptive rate algorithm. From the figure, when the bandwidth largely increases the proposed algorithm adapts the video bitrate by stepping up quickly. On the other hand this conservative way can improve QoE for video by allowing more segments be accumulated in video buffer so there is no interruption in video playback. Otherwise, Fig. 5 shows one of the important features of the adaptive rate algorithm under a sudden-drop condition in bandwidth. We can show how the proposed algorithm acts quickly by adapting the video bitrate to large drop in bandwidth. In this way the algorithm can avoid the risk of playback interruption and keep the QoE in acceptable level.

Figure 6 shows the comparison among different adaptive rate algorithms according to the number of playback interruptions. QDASH faces three interruptions while our proposed algorithm and AAA algorithm face one interruption. The reason is that QDASH depends on download time in adapting the video bitrate and since most of video streaming providers encode their videos in VBR (Variable Bit Rate), so each segment has a different size which means different segments would have different download times and it could not estimate the available bandwidth in accurate way. On the other hand the proposed algorithm and AAA algorithm can have less number of

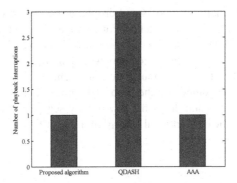

Fig. 6. Comparison of the number of playback interruptions among different adaptive rate algorithms

interruptions due to their accurate way in estimating the available throughput and administrate the video buffer. While Fig. 7 shows the comparison among different adaptive rate algorithms in term of the average video bitrates. From this figure, the proposed algorithm outperforms QDASH and AAA algorithms by 300 kbps and 200 kbps respectively due to the ability of the proposed algorithm in administrating the video buffer occupancy and keep it fill with good quality segments. The main work of the proposed algorithm is appending the video buffer with segments of high quality version (i.e. high video bitrate) and drops the downloaded segments with low quality version (i.e. low video bitrate). While AAA algorithm waits the video buffer level reaches a threshold value then stepping up or down the video bitrate for next segments.

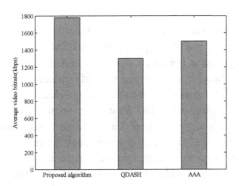

Fig. 7. Comparison of average video bitrate at different adaptive rate algorithms

Finally, Fig. 8 shows the comparison among different adaptive rate algorithms in term of the average number of video bitrates switches. From this figure the proposed algorithm outperforms the QDASH algorithm in minimizing the number of video bitrate switches because the estimated way that is used by our proposed algorithm for throughput could overcome the fluctuating video bitrate curve. Also appending the video buffer with high quality segments and dropping the low quality segments could reduce the number of video bitrate switches. For example if there is four video encoded versions: v1, v2, v3 and v4 where v1 < v2 < v3 < v4 in conventional algorithm if the available throughput decreases the algorithm would reduce the video bitrate to v3 followed by v2 and when the throughput condition is enhanced the algorithm rises the video bitrate to v4. On the other side the proposed algorithm appends the video buffer with high quality segments and drops the low quality segments (i.e. appends with v4 followed by v3) unlike the conventional algorithm it doesn't reduce the video bitrate to v2 so minimizing the number of switches.

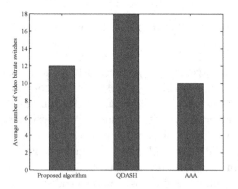

Fig. 8. Comparison of average number of video bitrate switches among

5   Conclusions

In this work, an adaptive rate algorithm is proposed to enhance the video quality through video streaming by monitoring the network conditions and administrating the video buffer occupancy. These network conditions include throughput stepping down gradually, long term throughput fluctuation and suddenly dropping of network throughput. Through the simulation results, we checked the effectiveness of the algorithm under these conditions. Our simulation results show that the proposed algorithm has a quick response to these cases through adapting the video bitrate accordingly and maintains the video buffer away from the risk of underflow. Also we compared the proposed algorithm with other algorithms suck as QDASH [10] and AAA [16] in terms of average video bitrates, number of video bitrate switches and number of playback interruptions. We found the proposed algorithm outperforms these algorithms in achieving high video bitrates and low number of video bitrate switches. This due to the main work of the algorithm based on enhancing the video quality through administrates the video buffer and maintains it fill with segments of high quality version while the conventional algorithms tend to download the segments quickly that fill the video buffer with segments of low quality version.

References

1. Petrangeli, S., Famaey, J., Claeys, M., Latré, S., De Turck, F.: QoE-driven rate adaptation heuristic for fair adaptive video streaming. ACM Trans. Multimedia Comput. Commun. Appl. (TOMM) **12**(2), 28 (2016)
2. Hossfeld, T., Seufert, M., Sieber, C., Zinner, T., Tran-Gia, P.: Identifying QoE optimal adaptation of HTTP adaptive streaming based on subjective studies. Comput. Netw. **81**, 320–332 (2015)
3. Stoekhammer, T.: Dynamic adaptive streaming over HTTP-design principles and standards. In: Proceedings of the Second Annual ACM Conference on Multimedia Systems, New York, USA, pp. 2–4 (2014)
4. Dobrian, F., Sekar, V., Awan, A., Stoica, I., Joseph, D., Ganjam, A., Zhan, J., Zhang, H.: Understanding the impact of video quality on user engagement. ACM SIGCOMM Comput. Commun. Rev. **41**(4), 362–373 (2011)
5. Ni, P., Eg, R., Eichhorn, A., Griwodz, C., Halvorsen, P.: Flicker effects in adaptive video streaming to handheld devices. In: Proceedings of the 19th ACM International Conference on Multimedia, pp. 463–472 (2011)
6. Jiang, J., Sekar, V., Zhang, H.: Improving fairness, efficiency, and stability in http-based adaptive video streaming with festive. In: Proceedings of the 8th International Conference on Emerging Networking Experiments and Technologies, pp. 97–108 (2012)
7. Thang, T.C., Ho, Q.D., Kang, J.W., Pham, A.T.: Adaptive streaming of audiovisual content using MPEG DASH. IEEE Trans. Consum. Electron. **58**(1) (2012)
8. Liu, C., Bouazizi, I., Gabbouj, M.: Rate adaptation for adaptive HTTP streaming. In: Proceedings of the Second Annual ACM Conference on Multimedia Systems, pp. 169–174 (2011)
9. Akhshabi, S., Begen, A.C., Dovrolis, C.: An experimental evaluation of rate-adaptation algorithms in adaptive streaming over HTTP. In: Proceedings of the Second Annual ACM Conference on Multimedia Systems, pp. 157–168 (2011)
10. Mok, R.K., Luo, X., Chan, E.W., Chang, R.K.: QDASH: a QoE-aware DASH system. In: Proceedings of the 3rd Multimedia Systems Conference, pp. 11–22 (2012)
11. Suh, D., Jang, I., Pack, S.: QoE-enhanced adaptation algorithm over DASH for multimedia streaming. In: International Conference on Information Networking (ICOIN), pp. 497–501 (2014)
12. ur Rahman, W., Chung, K.: Buffer-based adaptive bitrate algorithm for streaming over HTTP. KSII Trans. Internet Inf. Syst. (TIIS) **9**(11), 4585–4603 (2015)
13. Mok, R.K., Chan, E.W., Chang, R.K.: Measuring the quality of experience of HTTP video streaming. In: IFIP/IEEE International Symposium on Integrated Network Management (IM), pp. 485–492 (2011)
14. Singh, K.D., Hadjadj-Aoul, Y., Rubino, G.: Quality of experience estimation for adaptive HTTP/TCP video streaming using H.264/AVC. In: Consumer Communications and Networking Conference (CCNC), pp. 127–131 (2012)
15. Ni, P., Eg, R., Eichhorn, A., Griwodz, C., Halvorsen, P.: Spatial flicker effect in video scaling. In: Third International Workshop on Quality of Multimedia Experience (QoMEX), pp. 55–60 (2011)
16. Miller, K., Quacchio, E., Gennari, G., Wolisz, A.: Adaptation algorithm for adaptive streaming over HTTP. In: 19th International Workshop on Packet Video Workshop (PV), pp. 173–178 (2012)

Integrating Traditional Stores and e-Commerce into a Multi-tiered Recommender System Architecture Supported by IoT

Giancarlo Fortino[1,2], Antonio Guerrieri[2(✉)], Domenico Rosaci[3], and Giuseppe M. L. Sarné[4]

[1] DIMES, University of Calabria, Rende, Italy
giancarlo.fortino@unical.it
[2] ICAR-CNR, Rende, Italy
antonio.guerrieri@icar.cnr.it
[3] DIIES, University Mediterranea of Reggio Calabria, Reggio Calabria, Italy
domenico.rosaci@unirc.it
[4] DICEAM, University Mediterranea of Reggio Calabria, Reggio Calabria, Italy
sarne@unirc.it

Abstract. The use of Recommender Systems (RSs) to support customers and sellers in Business-to-Consumer activities is emerged in the last years and several RSs have been proposed on different e-Commerce platforms to provide customers with automatic and personalized suggestions. However, the information such tools catch in supporting B2C customers in their Web activities then are unused to support them on the traditional commerce. In other words, these two environments operate separately without implementing synergistic actions to share knowledge and experiences between these two modality of commerce. In this paper, we propose a distributed RS, called *ICR-IoT*, based on a multi-tiered agent architecture, conceived to realize such a synergy. The key of our idea is that of using a tier, based on the Internet-of-Things technology, designed to catch information about customers of traditional markets in order to generate very effective suggestions to support commercial activities both on a traditional store as well as on an e-Commerce site.

1 Introduction

The use of Recommender Systems (RSs) for supporting Business-to-Consumer (B2C) activities is quickly emerged in the last years [16,18] and several of such tools have been proposed on different e-Commerce (EC) platforms to provide customers with automatic and personalized recommendations. However, the information such tools catch in supporting B2C customers in their Web activities are unused to support them on the Traditional Commerce (TC). In other words, these environments operate independently without synergies to share knowledge and experiences between the two modalities of commerce.

G. Fortino et al. (Eds.): IDCS 2017, LNCS 10794, pp. 50–62, 2018.
https://doi.org/10.1007/978-3-319-97795-9_5

Currently, RSs fall in supporting customers and sellers mainly for an inadequate exploration of the whole market space, actually composed by (*i*) traditional stores and (*ii*) EC sites visited by customers. To face this issue, novel B2C systems, featuring high levels of automation, might exploit software agent technology to support EC actors along all their commercial activities are carried out both in a traditionally way and on the Web, with a high level of effectiveness.

More in detail, the goal of a RS is to provide its users with potentially useful suggestions for their purchases [20]. To this aim, intelligent software agents [21], by monitoring customers and sellers commercial activities, can build customers' profiles to represent their interests and preferences that RSs exploit across the steps of a B2C process to assist customers in a personalized way. To identify all the activities forming a commercial experience, more behavioral models have been proposed in the literature as the well-known Consumer Buying Behavior (CBB) model [9], derived by the traditional commerce, based on six stages, namely: (*i*) Need Identification; (*ii*) Product Brokering; (*iii*) Merchant Brokering; (*iv*) Negotiation; (*v*) Purchase and Delivery; (*vi*) Service and Evaluation.

Moreover, RSs active on the EC-sites can adopt a centralized or a distributed architecture, although a distributed approach, as in [14, 15], could be unacceptable on a mobile client due to its computational overheads. However, the main problem introduced in the literature for both these RSs is that of being conceived, in an exclusive manner, either for a TC or for an EC environment. This exclusivity does not allow that the information gathered by a RS on a traditional market to be also exploited into an online scenario, drastically limiting the effectiveness of the RS itself. For example, consider a customer that is visiting a traditional store, performing some CBB activities. The same customer could visit an EC-site, where the knowledge about his/her behavior in a traditional store could be useful to generate effective suggestions closer on his/her interests and preferences. Conversely, information on the customers behavior on an EC-site may be exploited in a traditional store to make suitable suggestions for him/her. This observation lead to the necessity of constructing an unique customer's profile, based on the overall set of his/her experiences on all the stores he/she frequented in the past, both traditional and online.

We argue that the key activity to build such a unique profile is to acquire useful information about the activities performed by the customer in traditional stores. Among the existing technologies, we suggest to use an Internet-of-Things (IoT) [1, 8] approach to acquire information about the customers behavior in traditional stores. More in detail, the IoT platform we propose consists of a customer agents set, living on the customers mobile phones, that by interacting with devices integrated with the products present in the store, and with other objects of the store itself (shopping trolleys, information boxes and so on) [10].

Summarizing, in this paper, we propose to integrate an IoT platform into a multi-tiered agent system, called Integrated Commerce Recommender using IoT (*ICR-IoT*), acting as a RS. This tier-based organization allows the distribution degree of the RS to be increased and to provide effective suggestions without onerous computational tasks on the client side and introducing advantages in terms of openness and privacy. In particular, the basic idea underlying our framework (Fig. 1) is that four software agents assist each customer. The first, named Information Agent, is devoted to catch information about interests and preferences of its associated customer when he/she visits an EC-site or a traditional store (by interacting with IoT objects) and transfers such information to the other customer agents, each one dealing with a different CBB stage. Each agent is running on a different thread in the customer's client, thus improving the efficiency of the overall process-making agent interactions specialized.

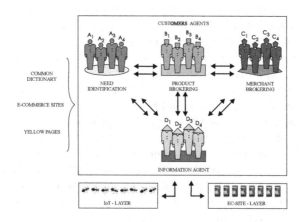

Fig. 1. The *ICR-IoT* architecture.

Each customer's agent, during its activity, can interact with the *ICR-IoT* sellers' nodes (associated with traditional stores and EC sites), while each seller is assisted by a seller agent provided with its product catalog and customers' profiles encoding the preferences of each customer visited the store. Such an interaction allows the customer agent to provide content-based (CB) suggestions for the customer and makes the seller agent able to generate personalized suggestions about its products to support the store visit. The customer agents also interact with the seller agents to reciprocally generate collaborative filtering (CF) suggestions. This way, if a customer c_1 needs to interact with a customer c_2 for need identification purposes, his/her Need Identification-agent interacts with the c_2's Need Identification-agent. The other agents of c_1 and c_2 are free to perform other activities, thus improving the system performances with respect to those systems where a unique agent can execute only one activity at time.

The rest of the paper is as follows. In Sect. 2, we present the *ICR-IoT* knowledge representation, while Sect. 3 presents the agents' behavior. Section 4 describes some related work and in Sect. 5 we discuss efficiency and some experimental results. Finally in Sect. 6 we draw some conclusions.

2 The *ICR-IoT* Knowledge Representation

Into the *ICR-IoT* framework, all the agents share a common dictionary containing the names of all the product categories and the relationships among categories. Furthermore, the profiles of the customers agents represent therein all the information involved in the associated CBB stage, while the profile of the Information Agent simply consists of the complete common dictionary. Similarly, the agent of each seller stores a catalogue of products organized in different categories. Moreover, in order to support the collaboration between different agents, a yellow page directory facilitator (DF) is active on the agent platform.

Dictionary of Categories. This dictionary, denoted as DC, stores the following information:

1. a list, named PC, of product categories;
2. a set CR of category relationships $\langle c_1; c_2; t \rangle$ where c_1 and c_2 belong to DC and t is the type of the relationship, that can be: ISA if all the products belonging to c_1 also belong to c_2; synonymy-linked, denoted by SYN, if both all the products belonging to c_1 also belong to c_2 and vice versa; overlap-linked, denoted by OVE, if there exists some product of c_1 that also belongs to c_2, and vice versa (note that if two categories are synonymy-linked, they are also overlap-linked); commercial-linked, denoted by COM, if we suppose that the customers usually purchase both products belonging to c_1 and c_2.

We represent the dictionary of categories DC as a direct labeled graph $G(DC) = \langle PC; CR \rangle$, where for each category $cat \in PC$ there is in the graph an associated node called nc; for each relationship belonging to CR there is an arc $\langle i; j; t \rangle$ oriented from i to j and labeled by t. Nodes represent product categories, which the products offered by the sellers belong to, and arcs represent existing relationships between categories. Moreover, we say that i and j belong to a category relationship ISA, SIN, OVE or COM if they are in the same dictionary and there is a path between i and j composed of arcs all labeled with that relationships. Moreover, we say that i and j belong to the category relationship GEN, if there is in DC a path between i and j independently of the specific arc-labels.

Agent and Site Profiles. To handle the Need Identification (resp. Product Brokering, Merchant Brokering) CBB stage in the *ICR-IoT* framework, each customer c is assisted in that stage by an agent, called *NI* (resp., *PB*, *MB*). Each customer agent dealing with a CBB stage stores in a profile, called *NI* (resp., *PB*, *MB*)-profile all the information about c necessary to handle the associated CBB stage. The profile is implemented by a dictionary of categories *NIP* (resp., *PBP*, *MBP*) where the nodes represent categories of interest (resp. product categories associated with products or merchants) for c, while the arcs represent relationships between categories and each category (resp. product of interest, merchant) is associated with a quantitative evaluation of the c's interest for it. Moreover, since a product (resp., merchant) search could be not activated for

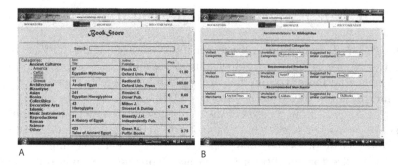

Fig. 2. (A) An example of an ICR-IoT site; (B) The personal agents recommendations.

each category (resp., product) of interest for c, the categories belonging to PBP (resp., MBP) are generally a subset of those in NIP (resp., PBP). Consequently, each arc of the PBP (resp., MBP) between categories corresponds to an arc belonging to the NIP (resp., PBP). Finally, each category belongs either to the common dictionary or to a *"personal"* customer's category (understandable to the other agents being in a general relationship with at least another category of DC). Remember that the Information Agent profile only stores a representation of DC.

Analogously, each seller s in the *ICR-IoT* platform is associated with a seller agent that represents into its site profile SP a catalog of products and information about the preferences of its past customers. Also SP is represented by the DC whose nodes represent product categories in which the seller s offers some products and whose arcs represent relationships between product categories.

We introduce in the framework a function $SP(cat)$, that accepts the category cat as input and yields as output the tuple $SP(cat) = \langle prod; cust \rangle$, where $prod$ is a list of products offered by the seller s in the category cat, and $cust$ is a list of users that purchased products belonging to cat. To access the elements of a list of products, we use a mapping $SP(cat).prod(p)$ that yields as input a product p and returns as output the tuple $SP(cat).prod(p) = \langle price; payment; format \rangle$, where $price$ is the price of p, $payment$ is the set of payment methods available for p and $format$ is the format available for p.

Directory Facilitator. The *Directory Facilitator* DF provides customers of the *ICR-IoT* platform with the possibility of publishing their interests. It consists of a set of category dictionaries $DC(c)$, one for each customer c. In particular, $DC(c)$ is a sub-graph of c's NI-profile, containing those categories cat in NI that are set as public by c.

3   The Information Agent Behavior in *ICR-IoT*

The *Information Agent* (IA) associated with c is a mobile agent, living on the devices of the customer c, having the capability of interacting both with each node of the IoT platform in the physical traditional commercial stores and with the EC-sites. This agent can interact with the *ICR-IoT* recommender framework when the user navigates on EC sites associated with the platform but it can also *"migrate"* to another customer's device for executing its tasks on that device.

3.1 Interacting with an EC Site

When c is interacting with an EC site, the *ICR-IoT*: (i) supports the Web site navigation of its user by acting as a normal browser; (ii) generates potentially useful recommendations for its user. To this end, the client interface is provided with two facilities, called Browse and Recommend, described below. Remember that each information related to the c's activities on the EC-site is caught by the *Information Agent* and sent to the other c's agents. For sake of simplicity, below this step is omitted. If c is a newcomer, his/her *NI* agent builds an initial *NI*-Profile *NIP* by adding the categories of his/her interest, together with their relationships, from *DC*. Moreover, c can choose to add to *NIP* some personal categories belonging to *DC* by specifying for each of them its name and path in *NIP* and joining *cat* with at least another category in *DC*. Besides, for each selected category *cat*, c should specify his/her interest degree $NIP(cat).interest$ and the visibility mode $NIP(cat).mode$ (in order to preserve his/her privacy).

Browsing EC Sites: Agents Working over the Shoulders. Each *ICR-IoT* site provides the customer c with the following capabilities:

1. Navigating through the categories by means of the tab *"Browser"* (Fig. 2-A);
2. Using the Search tool for a keyword-based search among the products sold at fixed price (i.e., *"Buy-It-Now"*) or with an auction (i.e., *"Make an Offer"*). For each product $p \in cat$, c can perform the tasks: T_a: Selecting the product to know the offer; T_b: Watching the product; T_c: Purchasing the product.

Each task T_a, T_b or T_c performed by c implies a call to the agents *NI*, *PB* and *MB* that automatically update their profiles and in particular:

- The *NI*-agent is invoked, feeding it the category *cat*. If *cat* is not in its profile, it is added therein and its interest value $NIP(cat)$ is set to an initial value *iniInt*. Then the *NI*-agent requires to the *PB* and *MB* agents to add *cat* and its interest value to their profiles. Otherwise, if $cat \in NIP$, its interest value is updated to $NIP(cat) = min(1; NIP(cat) + D_a)$, where D_a (with $a = T_a; T_b; T_c$) is a parameter arbitrarily set by c in $[0; 1]$. The value $NIP(cat)$ is then passed to the agents *PB* and *MB* to update their profiles.
- The client invokes the *PB*-agent for the product p. If p does not belong to *PB*-profile it is added to the list $PBP(cat).prod$ (with *iniInt* set as interest value) and its insertion in $MBP(cat).prod$ belonging to the *MB*-agent is required. Otherwise, if $p \in PBP$, then $PBP(cat).prod(p).i = min(1; PBP(cat).prod(p).i + D_a)$ and its value copied in $MBP(cat).p.i$.

– The client invokes the MB agent, sending as input the seller s. If $s \notin MBP$ it is added to the list $MBP(cat).sellers$ with $nT = 1$ and a score equal to $iniInt$. Otherwise, nT is increased by 1 and $MBP(cat).sellers(s).ev = min(1; MBP(cat) : sellers(s).ev + D_a)$. Periodically, the value $NIP(cat).i$ (resp., $PBP(cat).prod(p).i$, $MBP(cat).sellers(s).ev$) associated with the NI (resp., PB, MB)-profile, after a tNI (resp. tPB, tMB) time period it is decreased of rNI (resp. rPB, rMB), a parameter set by c in $[0; 1]$.

In addition, the seller agent of s updates its list $SPP(cat).customers \in SPP$ after each customer's task that involves a product p belonging to cat. In particular, if c belongs to $SPP(cat).customers$, then a new element $SPP(cat).customers(c)$ is added to it. Moreover, p is added to the list $SPP(cat).customers(c).prod$ and the number of transactions $SP(cat).customers(c).nT$ is increased. Otherwise, if c belongs to $SP.(cat).customers$, the seller agent updates the element $SPP(cat).customers(c)$ by increasing the number of transactions $SPP(cat).customers(c).nT$ and inserting p in $SPP(cat).customers(c).prod$ if it is currently absent.

Recommending Products: Exploiting Customer's Profiles. When the customer c selects the tab *"Recommender"* in his/her client, then some suggestions are generated for him/her and visualized in a page with a section for each supported stage (Fig. 2-B). Each agent in a cascade mode computes such suggestions. Firstly, the customer chooses a category from those belonging to the section *"Recommended Categories"*. Then, a set of products is suggested in the section *"Recommended Products"*. When a product is chosen, a set of merchants selling that product is suggested in the section *"Recommended Merchants"*.

The NI-agent recommends c with a set of categories visualized in the client section *"Recommended Categories"* in the three distinct list-boxes (Fig. 2-B):

– *Visited Categories*, containing categories selected with a *CB* approach from the NIP built by monitoring the c's activity (see Sect. 3).
– *Unvisited Categories* lists all the categories yet unknown for c, but supposed interesting for him/her by his/her NI-agent. This agent adopts a relationship-based mechanism to exploit the interaction between the c's NI-agent and those of the sites he/she visited in the past. The agent of a seller s, for each category cat visited by c (i.e., c belongs to $SPP(cat).customers$), determines all the categories $cat*$ belonging to SPP such that $cat*$ is unvisited by c and there exists a path in SPP between cat and $cat*$. All these categories are sent to the c's NI-agent, to be added to this list.
– *Suggested by Similar Customers*, where the categories are determined, with a CF technique, on the whole EC customer's navigation history by the c's NI-agent collaborating with the NI-agents of customers similar to c for interests. To this aim, it is exploited the directory facilitator DF (see Sect. 2) storing, for each customer x his/her public interest profile $IP(x)$. The c's NI-agent computes the similarity degree $s(c; x)$ between these two profiles by using the Jaccard measure of the set of nodes of NIP and $IP(x)$ for n different customers (where n is a parameter set by c). Then, the c's NI-agent determines,

for each similar customer x, those categories stored in the public profile $IP(x)$ that do not belong to NIP, and adds them to this list.

The PB-agent (resp., MB-agent) suggests, in the section "*Product Recommendations*" (resp., "*Merchant Recommendations*") a set of products (resp., sellers) of the category cat selected by c from the recommended categories (resp., products) on his/her client and visualized in the following listboxes:

- *Visited Products* (resp., *Sellers*): it shows products (resp., sellers) of the category cat belonging to PB-profile $P(PBc)$ (resp., MB-profile $P(MBc)$).
- *Unvisited Products* (resp., *Sellers*), this list is built by means of a collaboration between the c's PB (resp., MB)-agent and the seller agent of each site visited by c. For a PB-agent, each listed $p \in cat$ is unvisited by c and belongs to each site profile. Differently, for the MB-agent the set is formed by those sellers having cat in their profiles and are unvisited by c in the past.
- *Similar Customers Suggest*: these suggestions arise by the collaboration between the PB (resp., MB)-agents of c and those of other customers similar for interests (their list is provided by the c's NI-agent). Each of the PB (resp., MB)-agent of these customers sends to c's PB (resp., MB)-agent its set of products $PBP(cat).prod$ (resp., $sellersMBP(cat).sellers$) that is added to this list. The PB (resp., MB)-agent shows the products (resp. *sellers*) belonging to the listbox "*Visited Products*" (resp., "*Visited Sellers*") and the products (resp., *sellers*) belonging to the listboxes "*Unvisited Products*" (resp., "*Unvisited Sellers*") and "*Suggested by Similar Customers*".

Each seller agent SA associated with a seller s exploits its profile SP to personalize the site presentation for each customer c that is visiting it. When c finished to visit the site, then the element $SP(cat).customers(c)$ will be inserted in the SA profile. Using such an information, SA personalizes its home page for c by visualizing in a specific *Shop Window* all the products belonging to $SP(cat).customers(c).prod$, ordered by interest value. The seller agent SA uses this list as a sort of local profile related to c and at the same time, it increments the value $SP(cat).customers(c).numV$ to consider his/her current visit.

Interacting with the IoT Platform. When the *Information Agent* is interacting with a node of the underlying IoT platform, corresponding to a product situated in a physical traditional store, he/she performs the following actions:

(i) It acquires the information coming by the node (e.g., brand, price and so on) and updates the NI, PB and MB-profiles, accordingly to the description given above, where the tasks T_a (Selecting the product to know the offer), T_b (Watching the product) and T_c (Purchasing the product) are automatically revealed by the exploited IoT technology. For instance, if the cellular phone is close to the product provided by an RFID label, the action T_a is performed, while if the card associated to the product is visualized on the agent interface in the cellular phone, then the action T_b is performed. When the product will be purchased at the checkout, the action T_c is performed.

(ii) It displays the recommendations for its user generated by the other customers agents, accordingly with the description given above.

4   Related Work

Centralized RSs are widely exploited, and often embedded, in Web EC-sites. The well known is the Amazon site [2] adopts some RSs founded on the analysis of the customer's browsing history, past purchases and purchases carried out by other customers. The system drives a customer to buy something because it is linked to something that he/she already purchased, or for its popularity. Also eBay [7], as other auction sites [6], provides suggestions based on profile features. These cited centralized approaches generate, similarly to *ICR-IoT*, both CB and CF recommendations and store all the private information about customers and sellers necessary to generate recommendations. Differently to *ICR-IoT* they are not open and use pre-defined dictionaries of terms for the product categories, while *ICR-IoT* allows the users to define new terms in their personal ontologies.

Distributed RSs (DRSs) share their tasks among more computational entities. Notwithstanding, the greater complexity of DRSs in terms of design and performances optimization [12] with respect to CRSs, they are growing in diffusion for their potential scalability in time and space complexities, higher privacy and security and, finally, their robustness to faults due to the distributed nature.

Many DRSs exploit on the peer-to-peer (P2P) and agents technologies to exchange local data with other peer (e.g., Chord [19]) in a cooperative fashion. In CASy (Competitive Attention-space System) [4] learning agents, associated with the shops of a mall, monitor each transaction carried out therein and support each visiting customer, on the basis of the interests stored in his/her profile and suggestions coming from other shop agents. In [5] a P2P DRS adopting a user-based filtering algorithm optimizing scalability and privacy is introduced. It adapts its computations to the density of the user neighborhood. Another P2P DRS implementing a CF approach, in a computationally efficient way, is presented in [3] for auction systems like eBay [7]. It implements a highly scalable distributed algorithm adopting a P2P solution based on best-seller lists and tolerates malicious users, an important feature for P2P environments. This system, on average, has a time complexity of $\theta(n + mlog2m)$, where n is the total number of products and m is the total number of users in the system, with a significant advantage on usual the computational complexities of this RSs class of $\theta(m + n)$ and $\theta(m2n)$ [13]. A knowledge-based DSR managing tourism issues is proposed in [11] by using a multi-agent system, where agents support users searching travel packages by reciprocally exchanging information coming from their local knowledge-bases. Each user is supported by more agents, each one expert in a domain (hotel, flights, interchanges, and so on). Here each task is decomposed in more sub-tasks and each agent is free to choice the sub-task closer to its skills based on its experiences. All the resulting agent recommendations are then composed to form the best travel package as possible. MobHinter [17] is a CF DRS developed for mobile ad-hoc networks exploited by the devices

to collaborate with other devices not accessing to remote on-line data repositories when other communication channels are inaccessible. MobHinter searches
affinities among the neighbors to receive personalized suggestions.

All the referred DRSs take advantage of the distributed architectures in terms
of scalability, risks failure, privacy and security. Any of them, differently from
ICR-IoT, provides a specific support to a customer on the Need Identification,
Product or Merchant Brockering CBB stages based on his/her interests and
preferences (excepted [3] where agents can decide if using or not the information
stored in customers profile). Moreover, *ICR-IoT* generates both CB and CF
recommendations separately for each one of the considered CBB stages. All
these recommenders and *ICR-IoT* are (or should be, as in [5,17]) agent-based
and/or exploit a P2P platform to find similar neighbors, resources and exploit
predefined services. An agent specialization is considered in [11] and *ICR-IoT*,
but the first one refers to an item specialization while our system considers the
different phase involved into an EC activity (as described in the CBB model).

5   Efficiency and Effectiveness of *ICR-IoT*

In this Section, we discuss efficiency and some experimental results about the
advantages of our approach. In terms of efficiency, for a community of n customers and m sellers, a unique centralized agent managing all the three CBB
phases has computational cost of $NC = \sum_{i=1}^{3} n_i \cdot k_i$, where k_i and n_i are the
number of contemporary sessions activated and of operations needed for a user
to manage the *Need Identification, Product* and *Merchant Brokering* phases,
respectively. Instead, in *ICR-IoT*, for a given CBB stage, each user's agent can
deal with more different issues, which run on different threads.

Let α_i, be the multi-threading degrees for a specific CBB stage and let
$\beta = k_1 + k_2$ be the computational overhead due to the communications between
the local agents (i.e., the *Need Identification* agent calls the *Product Broker*
agent, that in its turn can call the *Merchant Broker* agent that does not run
any additional operation). In this way the computational cost for a CPU will
be $ND = \beta + \sum_{i=1}^{3} \alpha_i \cdot n_i \cdot k_i$ and the computational advantage (ρ), due to the
distribution in *ICR-IoT*, is equal to $\rho = \frac{\beta + \sum_{i=1}^{3} \alpha_i \cdot n_i \cdot k_i}{\sum_{i=1}^{3} n_i \cdot k_i}$, where if, for simplicity,
$a = a_1 = a_2 = a_3$ and $k = k_1 = k_2 = k_3$ and $N = n_1 + n_2 + n_3$, the above formula
becomes $\rho = \alpha + 2/N$. Therefore, the advantage of using *ICR-IoT* is perceivable
with a small multi-threading contribution (i.e. high values of α) in presence of
a reasonably high number of operations (i.e., an intense EC activity), while for
a high multi-threading activity the advantage shows up also for small N values.

In terms of effectiveness, the time exploited to perform B2C processes in serial
and multi-threading way has been compared by means of a software appositively
designed. To this aim, we considered a period of 2 h where a set of 500 customers
finalize all their B2C processes with a purchase dealing with a merchant population (M) of 10 units. Moreover, the merchant has to satisfy also the requests due
to other customers that could absorb significant merchants' servers resources.

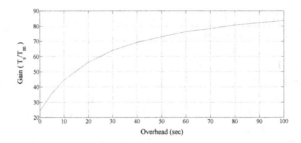

Fig. 3. The average serial (T_s) and multi-threading (T_m) times (in sec.) for carrying out a B2C process depending on the Overhead due to 500 Customers and 10 Merchants.

This is taken into account by means of an overhead (O) of 1100 requests for second, randomly shared among the merchants. Finally, a lot of different of communication, computational and behavioral parameters have been tuned to model realistic B2C processes. Obviously, in order to compute in average the time (in seconds) needed to perform a purchase process in a multi-threading (T_m) and in a serial (T_s) modality the same values for the parameters have been used. More in detail, T_m (i.e., T_s) has been computed as $T_m = \sum_{n=1}^{NP} T_{mn}/NP$, where NP is the number of purchases, randomly fixed, performed in the considered test session. The experimental results shown in Fig. 3 confirm that the *ICR-IoT* approach consumes in average about the 25% of time less than the serial approach in performing a purchase in absence of overhead and when the overhead grows also T_s grows with it while T_m is almost uniform. In Table 1 are reported the average gain (G) in percentage of T_s with respect to T_m for different values of the overhead. This behavior is because changes in the number of merchants, overheads and so on, have a minimal impact on T_m and very high impact on T_s. This because, in average, each merchant's server is busy to satisfy the customers' requests and T_s grows with the level of "*saturation*" of the merchants' servers worsening the quality of their service.

Table 1. The average gain ($G = T_s/T_m$) to carry out a B2C process depending on the number of Overhead by considering 500 Customers and 10 Merchants.

O	0	5	10	20	30	40	50	60	70	80	90	100
G	24.61	36.12	44.63	56.43	63.98	69.19	73.05	76.39	78.39	80.75	82.28	83.61

6   Conclusions

In this paper, we have presented advantages and limitations of the *ICR-IoT* distributed architecture that introduces novel, original characteristics with respect to other recommenders. *ICR-IoT* allows to the different CBB stages of an EC process to be assigned to a different agent creating a tier of specialized agents.

This architecture reduces the computational cost for the device on which the local agents run and the presence of specialized agents improves the users' knowledge representations, the openness of the system and the privacy degree.

Acknowledgment. This work has been developed within by the Networks and Complex Systems (NeCS) Laboratory, Dep. DICEAM, University Mediterranea of Reggio Calabria.

References

1. Aloi, G., Caliciuri, G., Fortino, G., Gravina, R., Pace, P., Russo, W., Savaglio, C.: Enabling iot interoperability through opportunistic smartphone-based mobile gateways. J. Netw. Comput. Appl. **81**, 74–84 (2017)
2. Amazon URL (2017). http://www.amazon.com
3. Awerbuch, B., Patt-Shamir, B., Peleg, D., Tuttle, M.: Improved recommendation systems. In: Proceedings of the 16th ACM-SIAM Symposium on Discrete Algorithms, pp. 1174–1183. Society for Industrial and Applied Mathematics (2005)
4. Bohte, S., Gerding, E., Poutré, H.: Market-based recommendation: agents that compete for consumer attention. ACM Trans. Internet Technol. **4**(4), 420–448 (2004)
5. Castagnos, S., Boyer, A.: Personalized communities in a distributed recommender system. In: Advances in Information Retrieval, pp. 343–355 (2007)
6. Culver, B.: Recommender system for auction sites. J. Comput. Sci. Coll. **19**(4), 355–355 (2004)
7. eBay URL (2017). http://www.ebay.com
8. Fortino, G., Trunfio, P.: Internet of Things Based on Smart Objects: Technology, Middleware and Applications. Springer, Cham (2014). https://doi.org/10.1007/978-3-319-00491-4
9. Guttman, R., Moukas, A., Maes, P.: Agents as mediators in electronic commerce. Electron. Mark. **8**(1), 22–27 (1998)
10. Karnouskos, S., Marrón, P.J., Fortino, G., Mottola, L., Martínez-de Dios, J.R.: Applications and Markets for Cooperating Objects. Springer, Heidelberg (2014). https://doi.org/10.1007/978-3-642-45401-1
11. Lorenzi, F., Correa, F., Bazzan, A., Abel, M., Ricci, F.: A multiagent recommender system with task-based agent specialization. In: AMEC, pp. 103–116 (2008)
12. Olson, T.: Bootstrapping and decentralizing recommender systems. Thesis (2003)
13. Papagelis, M., Rousidis, I., Plexousakis, D., Theoharopoulos, E.: Incremental collaborative filtering for highly-scalable recommendation algorithms. In: Hacid, M.-S., Murray, N.V., Raś, Z.W., Tsumoto, S. (eds.) ISMIS 2005. LNCS (LNAI), vol. 3488, pp. 553–561. Springer, Heidelberg (2005). https://doi.org/10.1007/11425274_57
14. Parikh, N., Sundaresan, N.: Buzz-based recommender system. In: Proceedings of the 18th International conference on WWW, pp. 1231–1232. ACM (2009)
15. Rosaci, D.: Sarnè, G.M.L., Garruzzo, S: MUADDIB: a distributed recommender system supporting device adaptivity. ACM Trans. Inf. Syst. **27**(4), 24:1–24:41 (2009)
16. Schafer, J., Konstan, J., Riedl, J.: E-commerce recommendation applications. Data Min. Knowl. Discov. **5**(1–2), 115–153 (2001)

17. Schifanella, R., Panisson, A., Gena, C., Ruffo, G.: Mobhinter: epidemic collaborative filtering and self-organization in mobile ad-hoc networks. In: Proceedings of the 2008 ACM Conference on Recommender Systems, pp. 27–34. ACM (2008)

18. Sivapalan, S., Sadeghian, A., Rahnama, H., Madni, A.: Recommender systems in e-commerce. In: World Automation Congress, pp. 179–184. IEEE (2014)

19. Stoica, I., Morris, R., Karger, D., Kaashoek, M., Balakrishnan, H.: Chord: a scalable peer-to-peer lookup service for internet applications. SIGCOMM Comput. Commun. Rev. **31**, 149–160 (2001)

20. Wei, K., Huang, J., Fu, S.: A survey of e-commerce recommender systems. In: 2007 International Conference on Service Systems and Service Management, pp. 1–5. IEEE (2007)

21. Wooldridge, M., Jennings, N.R.: Agent theories, architectures, and languages: a survey. In: Wooldridge, M.J., Jennings, N.R. (eds.) ATAL 1994. LNCS, vol. 890, pp. 1–39. Springer, Heidelberg (1995). https://doi.org/10.1007/3-540-58855-8_1

Smart Nutrition Monitoring System Using Heterogeneous Internet of Things Platform

Bahman Javadi[1]([✉]), Rodrigo N. Calheiros[1], Kenan M. Matawie[1],
Athula Ginige[1], and Amelia Cook[2]

[1] School of Computing, Engineering and Mathematics,
Western Sydney University, Sydney, Australia
b.javadi@westernsydney.edu.au
[2] School of Science and Health, Western Sydney University,
Sydney, Australia

Abstract. Poor nutrition impairs the health and wellbeing of the population and increases the risk of chronic diseases such as obesity and type 2 diabetes. Chronic diseases that require dietary management can be better managed if food and nutrition intake is monitored. Existing methods for measurement are inaccurate and not scalable as they are based on a person's ability to recall and self-report. In this paper, we propose a smart nutrition monitoring system based on Internet of Things (IoT) technologies to collect reliable nutrition intake data from heterogeneous sensors. The proposed method is non-invasive and consists of a combination of data sources from heterogeneous devices to increase accuracy. The system architecture is based on emerging Fog Computing concepts where data collection points are able to do the preprocessing and lightweight analytics before sending data to the Cloud. The system prototype is developed using various sensors including cameras to generate 3D images for food volume estimation.

1 Introduction

Healthy eating has a great impact on the lifestyle quality and can prevent diet-related diseases such as diabetes, obesity and cardiovascular disease [1]. Research data from the Institute for Health Metrics and Evaluation (IHME)[1] in 2015 revealed that dietary risks are the leading cause of disease burden in Australia and contributed to more health loss than smoking, alcohol, and drug use. There are also significant economic costs associated with diet-related chronic diseases. For instance, the estimated financial cost for type 2 diabetes alone is more than $14 billion per year in Australia[2]. This cost is about $200 billion per year in USA for obesity [2].

---

[1] http://www.healthdata.org/.
[2] https://www.diabetesaustralia.com.au/.

© Springer Nature Switzerland AG 2018
G. Fortino et al. (Eds.): IDCS 2017, LNCS 10794, pp. 63–74, 2018.
https://doi.org/10.1007/978-3-319-97795-9_6

The ability to manage food and nutrition is vital to a healthy and productive society. Self-monitoring food intake, with the provision of automated and tailored feedback, is an effective strategy to build awareness of one's current diet and eating patterns. This would require a smart nutrition monitoring system. Traditional dietary assessment methods (e.g., 24 h recalls, food frequency questionnaires) are either unable to provide individual level feedback with the necessary precision, or they are impractical for self-monitoring, largely due to participant burden and low scalability [3]. More advanced approaches for food intake monitoring are based on smart phones [4], but still they rely heavily on user memory and recall, which is not practical for many, especially for people with memory disorders.

Recently, many researchers have attempted to address these issues using wearable sensor devices [5]. The main advantage of this approach is removing the burden of self-report. Although there are several studies to adopt these sensors to monitor food intake, most of them have been tested in laboratory conditions for limited number of participants [6]. Moreover, almost all of them are based on a single sensor, which limits the accuracy of data collection and consequently data reliability. The average accuracy for nutrition intake using these sensors is about 90% in laboratory environments [7]. So an open challenge is to find a non-invasive solution to monitor nutrition intake in real-life scenarios with a high degree of accuracy.

In this paper, we investigate the use of Internet of Things (IoT) technologies to collect nutrition intake data. The Internet of Things is an emerging technology consisting of several heterogeneous devices that can exchange data without human interaction [8]. This will enable non-invasive measurement of food intake by collecting data from different devices including wearable and environmental sensors. To limit the scope of this project, we only focus on take-away foods for young adults. We consider young adults (ages 18–35) as they are at a heightened risk of harmful effects of unhealthy "meals out", because they spend, proportionately, even more on the "Meals out and fast food" category than any other age group [9].

The rest of this paper is organized as follows. Related work is described in Sect. 2. In Sect. 3, we present the problem statement of smart nutrition monitoring system. Section 4 includes the detail of the proposed system model and its components. The system prototype and its implementation details are presented in Sect. 5. Conclusions and future work are presented in Sect. 6.

2   Related Work

There are several research about measuring food and nutrition intake to manage and control the eating habit. There are two main approaches to address this challenge: manual and automatic techniques. Manual approaches are based on self-reports on paper [10], smart phones [9], or questionnaires [11]. In the paper-based methods, users need to provide the detail of the meals and beverages that they consumed during the day based on the personal recall. In a more advanced method, paper is replaced by smart phones so there will be a better user interface and faster response time from the dietitian or doctor. The last manual method is based on food frequency questionnaires where food consumption frequency is collected for a period of time (not for every single meal). All these manual methods are based on personal recall and might be imprecise. Moreover, these methods discourage people to continue recording due to lack of convenience and on average only 15% of the participants complete the program [12].

In order to address the issues in manual techniques, automatic methods based on environmental and wearable sensors are proposed [5]. The main advantage of the automatic approach is removing the burden of self-report. For instance, using environmental sensor such as cameras, automatic food intake detection from captured images of human faces during the eating process can be achieved [13]. However, this technique is not able to detect specific food types or food composition. Similar techniques based on motion sensors or pressure sensors have similar drawbacks while they have restriction to be used in free-living populations [14].

Automatic methods based on wearable sensors could be potential solutions as they do not rely on user's input and provide real time food intake monitoring. These sensors adapt various detection techniques such as chewing [15], swallowing [16] and wrist motion [17]. Although there are several studies to adopt these sensors to monitor food intake, most of them have been tested in laboratory conditions for limited number of participants [6]. The average accuracy for nutrition intake using these sensors is about 90% in laboratory environments [7]. Moreover, almost all of them are based on a single sensor, which limits the accuracy of data collection and consequently data reliability. So an open challenge is to find a non-invasive solution to monitor nutrition intake in real-life scenarios with a high degree of accuracy.

Because of the aforementioned limitations in existing methods for tracking nutrition intake, in this paper we investigate the use of Internet of Things (IoT) and Fog computing-based technologies to collect nutrition intake data from heterogeneous data sources. While using wearable sensors seem initially a better approach, they have many limitations in real-life scenarios, so our approach is based on environmental sensors. The approach is detailed in the next sections.

3   Smart Nutrition Monitoring System

We devise a Nutrition Smart Monitoring System that utilizes IoT, Fog computing, and hierarchical data analytics to provide an accurate understanding of the dietary habits of young adults, which can be used by users themselves as a motivator for change behavior and by dietitians to provide better guidance to their patients.

One of the main objectives when designing the system was *minimizing the amount of direct input and actions from users*, what may motivate continuous utilization of the system. Another objective of the system was achieving the goals of accurate data collection with inexpensive IoT devices. To circumvent limitations of such devices, we envision that *multiple and heterogeneous IoT devices will be used in a single data collection* and that statistical analysis will be carried out in the background to conciliate the information and increase accuracy. Finally, we aimed at leveraging emerging Fog Computing [18] capabilities in the architecture. By Fog Computing, we mean the capability of enabling some computation to occur in the edge of the network and the rest in the cloud. This decision is motivated by key capabilities of Fog Computing such as reduced communication latency (by enabling local computation) while taking advantage of the higher scale of cloud resources for heavier data analysis and computation.

The proposed smart nutrition monitoring system is composed of a kiosk where diverse sensors are installed. Since we are targeting take-away foods, this should be designed in a way that users can access that in the same place that they buy the food (e.g., restaurants). This kiosk will be equipped with various IoT sensors to collect weight, volume and structure (e.g., molecular pattern) of the food. The only action required from users is to authenticate with the kiosk (via a mobile app) and deposit the food in the kiosk for a couple of seconds while relevant information is obtained by the sensors. Once data is obtained, users can cease interaction with the kiosk and can proceed with their daily activities. Therefore, the data collection will be done with a non-invasive technique where the user does not need to enter any information about the food. The kiosk also has a built-in controller as part of Fog Computing system to process and communicate the collected data with other components of the system.

Data collected by the kiosks are sent to cloud servers where it is stored and processed. In a later time, reports and charts can be generated to the user (and optionally to their dietitian, if the user is the patient of a dietitian and wishes to share the information). Users and dietitians are the two actors in our envisioned system. Nevertheless, only users generate input data; dietitians can only generate reports and visualize their patients' information.

4   System Model and Architecture

Figure 1 presents the architecture of the Smart Nutrition Monitoring System. It is composed of two parts: the data collection points (kiosks) that analyze the presented food by user and the engine that carries out the relevant data storage, processing, reporting, and visualization. The kiosk has processing capabilities that enables it to play the role of edge device in a Fog Computing environment. Our system is complemented by two external components: cloud servers for data processing and an external database able to provide nutrition information about the food. Each component is discussed in the rest of this section. Implementation details of each component are discussed in Sect. 5.

4.1   Data Collection Points

The main interface between users and the system to enter information are the data collection points (i.e., kiosks). Users present the food in the kiosk and

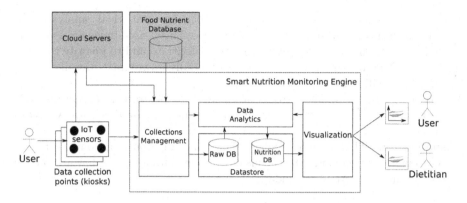

Fig. 1. Architecture of the smart nutrition monitoring system.

authenticate with the system via a mobile app. The same app triggers the process of activating the sensors so data is collected and send to the relevant systems.

Kiosks are designed to be modular: different kiosks can have different sensors in a given time. This gives flexibility to expand the units when new technologies are available and also enable data collection to progress even if some sensors are faulty. Regardless the particular sensors in operation, the concept behind kiosks is the following: kiosks are box-like structures that are large enough to accommodate a dish with food and sensors.

Data is collected by the heterogeneous sensors and aggregated before being transmitted. Cameras located in the kiosk also capture photos from the food from different angles and transmit them to the Cloud servers to generate a 3D model of the food, which will be used for food volume estimation.

4.2 Smart Nutrition Monitoring Engine

The Smart Nutrition Monitoring Engine has four components that are responsible for different aspects of the system, as follows.

Collections Management. This component provides an API that is accessed by the kiosks to upload food intake data and by the Cloud servers to return the results of computing-intensive operations (such as rendering of the 3D model of the food). In terms of functionality, it stores all the information in a raw database. The data that is stored is a combination of the information received by the other components and also nutritional value of the food that was presented. The latter is obtained from an external source which can be accessed, for example, via a nutrient database[3]. Another responsibility of the Collections Management is to request the Data Analytics module to perform specific operations when new data is collected from kiosks.

---

[3] See, for example, https://www.fatsecret.com, which maintains such a database that can be accessed via RESTful APIs.

Data Analytics. This module is responsible for statistical analysis and machine learning activities in the architecture. This is used to generate reports and analyses that are relevant to users and dietitians and to identify the food that has been presented by users (and potentially its volume). Details of such analysis are discussed in Sect. 4.4.

Datastore. This component stores both raw data (sourced from the user utilization of kiosks) and data that has been processed by the Data Analytics module.

Visualization. This module displays charts showing consumption of different nutrients over time and other forms of complex data analysis that are carried out by the Data Analytics module.

4.3   Cloud Servers

Cloud servers are adopted in the system for complex data processing such as 3D models rendering using multiple photos taken from different angles from the food deposited in the kiosk by users. The generation of the 3D model is a highly CPU-intensive application, and takes over 1 h even for very simple samples.

Our architecture does not specify if the server capabilities are obtained via dedicated private clouds or by using public cloud services. In fact, the latter enables on-demand scaling to enable generation of multiple models in parallel when necessary. Regardless the choice, a strategy for adaptive provisioning and scheduling of cloud nodes for the architecture needs to be adopted, such as the approach proposed by Cai et al. [19]. Another alternative for this component is a hybrid approach, where a private cloud is used and public cloud nodes are added dynamically when the queue for model generation in the private cloud reaches a certain size. This is known in the literature as cloud burst, and there are solutions available for the problem [20,21].

4.4   Data Analytics

Data collected for this project come from different sources and sensors applications, and can be complex and decomposite of different numerical and digital data. Integrating such multiple responses will greatly help to capture more accurate and valuable data that are useful to determine more significant statistical modeling and analysis that will serve different purposes in this area.

The automation of data collection will set the infrastructure and scale for machine learning tasks. This will include algorithms to integrate the data, detect objects, estimate volumes, and determine or estimate the associated nutritional composition values. Apart from visualization analysis and classification techniques used for object recognition, this analysis will involve various advanced statistical methodology such as Hidden Markov model, Support Vector machine, image and signal processing, clustering and prediction. Some of these techniques were used in wearable food intake monitoring, more details and review are given in [7].

The other part of this analytics is the accuracy and reliability of the collected data and the optimal form of the aggregated values. It is expected this will result in better and more significant predicted values that can be compared with standard nutritional calculations and tables. This will modify, update, and validate dietitians evaluation, interpretation, investigation, and accuracy of their values and recommendations. Daily and monthly food consumptions and other predictions based on this approach can also be used for time-series analysis and prediction of food consumption.

5   System Prototype

To demonstrate the viability and feasibility of our approach, we have developed a prototype of the Smart Nutrition Monitoring System as shown in Fig. 2. Details are discussed in the rest of this section.

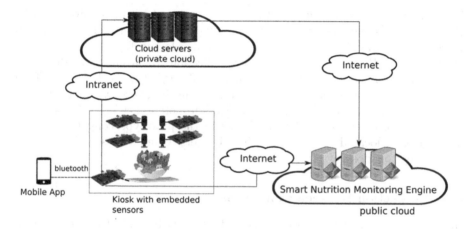

Fig. 2. Prototype of the smart nutrition monitoring system.

5.1   Data Collection Points Prototype

The prototype version of the Data Collection Points, e.g., the Kiosk, utilizes Raspberry Pi 3 Model B boards (Quad Core 1.2 GHz Broadcom BCM2837 CPU, 1 GB of RAM) to interact with sensors and the rest of the architecture. There are 5 cameras with 8 megapixel resolution, each of which is attached to one Raspberry Pi. As the sensor device, we used the SITU Smart Scale[4], which is a smart food scale that communicates with other devices via Bluetooth. The vendor provides an app for iOS and an SDK that Android developers can use to develop their own apps. Besides the Raspberry Pis connected to cameras, there is an extra board that has a *Master* role. The Master is used to connect

---

[4] http://situscale.com/.

to the scale, receive the photos from the Raspberry Pis connected to cameras, and to interface with the architecture. To better integrate with the scale, the Master Raspberry Pi in our prototype had its Operating system replaced by emteria.OS[5] (Android-compatible Operating System that is optimized to run in Raspberry Pi 3).

The process of information capture is triggered by users via a mobile app we developed. In this method, previously registered users of the system deposit the food dish in the kiosk, authenticate with the app, and tap a button on the app, which sends a message to a process running on the Master Raspberry Pi, indicating that the data collection process should start. The Master Raspberry Pi then collects the reading from the scale and from the other Raspberry Pis and sends all the relevant information to the Smart Nutrition Monitoring Engine via WiFi connection.

5.2   Smart Nutrition Monitoring Engine Prototype

The Smart Nutrition Monitoring Engine was designed with two key principles in mind (i) it should be built as a "cloud-first" application and (ii) it should leverage best practices in distributed software development.

To achieve these goals, the Engine's Collection Management module prototype has been developed in Java using the Jersey framework for RESTFul web services and is deployed on Tomcat 9.0. The Engine's Datastore module uses MySQL 5.7 and the Engine's Visualization module has been developed in ASP.Net. The external cloud servers used in the prototype consist of a computing cluster located at Western Sydney University and accessed via the local network by the kiosk.

5.3   Interaction Between Components

Interaction with the Engine occurs via a RESTful API, and is depicted in Fig. 3. Following best practices in the development of such APIs, this API is resource-centric: it is organized around the notion of a "collection" the represents a single use of the kiosk by a user to upload nutritional information.

When the kiosk is activated by the user (via the mobile app that also authenticates the user), it undertakes two actions: firstly, it uploads information and requests the creation of a unique endpoint (URL) that can be used later to upload the 3D model of the food. This step occurs via a POST request to a specific endpoint. The unique URL generated as a response to the initial data upload is determined by the kiosk rather than by the engine. This is because the URL needs to be communicated to the cloud servers so it knows where to send the 3D food model once it is generated.

On successful upload of the information and creation of the unique endpoint, the Engine, via its Collections Management module, sends the photos for processing to the cluster alongside with the information about the URL where the

---

[5] https://emteria.com/.

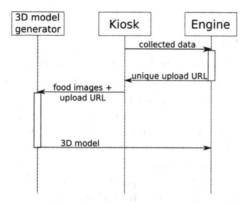

Fig. 3. Sequence diagram showing how the different components of the smart nutrition monitoring system interact to enable capture and manage nutrition intake of users.

model, once generated, needs to be uploaded. The successful creation of the unique URL address also enables that update, reading, and deletion of data related to this particular data collection can be carried out with PUT, GET, and DELETE HTTP operations, respectively.

Notice that the upload of the model is asynchronous with the rest of the data communication process. This is because of the huge difference in time scale in which the 3D model is created: while the rest of the data to be uploaded can be generated in seconds or milliseconds (depending on the sensors that collect the data and the latency to the cloud), the 3D model generator usually takes a few hours in servers with high CPU capacity.

Output of the operations are communicated via HTTP status codes. Table 1 lists the status codes and their meanings used in the prototype. The use of a generic 404 Not Found, rather than a more specific return, when the URL being accessed does not exist or when an invalid operation for the URL is attempted, aims to reduce the amount of information given to malicious users accessing the platform. In particular, malicious users will not be able to know whether a specific endpoint exists or not if they try to access in the incorrect form (what is an evidence that the access is not occurring via the expected ways).

The API is designed to enable data collected from all the different sensors installed in a kiosk to be sent in a single HTTP message. In the JSON file sent by the kiosk in the body of the message, one of the tuples has as a value a list. Each element of the list represents the data collected by one sensor, in the form a JSON object that contains the sensor ID, sensor type, what is being measured, value, and unit of the data collected. If a single sensor generates more than one data point, each data point becomes a different element (object) on the list, as shown in the code in Fig. 4.

When designing our system, we aimed at following the principle of being permissive with the input received and rigorous on the output provided. This means that the output generated by the Engine and sent to clients conforms

Table 1. HTTP status codes used in the engine prototype.

HTTP status code	Use
200 Ok	Successful read or update of a collection
201 Created	A new food intake collection was received and is valid
204 No Content	Collection successfully deleted
400 Bad Request	Data uploaded cannot be successfully decoded in information that can be included in the database (due to missing information that are keys in the database)
401 Unauthorized	Attempt to connect without authentication
404 Not Found	The URL being accessed does not exist or an invalid operation for the URL was attempted

```
{
"kioskId":"6947FA34B86",
"userId":"user@email.edu.au",
"scanId":"djklfj4980985fdsl",
"date":"13/09/2017",
"time":"15:30",
"items":[
{
"sensorId":"6874AB159",
"sensorType":"scale",
"metric":"weight"
"value":182.5,
"unit":"g"
},{
"sensorId":"C456D3450",
"sensorType":"composition",
"metric":"calories"
"value":397.5,
"unit":"kJ"}]
}
```

Fig. 4. Example of a JSON file representing the data being uploaded to the Engine.

strictly with the expected formats; while great effort is put on receiving the input to extract as much relevant information as possible to enable successful data collection. This means that the Engine tolerates any missing field in the input that is not strictly required (i.e., which are not keys in the database tables), and only generates a 400 Bad Request message if keys are missing or if the JSON file is malformed and thus relevant information cannot be extracted. One reason for tolerating missing fields is the fact that it is possible that in given moments some sensors in the kiosk might be faulty and may not generate output or generate meaningless output, and this should not compromise upload of measurements by non-faulty sensors in the same collection.

Besides data obtained from sensors in the kiosk, another source of data for the Engine is the external Food Nutrient Database. Our prototype utilizes the FatSecret database https://www.fatsecret.com, which is accessed via a RESTful API. The interaction with FatSecret is triggered when the Data Analytics module returns to the Collections Management Module a string with a food name (which can be the result of an analysis about the likely content of the food presented by the user). This name is used for a search in the FatSecret database (via the API) to determine nutrition facts about such food. This information is then stored in the Datastore.

All the nutrition data collected and stored in the database are used to generate daily, weekly, and monthly charts of intake of different nutrients and calories, for dietitians and users. Dietitians can only access data from users that are their patients (not patients from other dietitians).

6   Conclusions and Future Work

Understanding food habits and portion sizes consumed can form the basis to develop an information system to provide context-specific information to guide and improve these habits. This paper presented a novel smart nutrition monitoring system for take-away food. It contains a data collection module (kiosk) that contains heterogeneous sensors. Following a Fog Computing approach, data from such sensors are collected and pre-processed before being sent to the Smart Nutrition Monitoring Engine in the cloud for further processing, storage, and visualization. In contrast to previous approaches for food intake monitoring, this method is practical and non-invasive with minimum participants' burden.

As future work, we aim to develop new modules in the architecture to facilitate the addition of new sensors to the system with minimum burden for developers and administrators. We also aim to develop advanced analytics capabilities that can compensate for inaccuracy of individual sensors, increasing even further the accuracy of the data provided by the system.

References

1. Bazzano, L.A., et al.: Fruit and vegetable intake and risk of cardiovascular disease in us adults: the first national health and nutrition examination survey epidemiologic follow-up study. Am. J. Clin. Nutr. **76**(1), 93–99 (2002)
2. Volkow, N.D., Wang, G.J., Baler, R.D.: Reward, dopamine and the control of food intake: implications for obesity. Trends Cogn. Sci. **15**(1), 37–46 (2011)
3. Basiotis, P.P., Welsh, S.O., Cronin, F.J., Kelsay, J.L., Mertz, W., et al.: Number of days of food intake records required to estimate individual and group nutrient intakes with defined confidence. J. Nutr. **117**(9), 1638–1641 (1987)
4. Darby, A., Strum, M.W., Holmes, E., Gatwood, J.: A review of nutritional tracking mobile applications for diabetes patient use. Diabetes Technol. Therap. **18**(3), 200–212 (2016)
5. Fontana, J.M., Sazonov, E.: Detection and characterization of food intake by wearable sensors. In: Wearable Sensors, pp. 591–616 (2014)

6. Passler, S., Fischer, W.J.: Food intake monitoring: automated chew event detection in chewing sounds. IEEE J. Biomed. Health Inform. **18**(1), 278–289 (2014)
7. Vu, T., Lin, F., Alshurafa, N., Xu, W.: Wearable food intake monitoring technologies: a comprehensive review. Computers **6**(1), 4 (2017)
8. Gubbi, J., Buyya, R., Marusic, S., Palaniswami, M.: Internet of Things (IoT): a vision, architectural elements, and future directions. Future Gener. Comput. Syst. **29**(7), 1645–1660 (2013)
9. Hebden, L., Cook, A., van der Ploeg, H.P., Allman-Farinelli, M.: Development of smartphone applications for nutrition and physical activity behavior change. JMIR Res. Protoc. **1**(2), e9 (2012)
10. Block, G.: A review of validations of dietary assessment methods. Am. J. Epidemiol. **115**(4), 492–505 (1982)
11. Fallaize, R., et al.: Online dietary intake estimation: reproducibility and validity of the food4me food frequency questionnaire against a 4-day weighed food record. J. Med. Internet Res. **16**(8), e190 (2014)
12. Bingham, S.A., et al.: Comparison of dietary assessment methods in nutritional epidemiology: weighed records v. 24 h recalls, food-frequency questionnaires and estimated-diet records. Br. J. Nutr. **72**(4), 619–643 (1994)
13. Cadavid, S., Abdel-Mottaleb, M., Helal, A.: Exploiting visual quasi-periodicity for real-time chewing event detection using active appearance models and support vector machines. Pers. Ubiquit. Comput. **16**(6), 729–739 (2012)
14. Zhou, B., et al.: Smart table surface: a novel approach to pervasive dining monitoring. In: 2015 IEEE International Conference on Pervasive Computing and Communications (PerCom), pp. 155–162. IEEE (2015)
15. Amft, O., Kusserow, M., Tröster, G.: Bite weight prediction from acoustic recognition of chewing. IEEE Trans. Biomed. Eng. **56**(6), 1663–1672 (2009)
16. Sazonov, E.S., Makeyev, O., Schuckers, S., Lopez-Meyer, P., Melanson, E.L., Neuman, M.R.: Automatic detection of swallowing events by acoustical means for applications of monitoring of ingestive behavior. IEEE Trans. Biomed. Eng. **57**(3), 626–633 (2010)
17. Dong, Y., Hoover, A., Scisco, J., Muth, E.: A new method for measuring meal intake in humans via automated wrist motion tracking. Appl. Psychophysiol. Biofeedback **37**(3), 205–215 (2012)
18. Mehdipour, F., Javadi, B., Mahanti, A.: FOG-engine: towards big data analytics in the Fog. In: 2016 IEEE 14th International Conference on Dependable, Autonomic and Secure Computing, 14th International Conference on Pervasive Intelligence and Computing, 2nd International Conference on Big Data Intelligence and Computing and Cyber Science and Technology Congress (DASC/PiCom/DataCom/CyberSciTech), pp. 640–646. IEEE (2016)
19. Cai, Z., Li, X., Ruiz, R., Li, Q.: A delay-based dynamic scheduling algorithm for bag-of-task workflows with stochastic task execution times in clouds. Future Gener. Comput. Syst. **71**, 57–72 (2017)
20. Calheiros, R.N., Buyya, R.: Cost-effective provisioning and scheduling of deadline-constrained applications in hybrid clouds. In: Wang, X.S., Cruz, I., Delis, A., Huang, G. (eds.) WISE 2012. LNCS, vol. 7651, pp. 171–184. Springer, Heidelberg (2012). https://doi.org/10.1007/978-3-642-35063-4_13
21. Duan, R., Prodan, R., Li, X.: Multi-objective game theoretic scheduling of bag-of-tasks workflows on hybrid clouds. IEEE Trans. Cloud Comput. **2**(1), 29–42 (2014)

Towards a Reference Architecture for Swarm Intelligence-Based Internet of Things

Ouarda Zedadra[1(✉)], Claudio Savaglio[2], Nicolas Jouandeau[3],
Antonio Guerrieri[4], Hamid Seridi[1], and Giancarlo Fortino[2,4]

[1] LabSTIC, 8 may 1945 University, P.O. Box 401, 24000 Guelma, Algeria
`zedadra_nawel1@yahoo.fr`, `seridihamid@yahoo.fr`
[2] DIMES, Università della Calabria, Via P. Bucci, cubo 41c, 87036 Rende, Italy
`csavaglio@dimes.unical.it`, `giancarlo.fortino@unical.it`
[3] LIASD, Paris 8 University, 93526 Saint Denis, France
`n@ai.univ-paris8.fr`
[4] CNR - National Research Council of Italy Institute for High Performance
Computing and Networking (ICAR), Via P. Bucci 7-11C, 87036 Rende, CS, Italy
`antonio.guerrieri@icar.cnr.it`

Abstract. The Internet of Things (IoT) represents the global network which interconnects digital and physical entities. It aims at providing objects with intelligence that allows them to perceive, decide and cooperate with other objects, machines, systems and even humans to enable a whole new class of applications and services. Agent-Based Computing paradigm has been exploited to deal with the IoT system development. Many research works focus on making objects able to think by themselves thus imitating human brain. Swarm intelligence-based systems provide decentralized, self-organized and robust systems with consideration of coordination frameworks. We explore in this paper the exploitation of swarm intelligence-based features in IoT-based systems. Therefore, we present a reference swarm-based architectural model that enables cooperation among devices in IoT systems.

1 Introduction

The Internet of Things (IoT) is a highly dynamic and distributed networked system, composed of several cyberphysical objects producing and consuming information [1]. The IoT enables objects to communicate and to cooperate with each other [2], sensing and analyzing the environment and subsequently performing reasoned actions to achieve their objectives, being therefore defined Smart Objects (SO) [3]. However, such SO-oriented IoT raises many issues involving SO programming, IoT system architecture/middleware and methods/methodologies for the development of SO-based applications [4]. Agent-Based Computing (ABC) paradigm has been used to deal with such issues [5]. A first use of agents is to exploit smart agents to mitigate the lack of reasoning and intelligence in things in the IoT systems [6]. The basic idea is to embed reasoning and

© Springer Nature Switzerland AG 2018
G. Fortino et al. (Eds.): IDCS 2017, LNCS 10794, pp. 75–86, 2018.
https://doi.org/10.1007/978-3-319-97795-9_7

intelligence capabilities in each thing or to imitate Swarm Intelligence (SI)-based systems by modeling the system as a collection of simple interacting individuals.

SI envelops a wide variety of algorithms seeking self organization in biological systems inspired by the collective behavior of social insects. It considers simple individuals with limited computational and perception capabilities, indirect and efficient communication tools. In recent years, there has been increased research interest into swarm-based approaches and they have been found to be effective in dealing with several NP-hard problems [7].

The existing IoT architectures do not consider some of the important features in complex systems such as: self-organized and self-adaptive control, the modeling of components as heavyweight agents produce expensive costs and complex implementation, coordination mechanisms used are complex. SOs do not allow cooperation in complex IoT systems. Moreover, the existing SI-based architecture are domain oriented (health, smart cities etc.) and there exists a lack on a reference SI-based architecture in literature. To this purpose, a reference model is required to support seamlessly the use of SI features and the integration of SI-based algorithms within IoT systems.

To address the needs above, this paper introduces a new reference swarm-based model for IoT-based systems. We propose to use: (1) Multi-Agents Systems (MAS) technology (stationary and mobile, heavyweight and lightweight agents) to mitigate the lack of reasoning and intelligence in things and to exploit the benefits of edge computing by processing data in local, (2) Cloud Computing environment (CC) for its benefit in storage and computational resources, (3) stigmergic communication through shared workplace (agents) to provide cooperation between SOs without the need to know each other, to overcome the limited memory in things, to lower costs and reduce bandwidth requirements, (4) self-adaptive and self-organized behaviors in different layers in order to meet the fast changes in IoT data flow and device integration. This architecture aims to hide heterogeneity between devices and to cope with complexity and real-time issues. Since this work is a preliminary contribution, adaptive and decentralized algorithms could be included in the MASs of each layer for developing large-scale cyberphysical applications.

This paper is organized as follows. In Sect. 2 related works on SI-based algorithms and agent-based IoT architecture are briefly introduced. In Sect. 3, details of the proposed SI-based IoT architecture are discussed, in which stigmergic interaction among MASs in different layers is emphasized. Concerns and challenges of IoT are discussed in Sect. 4 followed by a conclusion in Sect. 5.

2   Related Work

We divide this Section into three Sections. In Sect. 2.1 we briefly introduce the SI paradigm. In Sect. 2.2, we give an overview about SI-based algorithms and their use in IoT-based systems. In Sect. 2.3, we present the most relevant agent-based IoT architectures and framework.

2.1   SI Paradigm

SI is an artificial intelligence technique based around the study of collective behavior in decentralized, self-organized systems [8]. It is defined as any attempt to design algorithms or distributed problem-solving devices inspired by the collective behavior of some social living beings, such as ants, termites, birds, and fishes [9]. The main features of SI-based algorithms that make them appealing for the development of IoT applications include scalability, robustness, parallel action, flexibility [10].

2.2   SI-Based Algorithms

Several algorithms inspired by the collective behavior of social insects or flocking birds have been proposed in the literature and applied successfully to many real world applications such as the benchmark mathematical problems, optimization tasks, routing network, image processing, data mining, scheduling tasks, and collective robotics.

The Ant Colony (AC) algorithm is an example of SI which is inspired by the classical ant system. The pheromone deposit and pheromone evaporation are used in [11] to calculate the trust value in the process of selecting trustable objects [12] in order to solve the path routing problem of the urban traffic in an IoT system [13].

The Ant Colony Optimization (ACO) is a population-based meta-heuristic [14] that can be used to find approximate solutions to difficult optimization problems. In [15], MAS architecture and ACO algorithm are used to solve routing problems. Authors in [16] use the classical ACO with some adjustments to pheromone trail to deal with disruption.

Particle Swarm optimization (PSO) is a population-based stochastic optimization technique for the solution of continuous optimization problems. Its mechanism is inspired by the coordinate movement of fish schools and bird flocks [17]. PSO is used in [18] to provide a fast recovery mechanism from path failure due to energy depletion or physical damage with an alternative path. It chooses a path with the optimal fitness from the optimal sensor nodes. In [19], The inertia weight method of PSO is applied in the encoding scheme to evaluate the total revenue to find good solutions where a particle is represented by the raw material inventory level in manufacturer.

Artificial Bee Colony algorithm is an optimization algorithm inspired by the intelligent foraging behavior of honey bee swarm [20]. In [21], Artificial Bee Colony algorithm is used to achieve the optimal solution services in an acceptable time and high accuracy where authors propose a service model and use Artificial Bee Colony algorithm to accomplish its instantiation. In [22], authors consider service optimization problem. They propose a set of service domain-oriented Artificial Bee Colony algorithms based on the optimization mechanism of Artificial Bee Colony and the influence of the service domain features.

Honey Bee Mating Optimization (HBMO) is considered as a typical swarm-based approach to optimization, in which the search algorithm is inspired by the process of marriage in real honey-bee [23]. In [24], it is used in routing problem in cognitive radio sensor networks.

2.3   Agent-Based IoT Architectures and Framework

Fortino et al. [25] propose a multi-layered agent-based architecture which allows for developing proactive, context-aware smart objects, atop heterogeneous computing and sensor/actuator platforms and coordinate them through a well-defined Jade-based middleware. In [26], authors propose a cloud-assisted and agent-oriented IoT architecture that will be realized through ACOSO [27] and agent-oriented middleware for cooperating smart objects, and body cloud, a sensor-cloud infrastructure for large scale sensor-based systems. A scalable architecture capable of dealing with all kinds of sensors in a smart city regardless of the technology used is proposed in [28]. Authors consider lightweight and heavyweight agents for the integration of heterogeneous sensors and for information fusion respectively. Authors in [29] present iSapiens, which is an IoT-based platform for the development of general cyberphysical systems suitable for the design and implementation of smart city services and applications. The iSapiens platform implements the edge computing paradigm through both the exploitation of the agent metaphor and a distributed network of computing nodes directly scattered in the urban environment.

Godfrey et al. [30] propose a mobile agent framework to achieve communication between heterogeneous devices, search for resources and provide services to devices in the network. The mobile agent is either runs on a dedicated node or computer connected to the network, or embedded in the device itself. Each mobile agent migrate from a node to another using a pheromone-based mechanism [31]. Authors in [32] present Rainbow, an architecture that permits an easy development of smart city applications. It combines MAS and fog computing, so as to allow the creation of distributed and swarm intelligence applications which can interact directly and in real time with the physical world. In [33], a three layered architecture based on multi-agent technology framework to achieve a self-organization and self-adaptation for the future intelligent shopfloor is proposed. It aims at quick organization of production, discovering and dealing autonomously with abnormalities. Authors in [34] propose a three layers framework for IoT (FIoT) based on MAS and machine learning techniques. They use three types of agents: god, adaptive and observer. God agent is used to detect new things, and to associate to each detected thing an adaptive agent. Adaptive agent is embodied with a thing (the things forms the body, while the agent forms the controller), it makes decisions based on Finite State Machine (FSM) or Artificial Neural Networks (ANN) technologies. Observer agent examines the environment to determine if the system meets its global goals, otherwise it defines new behaviors to adaptive agents. Two different applications are used: quantified things and smart traffic control. Authors in [35] propose ANT, a guiding system for tourists based on the foraging mechanism of ants. ANT enables unique features for tourist navigation by using an artificial stigmergy algorithm.

It allows tourists to: (1) the serendipitous discovery while providing the information to the rest of participants, and (2) make route decisions using the data provided by the server. It is based on MAS and uses three software agents: Final user ANT's agent, Objects ANT's Agent and ANT server.

3 Proposed Reference Architecture for SI-Based IoT

The proposed architecture is based on Multi-Agent Systems (MAS) and swarm intelligence. One basic feature is to introduce self-organized and self-adaptive behaviors in each layer through stigmergic communication. We present in Sect. 3.1 the building blocks of the proposed architecture. We describe in Sect. 3.2 the three layers of the architecture. In Sect. 3.3 we discuss the common features and novelties regarding the existing architectures.

3.1 Architectural Building Blocks

We use two types of agents (lightweight and heavyweight) and Smart Objects (SOs). Figure 1 shows the class diagram representing the main components of the proposed model and the relations between them.

Smart Object (SO) is modeled as lightweight agent which can perceive its environment, act on it, and share information with other SOs. They do not know each other, but they cooperate and communicate indirectly through sharing messages in the shared memory in Local Multi-Agent System (LMAS). SOs have inherent hardware and software constraints, e.g., low processing and transmission power, memory, and battery life. Hence, to have a seamless operation in the IoT, the communication process must support the exchange of information between heterogeneous devices and across heterogeneous networks. Each SO need to subscribe with a subject (a set of key words that trigger some of its behaviors) to the closest LMAS. A SO can; (1) perceive or collect data from its environment, (2) act on its environment, (3) pass on collected data to shared memory in LMASs, (4) update data stored in the shared memory, (5) retrieve stored data in shared memory.

Local Multi-Agent System (LMAS) it is a MAS composed of three agents: A shared memory agent, an Observer agent, and an Adaptive agent. The shared memory agent is a storage memory used to store data sent by different devices. It can be updated by devices or adaptive agents. Data streams provided by SOs can be interpreted as task progress, state indicators or triggers to other SOs. The Observer is a lightweight agent which uses a simple FSM to achieve its tasks. It is responsible of observing the changes in the shared memory agent, whenever there is a new message, it notifies the particular SOs if they are directly connected to it, else it adapts its behavior to a mobile agent, it migrates to the appropriate LMAS with the corresponding data. The Adaptive agent is a heavyweight agent, responsible of transforming the received information to meet sensors requirements, in order to provide the architecture with openness regarding the connection to sensor networks of different nature and to be uniform in the upper layers.

Adaptive Multi-Agent System (AMAS) it is a MAS composed of homogeneous adaptive agents. They are responsible of the processing, filtering and extraction of meaning information from a data flow. They deliver the resulting data to specific gateways. Adaptive agents in MAFs do not need to communicate, but rather they share a common memory agent to retrieve data provided by LMASs from the lower-layer. Adaptive agents need to be augmented with learning capabilities, logical reasoning, SI-based algorithms or use domain ontology to self-adapt and produce intelligent behaviors. MAF produce self-organize and self-adaptive behaviors. In a MAF, self-organizing behaviors can be produced by shared memory agent which controls the flow of data, each time it changes the organization of MAF to meet the requirements. Also self-adaptive behaviors are produced by AMAS, which requests new learning, ontology, algorithms whenever a new unknown data is retrieved.

Local Agent Framework (LAF) is a set of LMASs connected through an internet connection. It is located in the local environment besides the devices.

Middleware Agent Framework (MAF) is a set of AMASs which share a common memory agent. It is located in the middleware layer and deployed in the CC.

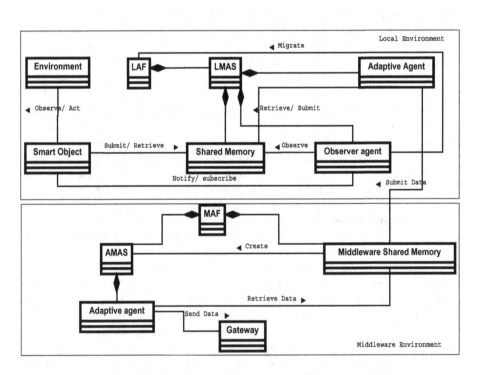

Fig. 1. Class diagram of the proposed SI-based model

3.2   Architectural Layers

The architecture is divided into three layers as shown in Fig. 2: physical layer, middleware layer and application layer. We describe these layers below:

- **Physical layer:** consists in everyday objects and devices (represented by a SO) connected to LMAS's agents through diverse communication technologies (RFID, WI-FI, ZigBee...). LMAS's agents are connected among them via a local network. SOs sense changes in the environment and transmit a raw of data to LMAS's agents in order to share them with other SOs to allow a cooperation between them. Recorded data is processed in local via adaptive agents in order to transmit it to other SOs and to upper layers. Using agent technology provides this layer with: (1) an open environment that allows the dynamic addition of new sensor systems and technologies, thus allowing a simple device-to-device communication, (2) a tight conjoining of the top-level intelligent models and the bottom-level physical resources, (3) a local process of data (edge computing), thus reducing costs and bandwidth.
- **Middleware layer:** this layer gathers data from LMAS's agents in the lower layer. It consists in a set of AMAS's agents which use a shared memory to retrieve data submitted by LMAS's agents. A strategy to create dynamically other AMASs is used to self-organizing to data changes. AMAS's agents benefit from SI-based algorithms, machine learning, logical reasoning and ontology to transform the collected data into the expected intelligence. This layer is also responsible of the right forwarding of data to its particular gateways to meet their authorized application entities.
- **Application layer:** includes a variety of potential applications and services enabled by the SI-based IoT systems. Low-level AMASs encapsulate data in the form of web services sensitive to context.

3.3   Discussion

As pointed out earlier, the focus of this research is towards evolving swarm intelligence control mechanisms in IoT systems. Hence, developing self-organized and self-adaptive behaviors to control the IoT system. Some of the challenging points addressed in this work and common to existing architectures include:

- Scalability: modeling IoT systems as a swarm provide scalability of the system because the control mechanisms do not depend on the number of devices within the system.
- Service times and bandwidth management: the distributed strategy edge computing allows data processing locally in smart devices rather than being sent to the cloud. It provides action in real time and working within the limits of available bandwidth [32,36].
- Heterogeneity: in order to solve the problem of heterogeneity among the communicating devices, regardless of the technology used, we use heavyweight agents to release the corresponding transformations [28].

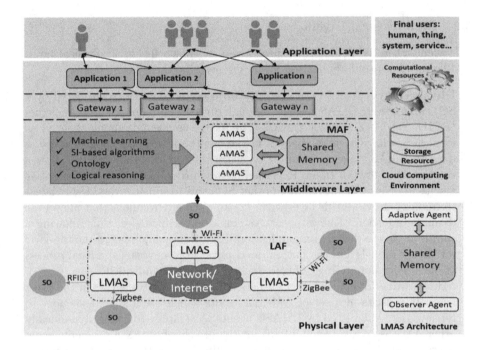

Fig. 2. General design for the proposed SI-based IoT system

- Intelligence: SI-based algorithms can be used in data processing, such as ACO [14], PSO [17], BFO [37], ABC [20], FFA [38], HBMO [23].
- Big data: CC computational and storage resources will enable storage, access, and processing of the huge amount of data produced by IoT systems [28].
- Devices communication: the proposed architecture allows device-to-device indirect communication between SOs which enables efficient use of network resources [39].
- Coordination: MAS technology provides best solutions to coordinate numerous devices [31,32].

The proposed architecture considers some features which are not considered in the existing SI-based and non-SI-based ones:

- Coordination: we use stigmergic communication through shared memory to allow cooperation between different components of the IoT system (SOs and agents). The implemented coordination mechanism allows devices and agents to communicate and cooperate without the need of mutual knowledge.
- Self-adaptive behaviors: agents in LMASs are stationary, but can change to be mobile and migrate to other LMASs to transmit data to SOs from other LMASs. Also, the shared memory can manage the number of agents in each AMAS in order to adapt to the dynamic changing of data flow.

4 Key Challenges and Concerns

The well known challenges and issues common to most of the research literature on IoT include: standardization, scalability and flexibility, power and energy efficiency, identification, authentication, security and privacy, integration, big data, network communications, inter-operability. Issues related to SI-based IoT systems may include:

- The adaptation and integration of SI-based algorithms in IoT-based environment to deal with the continue increasing in collected data, to extract meaning data in order to reduce the amount of stored and transmitted data, processing and filtering the huge and heterogeneous data coming from various sensors.
- Network structure of the proposed MAS should allow self-organization of the connected devices [40].
- The co-existence and interaction between physical space and the virtual (data) space in an IoT environment require the development of new technologies to allow data to be processed and manipulated between the real and digital spaces [41].
- The stigmergic communication provides self-organized solutions with lower costs, but its implementation needs somehow the integration of message passing mechanisms. In order to lower costs, resolve congestion and connectivity problems, coordination mechanisms need to avoid the message passing.
- Since IoT connects everyday objects to the Internet, online social networks with personal things information may incur social concerns as well [41].
- In order to meet the IoT system requirements specifically in costs and network efficiency, self-organizing behaviors to manage the number of agents in different layers need to be explored.
- Coordination issues have been widely considered in swarm robotics field and can constitute inspiration to SI-based IoT systems [42].

5 Conclusion

The IoT is attracting more and more attentions currently. It involves high-dimensional problems and a large amount of data. SI-based algorithms have proven to be the best algorithms applied to complex, dynamic and large scale systems such those of IoT.

We presented in this paper a reference SI-based model for IoT systems. The model is divided into three layers (physical, middleware and application). We used MAS technology, SI paradigm and edge computing. We modeled the IoT system as a swarm of simple SOs with limited computational and storage capabilities which use stigmegic communication to produce cooperative and complex behavior at the system level. SOs collect and transmit data and act in their environment when necessary. They can cooperate with each other through sharing collected information in a shared memory located in LMASs. Agents are responsible of notifying SOs, transmitting data to other LMASs, adapting and processing data coming from different devices. They use self-organized and self-adaptive behaviors to meet the IoT system requirements.

SI-based algorithms have been considered in numerous research works and they are very promising to integrate intelligence into IoT systems. Modeling IoT systems as a swarm of simple devices with stigmergic communication can provide cheaper and robust development solutions. As future work, we intend to implement the proposed reference model and to investigate its application to different IoT systems.

References

1. Miorandi, D., Sicari, S., De Pellegrini, F., Chlamtac, I.: Internet of Things: vision, applications and research challenges. Ad Hoc Netw. **10**(7), 1497–1516 (2012)
2. Fortino, G., Guerrieri, A., Lacopo, M., Lucia, M., Russo, W.: An agent-based middleware for cooperating smart objects. In: Corchado, J.M., et al. (eds.) PAAMS 2013. CCIS, vol. 365, pp. 387–398. Springer, Heidelberg (2013). https://doi.org/10.1007/978-3-642-38061-7_36
3. Fortino, G., Guerrieri, A., Russo, W., Savaglio, C.: Towards a development methodology for smart object-oriented IoT systems: a metamodel approach. In: International Conference on Systems, Man, and Cybernetics, pp. 1297–1302 (2015)
4. Fortino, G., Trunfio, P. (eds.): Internet of Things Based on Smart Objects. IT. Springer, Cham (2014). https://doi.org/10.1007/978-3-319-00491-4
5. Fortino, G.: Agents meet the IoT: toward ecosystems of networked smart objects. IEEE Syst. Man Cybernet. Mag. **2**(2), 43–47 (2016)
6. Fortino, G., Russo, W., Savaglio, C.: Agent-oriented modeling and simulation of IoT networks. In: FedCSIS, pp. 1449–1452 (2016)
7. Sabar, N.R., Ayob, M., Kendall, G., Qu, R.: A honey-bee mating optimization algorithm for educational timetabling problems. Eur. J. Oper. Res. **216**(3), 533–543 (2012)
8. Dorigo, M., Birattari, M.: Swarm intelligence. Scholarpedia **2**(9), 1462 (2007)
9. Bonabeau, E., Dorigo, M., Theraulaz, G.: Swarm Intelligence: From Natural to Artificial Systems, vol. 1, no. 7. Oxford University Press (1999)
10. El Zoghby, N., Loscri, V., Natalizio, V., Cherfaoui, V.: Robot cooperation and swarm intelligence. In: Wireless Sensor and Robot Networks: From Topology Control to Communication Aspects, pp. 168–201 (2014)
11. Suryani, V., Sulistyo, S., Widyawan, W.: Trust-based privacy for Internet of Things. Int. J. Electr. Comput. Eng. **6**(5), 2396–2402 (2016)
12. Lu, Y., Hu, W.: Study on the application of ant colony algorithm in the route of Internet of Things. Int. J. Smart Home **7**(3), 365–371 (2013)
13. Sabbani, I., Youssfi, M., Bouattane, O.: A multi-agent based on ant colony model for urban traffic management. In: International Conference on Multimedia Computing and Systems (ICMCS), pp. 793–798 (2016)
14. Dorigo, M., Di Caro, G.: Ant colony optimization: a new meta-heuristic. In: Congress on Evolutionary Computation, vol. 2, pp. 1470–1477 (1999)
15. Said, O.: Analysis, design and simulation of Internet of Things routing algorithm based on ant colony optimization. Int. J. Commun. Syst. **30**(8), 1–20 (2016)
16. Jiang, Y., Ding, Q., Wang, X.: A recovery model for production scheduling: combination of disruption management and Internet of Things. Sci. Program. **2016**, 1–9 (2016). Article ID 8264879

17. Kennedy, J., Eberhart, R.C., Shi, Y.: Swarm Intelligence, vol. 1, pp. 700–720. Kaufmann, San Francisco (2001)
18. Luo, S., Cheng, L., Ren, B.: Practical swarm optimization based fault-tolerance algorithm for the Internet of Things. KSII Trans. Internet Inf. Syst. (TIIS) 8(4), 1178–1191 (2014)
19. Fang, C., Liu, X., Pardalos, P.M., Pei, J.: Optimization for a three-stage production system in the Internet of Things: procurement, production and product recovery, and acquisition. Int. J. Adv. Manuf. Technol. 83(5–8), 689–710 (2016)
20. Karaboga, D.: An idea based on honey bee swarm for numerical optimization, Technical report-tr06, Erciyes University, Engineering Faculty, Computer Engineering Department, vol. 200 (2005)
21. Huo, L., Wang, Z.: Service composition instantiation based on cross-modified artificial bee colony algorithm. China Commun. 13(10), 233–244 (2016)
22. Xu, X., Liu, Z., Wang, Z., Sheng, Q.Z., Yu, J., Wang, X.: S-ABC: a paradigm of service domain-oriented artificial bee colony algorithms for service selection and composition. Future Gener. Comput. Syst. 68, 304–319 (2017)
23. Selva Rani, B., Aswani Kumar, C.: A comprehensive review on bacteria foraging optimization technique. In: Dehuri, S., Jagadev, A.K., Panda, M. (eds.) Multiobjective Swarm Intelligence. SCI, vol. 592, pp. 1–25. Springer, Heidelberg (2015). https://doi.org/10.1007/978-3-662-46309-3_1
24. Fadel, E., et al.: Spectrum-aware bio-inspired routing in cognitive radio sensor networks for smart grid applications. Comput. Commun. 101, 106–120 (2017)
25. Fortino, G., Guerrieri, A., Russo, W.: Agent-oriented smart objects development. In: International Conference on Computer Supported Cooperative Work in Design (CSCWD), pp. 907–912 (2012)
26. Fortino, G., Guerrieri, A., Russo, W., Savaglio, C.: Integration of agent-based and cloud computing for the smart objects-oriented IoT. In: International Conference on Computer Supported Cooperative Work in Design (CSCWD), pp. 493–498 (2014)
27. Fortino, G., Guerrieri, A., Russo, W., Savaglio, C.: Middlewares for smart objects and smart environments: overview and comparison. In: Fortino, G., Trunfio, P. (eds.) Internet of Things Based on Smart Objects. IT, pp. 1–27. Springer, Cham (2014). https://doi.org/10.1007/978-3-319-00491-4_1
28. Chamoso, P., De la Prieta, F., De Paz, F., Corchado, J.M.: Swarm agent-based architecture suitable for Internet of Things and smartcities. In: Omatu, S., et al. (eds.) Distributed Computing and Artificial Intelligence. AISC, vol. 373, pp. 21–29. Springer, Cham (2015). https://doi.org/10.1007/978-3-319-19638-1_3
29. Cicirelli, F., Fortino, G., Guerrieri, A., Spezzano, G., Vinci, A.: An edge-based platform for dynamic smart city applications. Future Gener. Comput. Syst. (FGCS) 76, 106–118 (2017)
30. Godfrey, W.W., Jha, S.S., Nair, S.B.: On a mobile agent framework for an Internet of Things. In: International Conference on Communication Systems and Network Technologies (CSNT), pp. 345–350 (2013)
31. Godfrey, W.W., Nair, S.B.: A bio-inspired technique for servicing networked robots. Int. J. Rapid Manuf. 2(4), 258–279 (2011)
32. Giordano, A., Spezzano, G., Vinci, A.: Smart agents and fog computing for smart city applications. In: Alba, E., Chicano, F., Luque, G. (eds.) Smart-CT 2016. LNCS, vol. 9704, pp. 137–146. Springer, Cham (2016). https://doi.org/10.1007/978-3-319-39595-1_14

33. Zhang, Y., Qian, C., Lv, J., Liu, Y.: Agent and cyber-physical system based self-organizing and self-adaptive intelligent shopfloor. IEEE Trans. Industr. Inf. **13**(2), 737–747 (2017)
34. do Nascimento, N.M., de Lucena, C.J.P.: An agent-based framework for self-adaptive and self-organizing applications based on the Internet of Things. Inf. Sci. **378**, 161–176 (2017)
35. López-Matencio, P., Vales-Alonso, J., Costa-Montenegro, E.: ANT: Agent stigmergy-based IoT-Network for enhanced Tourist mobility. Mob. Inf. Syst. **2017**, 1–15 (2017). Article ID 1328127. Hindawi
36. Bonomi, F., Milito, R., Zhu, J., Addepalli, S.: Fog computing and its role in the Internet of Things. In: MCC Workshop on Mobile Cloud Computing, 1st edn., pp. 13–16 (2012)
37. Passino, K.M.: Biomimicry of bacterial foraging for distributed optimization and control. IEEE Control Syst. **22**(3), 52–67 (2002)
38. Yang, X.S., He, X.: Firefly algorithm: recent advances and applications. Int. J. Swarm Intell. **1**(1), 36–50 (2013)
39. Bello, O., Zeadally, S.: Intelligent device-to-device communication in the Internet of Things. IEEE Syst. J. **10**(3), 1172–1182 (2016)
40. Gaikwad, P.P., Gabhane, J.P., Golait, S.S.: A survey based on smart homes system using Internet-of-Things. In: International Conference on Computation of Power, Energy Information and Communication (ICCPEIC), pp. 330–335 (2015)
41. Qin, Y., Sheng, Q.Z., Falkner, N.J., Dustdar, S., Wang, H., Vasilakos, A.V.: When things matter: a survey on data-centric Internet of Things. J. Netw. Comput. Appl. **64**, 137–153 (2016)
42. Hoff, N., Wood, R., Nagpal, R.: Distributed colony-level algorithm switching for robot swarm foraging. In: Martinoli, A., et al. (eds.) Distributed Autonomous Robotic Systems. Springer Tracts in Advanced Robotics, vol. 83, pp. 417–430. Springer, Heidelberg (2013). https://doi.org/10.1007/978-3-642-32723-0_30

A Sensor-Based Human Activity Recognition System via Restricted Boltzmann Machine and Extended Space Forest

Jingjing Cao, Wenfeng Li[(✉)], Qiang Wang, and Meng Yu

School of Logistics Engineering, Wuhan University of Technology,
Wuhan 430077, China
{bettycao,liwf}@whut.edu.cn

Abstract. This paper presents a classification system for activity recognition (AR) based on information gained from multi-sensors. Normally, the activity data received from different sensors are employed to construct features with high dimensionality. To automatically extract informative features from complex activities data set, an approach integrating feature extraction and ensemble learning is designed. Specifically, the restricted Boltzmann machines (RBM) and extended space forest (ESF) algorithms are combined in a suitable manners to generate accurate and diverse classifiers. The system conducts experiments on two real-world activity recognition data sets and the results show the effectiveness of the proposed system.

1 Introduction

With the advance of pervasive computing and Internet of Things (IoT) technologies, sensor-based human activity recognition has received considerable attention in many application fields, such as health care [1], monitoring and coaching [2], rehabilitation [3] and so forth. In general, multiple sensors are employed for body sensor network or smart home, which can acquire a great deal of sensor signals. From these sensory data, state-of-the-art activity recognition systems generate many features including statistical features (mean, standard deviation, correlation coefficients, entropy, kurtosis and skewness etc.), Fourier transform and wavelet transform of sensor signals and so on [4]. However, it is difficult to directly gained classification decision boundary on such massive and raw hand-crafted features. It is apparent that the key step in AR is extracting suitable feature representations and designing appropriate classification framework to improve the recognition performance.

In machine learning field, the popularity of ensemble learning [5] since it can remarkably improve the generalization capability by combining multiple homogeneous base/component classifiers. There are a large number of ensemble algorithms can be nicely utilized, such as Bagging, Random Subspaces, Random

© Springer Nature Switzerland AG 2018
G. Fortino et al. (Eds.): IDCS 2017, LNCS 10794, pp. 87–94, 2018.
https://doi.org/10.1007/978-3-319-97795-9_8

Forest, Rotation Forest, Boosting, and so forth. These ensemble methods can create base training data set in different way by generating new instances or new features. Recently, a novel algorithm named extended space forest (ESF) [6] is proposed to improve the diversity and accuracy of original ensemble algorithm (e.g., bagging) by adding new operated features into raw features.

With the rapid development of deep learning (DL) technologies [7], restrict Boltzmann machine (RBM), a significant feature representation tool that used to construct Deep Belief Networks (DBN), has attract much attention in recent years. Besides as a hierarchy component of DBN, the RBM is often utilized as a promising feature extractor due to its strong representation capability. Chunxia Zhang et al. [8] present a preliminarily framework to combine the RBM and bagging on 31 UCI real-world data sets and gives some interesting conclusions. For instance, 2RBM works worst among all ensemble methods, they believe that the final obtained features contains less discriminative information after extracting feature twice. Qi et al. [9] design a novel combination between deep support vector machine and Ex-Adaboost learning methods and discuss the effect by integrating these two schemes according to the experimental results. By applying DL in activity recognition, Zeng et al. [10] employ convolutional neural networks (CNN) as a feature extractor to recognize human action based on data collected from mobile sensors. Ronao et al. [11] design a deep convolutional neural networks (convnets) to perform efficient, effective, and data-adaptive human activity recognition (HAR) using the accelerometer and gyroscope on a smartphone.

In this paper, we design an ESF approach based framework by employing the different combinations of RBM, and it is called ESF_RBM model. Further, we investigate the performance of ESF_RBM variants in the applications of sensor-based human activity recognition. The performance of proposed model is evaluated by accuracy compared with traditional feature extraction method.

This paper is organized into four sections. Section 2 gives the methodology and proposed algorithm Sect. 3 conducts experiments to investigate the performance of the proposed methods on two AR data sets. Finally, Sect. 4 gives conclusion and future work.

2   Methodology

2.1   Restricted Boltzmann Machines

Restricted Boltzmann Machines can be regarded as an energy-based model. In general, it contains a visible layer v and a hidden layer h. The visible layer represent observable data and hidden layer can be employed as feature detectors. A standard RMB has full connections between the hidden and visible layer but no connections between two units within the same layer. For a given state $(\mathbf{v}, \mathbf{h})$, suppose they all satisfied Bernoulli distribution, then the energy function is defined as Eq. (1):

$$E(\mathbf{v}, \mathbf{h}; \boldsymbol{\theta}) = -\sum_{i=1}^{m} \sum_{j=1}^{n} w_{ij} v_i h_j - \sum_{i=1}^{m} b_i v_i - \sum_{j=1}^{n} a_j h_j, \tag{1}$$

where $\boldsymbol{\theta} = \{w_{ij}, a_i, b_j\}$ is model parameter and w_{ij} is the weight between visible unit v_i and hidden unit h_j, a_i and b_j denote bias of visible unit i and hidden unit j respectively. Due to the particular structure of RBM, when visible unit is given, the activation state of each hidden layer is conditionally independent. Then the binary state h_j of each hidden unit j is set to be one with probability:

$$p(h_j = 1|\mathbf{v}; \boldsymbol{\theta}) = \sigma(\sum_{i=1}^{m} w_{ij} v_i + a_j) \qquad (2)$$

where $\sigma(x) = \frac{1}{1+exp(-x)}$. Since the structure of RBM is symmetrical, then when hidden unit is given, the binary state v_i of each visible unit i is set to be one with probability:

$$p(v_i = 1|\mathbf{h}; \boldsymbol{\theta}) = \sigma(\sum_{j=1}^{n} w_{ij} h_j + b_i). \qquad (3)$$

To obtain model parameters $\boldsymbol{\theta}$, one can calculate the maximization of $logp(\mathbf{v}; \boldsymbol{\theta})$. Then the weight update formula is gained through contrastive divergence (CD) algorithm proposed by Hinton [] in 2002:

$$\Delta w_{ij} = E_{data}(v_i h_j) - E_{model}(v_i h_j) \qquad (4)$$

where $E_{data}(v_i h_j)$ is the expectation of observable data in training set, and $E_{model}(v_i h_j)$ represents the expectation obtained by running Gibbs sampling, initialized at the data v_i.

2.2   Extended Space Forest

The extended space forest (ESF) algorithm [6] is proposed based on the observation that traditional ensemble methods normally deleting/retain/rotating features. Contrarily, the algorithm adding new features by utilizing original features. Specifically, 12 operators(sum, difference, comp, divide, divide tanh, multiply, multiply tanh, single, two linear, uniform random matrix, gaussian random matrix and mix) are employed between two original features to gain new features. The detail procedure of the ESF is shown in Algorithm 1.

2.3   Integrating ESF with RBM

To incorporate ESF and RBM, we employ the framework proposed in [8]. Suppose we have a data set S described as the input of Algorithm 1. Six different combinations ESF_1RBM, ESF_1RBM_ORG, ESF_2RBM, ESF_12RBM, ESF_2RBM_ORG and ESF_12RBM_ORG are designed in this paper and the detailed process is illustrated in Fig. 1. ESF_1RBM carry out RBM as a feature extractor and ESF_2RBM making us of RBM twice. As a matter of fact, ESF_2RBM can form a simple structure of DBN, i.e. the output of the first RBM is treated as the input of the second RBM to obtain the input layer of features for ESF. Regarding the ESF_12RBM, both the outputs of 1RBM and 2RBM are

---

Algorithm 1. Extended space forest

Input: A set of labeled training instances $S = \{X, y\}$, where $X = \{x_i\}_{(i=1,...n)}$ is a training set with n instances and d features, $y = \{y_i\}_{(i=1,...n)}$ is class label set; ensemble size T; feature generation operator $\bigotimes$; base classifier H; the ensemble algorithm E and the proportion of new feature number to original feature number P.

Output: Training accuracy TrA; testing accuracy TeA.

Training phase: Initialization: $X' = X$.

for $t = 1, ..., T$ **do**

 Randomly generate $r = round(2 * P * d)$ paired original features and store them in matrix M and m_j is the jth column of M.

 for *each pair index* $j = 1 : 2 : r$ **do**

  The jth new feature $m'_j = m_j \bigotimes m_{j+1}$ $X' = [X'; m'_j]$

 Train base classifier H_t on X'

Obtain training accuracy TrA based on $\{H_t\}(t = 1, ..., T)$ and E.

Testing phase:

for $t = 1, ..., T$ **do**

 Extend the feature space of test instances x. Classify the extended test instance based on $\{H_t\}(t = 1, ..., T)$ and E.

Obtain testing accuracy TeA.

---

cooperated as the input training set of ESF method. As for ESF_1RBM_ORG, ESF_2RBM_ORG and ESF_12RBM_ORG, original features are also applied in the proposed algorithm since RBM may not functional enough to solve the supervised learning problem. Besides all other procedures are the same as ESF_1RBM, ESF_2RBM and ESF_12RBM respectively.

3　Experiment

3.1　Dataset and Experiment Setup

• Daily and Sports Activities Data Set (DSA) [12]: This dataset consists of five body-worn miniature inertial sensor units: MTx 3-DOF orientation trackers. Each MTx unit contains a accelerometer, a gyroscope and a magnetometer sensor, and all the sensors are tri-axial. They are placed on the chest, left wrist, right wrist, left size of the left knee and right size of the right knee on the subject's body. The 19 Activities are performed by 8 different subjects (4 female, 4 male, between the ages 20 and 30) for 5 mins: sitting (A1), standing (A2), lying on back and on right side (A3 and A4), ascending and descending stairs (A5 and A6), standing in an elevator still (A7) and moving around (A8), walking in a parking lot (A9), walking on a treadmill with a speed of 4 km/h (in flat and 151 inclined positions) (A10 and A11) and so on. The subjects are asked to perform the activities in their own style and were not restricted on how the activities should be performed. Sensor units are calibrated to acquire data at 25 Hz sampling frequency. The 480(= 60 × 8) signal segments are obtained for

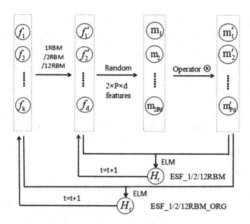

Fig. 1. Flowchart of ESF_RBM system

each activity by the way that 5-min signals are divided into 5-s segments, from which certain features are extracted.

• Human Activity Recognition Using Smartphones Dataset (HARS) [13]: It contains data gained from accelerometer and gyroscope with sampling rate of 50 Hz, and with fixed-width sliding windows of 2.56 s and 50% overlap (128 readings/window. 30 subjects using a smartphone on the waist to perform 6 activities: walking, walking_upstairs, walking_downstairs, sitting, standing and laying. In this work, only 7300 (about 70%) data are utilized as training data and 30% are treated as testing data. All the data are labeled manually according to the video-recorded.

The extreme learning machine (ELM) [14] is utilized in this work due to its simple structure and low computational complexity. It is designed as a least square based learning classifier by training a generalized single hidden layer feedfoward neural networks (SLFNs). Compared with conventional SLFNs algorithms, ELM trains much faster and tends to reach a smaller norm of weights, which implies a better generalization performance. As the base learner of ESF, ELM is employed for all the experiments. Regarding the training and testing data, the repeated random sub-sampling (RRSS) [4] are used for both two data sets. Specifically, 80% of the instances are used for training and 20% for testing for each subject.

3.2   Experimental Result

In order to choose the most suitable ESF operator for AR data sets, Tables 1 and 2 respectively report the means and standard deviations of training and testing accuracy with respect to four different operators among six ESF_RBM based methods on DSA data set. The bold part of the tables exhibit the best result of each row, which imply the best operator for each method. We observe that for both tables, multiply and multiply tanh can achieve better results than sum and different operators, and they show similar result. For the purpose of providing the best operator, the last row of these two tables calculate the average accuracy result of each operator column. As a result, multiply operator perform better than multiply operator, though the difference is limited, and the multiply operator is selected in this work.

Table 1. Comparison among average and stand deviation of training results on four ESF operators

	Different	Sum	Multiply	Multiply tanh
ESF_1RBM	0.8049 ± 0.0250	0.7993 ± 0.0268	**0.8092 ± 0.0259**	0.8050 ± 0.0260
ESF_1RBM_ORG	0.9620 ± 0.0077	0.9635 ± 0.0074	**0.9665 ± 0.0055**	**0.9665 ± 0.0068**
ESF_2RBM	0.7892 ± 0.0217	0.7877 ± 0.0211	0.7899 ± 0.0216	**0.7900 ± 0.0220**
ESF_12RBM	0.8154 ± 0.0242	0.8094 ± 0.0246	**0.8180 ± 0.0231**	0.8159 ± 0.0233
ESF_2RBM_ORG	0.9696 ± 0.0065	0.9687 ± 0.0056	**0.9713 ± 0.0052**	0.9708 ± 0.0056
ESF_12RBM_ORG	0.9595 ± 0.0074	0.9617 ± 0.0066	0.9649 ± 0.0072	**0.9657 ± 0.0059**
Average	0.8834	0.8817	**0.8866**	0.8856

Table 2. Comparison among average and stand deviation of testing results on four ESF operators

	Different	Sum	Multiply	Multiply tanh
ESF1_1RBM	0.7876 ± 0.0378	0.7764 ± 0.0388	**0.7889 ± 0.0394**	0.7856 ± 0.0355
ESF1_1RBM_ORG	0.9553 ± 0.0193	0.9577 ± 0.0162	0.9614 ± 0.0158	**0.9615 ± 0.0146**
ESF1_2RBM	0.7729 ± 0.0343	0.7723 ± 0.0331	0.7733 ± 0.0336	**0.7743 ± 0.0353**
ESF1_12RBM	0.7961 ± 0.0323	0.7886 ± 0.0330	**0.7992 ± 0.0336**	0.7983 ± 0.0342
ESF1_2RBM_ORG	0.9639 ± 0.0147	0.9636 ± 0.0157	0.9653 ± 0.0129	**0.9662 ± 0.0133**
ESF1_12RBM_ORG	0.9535 ± 0.0191	0.9551 ± 0.0169	**0.9606 ± 0.0155**	0.9592 ± 0.0170
Average	0.8715	0.8689	**0.8747**	0.8741

From the Table 3, it can be easily seen that if the ESF+RBM based methods do not include original features, their performance are worse than the single ELM. Contrarily, ESF_1RBM_ORG, ESF_2RBM_ORG, ESF_12RBM_ORG are perform better than ELM, and ESF_2RBM_ORG performs best. As for PCA, it should be noted that though the training accuracy of PCA method is greater than all ESF+RBM based methods, its testing accuracy is much lower than all other methods and the value is only 44.73%. It may implies that PCA has powerful capability to extract discriminative information from original data set, however, when ELM implement on such training data, overfitting has occurred. From the Table 4, the testing accuracies of ESF_1RBM, ESF_2RBM, ESF_12RBM drastically drop from 69.65% to about 50%. PCA also performs well on training data but fail on testing data, and its performance on testing data is similar as ESF_RBM group methods.

Table 3. Comparison among average and stand deviation of training and testing results on DSA data set

Methods	Training	Testing
ELM	0.9408 ± 0.0062	0.9292 ± 0.0069
PCA	0.8978 ± 0.0071	0.4473 ± 0.0411
ESF_1RBM	0.8071 ± 0.0244	0.7882 ± 0.0398
ESF_1RBM_ORG	0.9670 ± 0.0063	0.9615 ± 0.0163
ESF_2RBM	0.7853 ± 0.0254	0.7642 ± 0.0346
ESF_12RBM	0.8165 ± 0.0239	0.7967 ± 0.0371
ESF_2RBM_ORG	**0.9712 ± 0.0052**	**0.9658 ± 0.0168**
ESF_12RBM_ORG	0.9663 ± 0.0057	0.9592 ± 0.0163

Table 4. Comparison among average and stand deviation of training and testing results on HARS data set

Methods	Training	Testing
ELM	0.7190 ± 0.0284	0.6965 ± 0.0437
PCA	0.8526 ± 0.0057	0.5030 ± 0.0369
ESF_1RBM	0.5097 ± 0.0439	0.4952 ± 0.0541
ESF_1RBM_ORG	0.8598 ± 0.0056	0.8261 ± 0.0075
ESF_2RBM	0.5206 ± 0.0798	0.5129 ± 0.0656
ESF_12RBM	0.5312 ± 0.0859	0.5238 ± 0.0744
ESF_2RBM_ORG	**0.8632 ± 0.0041**	**0.8273 ± 0.0088**
ESF_12RBM_ORG	0.8549 ± 0.0054	0.8212 ± 0.0106

Compared with the experimental result in zhang's work [8], it is interesting that though ESF_2RBM works worse then single ELM or PCA based methods, it shows effect on two activity recognition data sets when combined with original features. Furthermore, the performances decrease by adding 1RBM into ESF_2RBM_ORG for both data sets but they still better than ELM and PCA. ESF_2RBM_ORG and ESF_1RBM_ORG shows similar behavior. From the above analysis, we infer that compared with 1RBM, 2RBM works more effective for our proposed framework when incorporating with original data information.

4   Conclusions

In this paper, we have investigated the effect by combining ensemble learning method and deep learning method for the field of sensor-based human activity recognition. The RBM and its variants are utilized as the feature extractor and integrated with extended space forest framework. For experiment, different operators of ESF algorithm are first compared to choose the appropriate operator. Then the different ESF_RBM based methods are also analyzed and several interesting conclusions have been made. In future, we will emphasis on training different deep learning methods to improve the HAR performance with different evaluation measures.

Acknowledgment. The work described in this paper was partially supported by National Natural Science Foundation of China under the Grant No. 61502360, No. 61571336, No. 71672137 and No. 61503291.

References

1. Zhu, C., Sheng, W.: Wearable sensor-based hand gesture and daily activity recognition for robot-assisted living. IEEE Trans. Syst. Man Cybern. Part A Syst. Hum. **41**(3), 569–573 (2011)
2. Ordez, F.J., Englebienne, G., Toledo, P.D., Kasteren, T.V.: In-home activity recognition: Bayesian inference for hidden markov models. IEEE Pervasive Comput. **13**(3), 67–75 (2014)
3. Chernbumroong, S., Cang, S., Yu, H.: A practical multi-sensor activity recognition system for home-based care. Decis. Support Syst. **66**(C), 6170 (2014)
4. Altun, K., Barshan, B., Tunel, O.: Comparative study on classifying human activities with miniature inertial and magnetic sensors. Patt. Recogn. **43**(10), 3605–3620 (2010)
5. Zhou, Z.-H.: Ensemble Methods: Foundations and Algorithms. Taylor & Francis (2012)
6. Amasyali, M.F., Ersoy, O.K.: Classifier ensembles with the extended space forest. IEEE Trans. Knowl. Data Eng. **26**(3), 549–562 (2014)
7. Zhang, H., Cao, X., Ho, J.K.L., Chow, T.W.S.: Object-level video advertising: an optimization framework. IEEE Trans. Ind. Inform. **PP**(99), 1 (2016)
8. Zhang, C.X., Zhang, J.S., Ji, N.N., Guo, G.: Learning ensemble classifiers via restricted boltzmann machines. Patt. Recogn. Lett. **36**(1), 161–170 (2014)
9. Qi, Z., Wang, B., Tian, Y., Zhang, P.: When ensemble learning meets deep learning: a new deep support vector machine for classification. Knowl.-Based Syst. **107**, 54–60 (2016)
10. Zeng, M., Nguyen, L.T., Yu, B., Mengshoel, O.J.: Convolutional neural networks for human activity recognition using mobile sensors. In: International Conference on Mobile Computing, Applications and Services, pp. 197–205 (2014)
11. Ronao, C.A., Cho, S.B.: Human activity recognition with smartphone sensors using deep learning neural networks. Expert Syst. Appl. Int. J. **59**(C), 235–244 (2016)
12. Barshan, B., Yksek, M.C.: Recognizing daily and sports activities in two open source machine learning environments using body-worn sensor units. Comput. J. **57**(11), 1649–1667 (2014)
13. Anguita, D., Ghio, A., Oneto, L., Parra, X., Reyes-Ortiz, J.L.: A public domain dataset for human activity recognition using smartphones (2013)
14. Liu, N., Wang, H.: Ensemble based extreme learning machine. IEEE Sig. Process. Lett. **17**(8), 754–757 (2010)

Exploiting the SEM Framework
for Modeling Smart Cities

Franco Cicirelli[1], Giancarlo Fortino[1,2], Antonio Guerrieri[1(✉)],
Alessandro Mercuri[1], Giandomenico Spezzano[1], and Andrea Vinci[1]

[1] Institute for High Performance Computing and Networking (ICAR),
CNR - National Research Council of Italy, Via P. Bucci 7-11C,
87036 Rende, CS, Italy
{franco.cicirelli,antonio.guerrieri,alessandro.mercuri,
giandomenico.spezzano,andrea.vinci}@icar.cnr.it
[2] Dipartimento di Ingegneria Informatica Modellistica, Elettronica e Sistemistica,
Università della Calabria, 87036 Rende, CS, Italy
g.fortino@unical.it

Abstract. Smart Cities are smart environments extending over a wide
geographical area having the aim of improving the quality of life of the
citizens and optimizing the management of city resources. Despite the
paramount interest towards these systems, there is a lack of approaches
for their design. The Smart Environment Metamodel (SEM) is a framework which is well suited for the development of smart environments in
general, and Smart Cities in particular. SEM allows the design of such
systems by offering two different perspective focusing on functional and
data requirements. This paper aims at showing the effectiveness of SEM
by exploiting the framework for the design of a case study referring to a
realized Smart City application developed in the city of Cosenza, Italy.

Keywords: Smart Cities · Internet of Things
Modeling · Implementation · Meta-modeling · Smart Street Cosenza

1 Introduction

Smart Cities [1,2], are complex Smart Environments (SEs) [3–6] enabling the
possibility to offer high-quality ICT-based services to both citizens and city
administrators. Basic building blocks of such services comprehend sensing the
city environment and controlling it through actuation devices. On these blocks,
more complex functionalities related, for instance, to monitoring, recognition,
knowledge discovery, and prediction can be carried out [7]. The overall goal is
improving the quality of life of the citizens while optimizing the use of city
resources and reducing expenses of public administrations [8]. In the Smart City
field, an important enabling technology is constituted by the so called Internet of Things (IoT) [9] in which smart objects, pervasively distributed in an
environment, cooperate to reach specific goals.

© Springer Nature Switzerland AG 2018
G. Fortino et al. (Eds.): IDCS 2017, LNCS 10794, pp. 95–106, 2018.
https://doi.org/10.1007/978-3-319-97795-9_9

Several real Smart Cities are already running in different city contexts. Examples of such systems comprehend the Smart City of Oulu [10], where a system for traffic monitoring has been implemented; the Cambridge Smart City [11], where sensor nodes have been deployed to sample and gather environmental data; the city of Padua [8], where IoT sensors monitor temperature, humidity, light, and benzene concentration in the air; the SmartSantander project [12], where environment pollution, outdoor parking, and automated irrigation systems have been controlled; and the Chicago Array of Things (AoT) urban sensing project[1], which proposes a network of interactive, modular sensor boxes installed to collect real-time data on the city's environment, infrastructure, and activity for research and public use. AoT essentially serve as a "fitness tracker" for the city, measuring factors that impact livability in Chicago such as climate, air quality and noise.

Despite the growing interest around Smart Cities, the development of such systems still needs proper solutions in terms of both development platforms and design approaches.

With this aim, for instance, in [13] the Syndesi framework is proposed. Syndesi has been designed for profiling people behavior in an environment and realizing customized services following their needs and preferences. While it takes into account the issue of modeling specific SEs, it does not consider a design approach starting from a metamodeling perspective. Authors of [14] provide a metamodel framework based on UML for supporting the development of systems based on smart objects. This metamodel has been purposely proposed for modeling ecosystems of objects but it does not provide specific abstractions for modeling SEs.

This paper shows how the Smart Environment Metamodel (SEM) [14] framework can be effective for the modeling of Smart City applications. SEM has been purposely conceived for modeling smart environments by offering two different perspectives for capturing both the functional and the data requirements of such systems. The usefulness of the SEM framework is demonstrated through a case study involving the development of the Smart Street Cosenza (SSC). The SSC is a smart city application realized in the city of Cosenza (Italy).

The rest of the paper is structured as follows: Sect. 2 summarizes the SEM framework, while Sect. 3 reports the design of the case study along with same details about system implementation and deployment. Finally, conclusions are drawn and ongoing work is reported.

2   The SEM Metamodel

In this section we describe the Smart Environment Metamodel (SEM) framework specifically developed for modeling SEs. SEM can be used both for the development and the analysis of new SEs as well as for the reverse engineering of existing ones. The framework is composed by two different perspective, that

---

[1] https://arrayofthings.github.io/#.

are the *functional metamodel* and the *data metamodel*. The former focuses on the services a SE has to provide to final users. The latter is used to describe properties and relationships existing among data sources belonging to an SE. The modeling entities introduced by the framework can be considered as basic building blocks which require to be specialized in order to meet constrains and needs of the SE under development.

The two metamodels rely on the UML class-diagrams [15] and, in particular, they use the UML stereotypes [16] which are mechanisms useful to extend the UML language. UML was chosen because it is the standard de-facto for designing computer-based applications so as to make SEM metamodels exploitable by a large audience. Both functional and data metamodels are described in the following subsections. A deeper discussion about SEM has been already provided in [7].

2.1   The SEM Functional Metamodel

Two are the concepts on which the functional metamodel relies, namely the *smart environment* and the *smart functionality*. Such metamodel, portrayed in Fig. 1, shows all the relevant features that a smart environment needs to have.

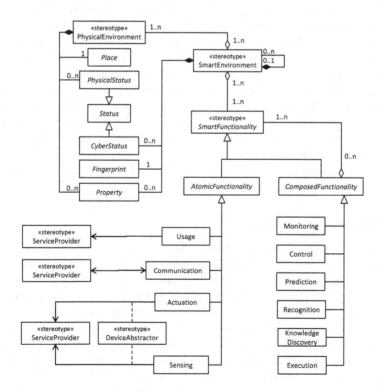

Fig. 1. The SEM functional metamodel.

In particular, the smart environment is identified through the *SmartEnvironment* stereotype and can be considered as composition of a set of nested *SmartEnvironment*s. This is because a specific environment can be composed by other smaller environments. A *SmartEnvironment* is characterized by: (i) a *PhysicalEnvironment*, indicating the physical part of an SE; (ii) some *CyberStatus* entities, modeling the status of all the cyber entities in the SE; (iii) some *Property*s, showing requirements and attributes of the SE; and (iv) a *Fingerprint*, representing the signature of the SE.

As for the cyber part, the *PhysicalEnvironment* is represented by a *PhysicalStatus* and some *Property*s. The *Place* attribute is supposed to offer information about the *PhysicalEnvironment* site.

All the functionalities that an SE can offer have been highlighted in the metamodel through the *SmartFunctionality* stereotype. It's worth noting that, by model, any SE has to offer at least one functionality while the same functionality can be offered by more then one SE.

In the functional metamodel presented in Fig. 1 functionalities are categorized as atomic or composed. More in particular, the atomic functionalities are further specialized as: (i) *Actuation* and *Sensing*, which sense and control the environment through the use of *Embedded Devices*. The *Device Abstractor* is in charge of mediating and abstracting interactions towards hardware equipments; (ii) *Usage*, which permits the exploitation of other external functionalities that are third-party provided (by a *ServiceProvider*); (iii) *Communication*, which allows data exchange with external entities identified through the *Target* stereotype.

By combining *SmartFunctionality*s we achieve what is defined as *ComposedFunctionality*. Six specializations of *ComposedFunctionality* have been identified. They are respectively devoted to: (i) monitor and control the enhanced environment (*Monitoring* and *Control* smart functions); (ii) make predictions about some events that can occur (*Prediction*); (iii) make aware the SE about known situations occurring in the SE itself (*Recognition*); (iv) discovery unknown relevant situations occurring in the SE (*KnowledgeDiscovery*); and (v) executing general purpose operations not included in the previous ones (*Execution*).

2.2   The Data Metamodel

All the relationships existing between a data source, abstracted by the *DataSource* stereotype, and the corresponding physical environment are captured by the data metamodel (see Fig. 2). Such metamodel is useful for specifying properties and characteristics of managed data. A *DataSource* is not related to a physical device, but to a *SmartFunctionality* producing data.

For a *DataSource* it is possible to specify: its data type (e.g. integer), if it is persistent or volatile, and if the produced data is event-based or stream-based. The physical entities interacting/affecting the *DataSource* is identified by the *Actor* stereotype. The position of the *DataSource* with respect to the SE is identified by the *Location*. Finally, *Relation* models important relationships existing among the *DataSource*s (e.g. proximity and statistical correlations).

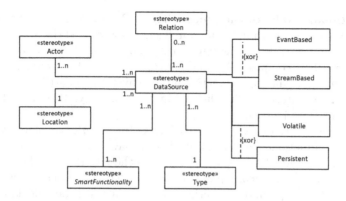

Fig. 2. The SEM data metamodel.

3   Exploiting SEM for Modeling Smart Cities

This section aims at demonstrating the real effectiveness of the SEM framework for the design of a wide-area SE like a Smart City one. In particular, as a case study, we discuss the development of the Smart Street actually deployed in the city of Cosenza (Italy) [6]. The Smart Street Cosenza (SSC) was purposely designed for offering a set of smart services to make aware the Cosenza citizens and administrators about the environmental status and anomalies occurring in the instrumented area.

3.1   The Smart Street Cosenza

The Smart Street instrumented within the considered SE extends for about 2.5 Km and covers: (i) *Corso Mazzini*, which is the main business street of the city, it is a pedestrian area hosting restaurants, cafes, shops, banks, and other commercial activities; (ii) the main bus station of the city located in *Via delle Medaglie D'Oro*; (iii) *Piazza Bilotti*, which is a square hosting an important toll parking; (iv) *Piazza Giacomo Mancini*, which is a square hosting a mall; and (v) *Viale Giacomo Mancini*, which is an high-traffic road in the heart of Cosenza. Such listed areas are monitored through sensors gathering data about pollutant gases, noise, and climatic comfort levels (measured in terms of temperature and humidity).

3.2   Modeling the Smart Street Cosenza

The SSC has been modeled by using the SEM framework and following a top-down design schema. In a first stage, the design has been focused on the functionalities that the SSC has to provide to citizens/administrators and, subsequently, on the data produced and managed in the SSC itself. All of this is described in the following subsections.

The Functional Model of the Smart Street Cosenza. By instantiating the SEM functional metamodel introduced in Sect. 2 we obtained the SSC functional model shown in Fig. 3. From the figure, the modeled *SmartEnvironment* is the *SmartCity* which is composed by the *SmartStreet* SmartEnvironment (top-left part of the figure). The main functionalities which the SmartStreet offers are classified in three categories (highlighted in grey), namely: *Wellness, Anomaly-Detection,* and *DataAggregation.*

DataAggregation is an abstract entity having the *Monitoring* stereotype indicating that the functionalities inheriting from it have the role of monitoring the environment. The term "Aggregation" refers to the fact that all the data gathered are aggregated on a geographical basis in order to create synthetic values. In our case the average and the variance of the data will be calculated. Each *DataAggregation* makes use of the *Persistence* entity (having the *Usage* stereotype) which has the goal to make explicit that all the aggregated data has to be permanently stored. This last service has been provided by a *SmartStreetServer* (*ServiceProvider* stereotype). In the figure are highlighted the specific monitoring activities/functionalities which are designed to be provided by the SSC. These are modeled by the entities extending *DataAggregation* and specifically they refer to the monitoring of temperature, humidity, atmospheric pressure, CO, CO_2, NO_2, O_3, noise, and luminosity. Each Monitoring functionality is related to a specific *Sensing* functionality. In the Fig. 3 this is modeled through aggregation relationships (e.g., between the *Temperature* monitoring and the *TempMeasure* sensing entities).

Wellness is another abstract entity having the *Recognition* stereotype indicating that the functionalities inheriting from it have the role of recognize specific events occurring in the system. More in particular, the *ClimateWellness* entity aims at analyzing data coming from sensors deployed in the environment to determine if the climate in a specific area is comfortable or not. The *EnvWellness* entity, instead, is devoted to assess if pollution is too high in a given place. Both *ClimateWellness* and *EnvWellness* are related to precise values read from sensors belonging to a specific place, so aggregated measures are not involved.

The *AnomalyDetection* is a concrete entity modeling a functionality devoted to detect anomalous events in the SSC. In particular, in the system such entity is related to the recognition of anomalous roars/sounds. In the SSC, a roar/sound is considered as an anomaly when a detected peak of noise is out of the 99th percentile of the noise probabilistic distribution, here modeled as a Gamma distribution having as average and variance the values computed by the *Noise* Monitoring functionality.

For this reason, the anomaly detection functionality depends on both aggregate and precise measures (see in Fig. 3 the aggregation relationships existing between the *AnomalyDetection, Noise,* and *NoiseMeasure*). It's worth of noting that, beside *Persistence,* both *Wellness* and *AnomalyDetection* make use of the *Notification* functionality offered by the *SmartStreetServer. Notification* is used to notify event of interest related to wellness and anomalies.

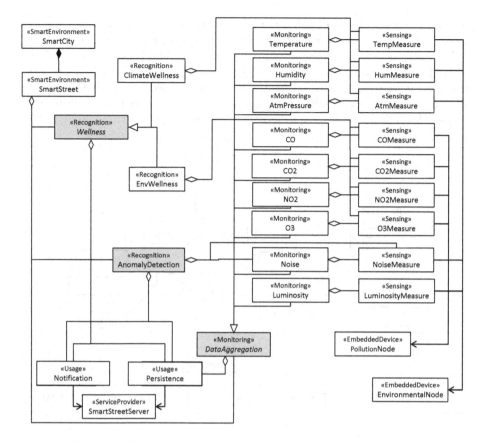

Fig. 3. An instantiation of the functional metamodel for the Smart Street Cosenza.

Finally, in Fig. 3, each Sensing entity is related to the relevant EmbeddedDevice used to acquire data. Here, two kind of devices are considered. Such devices comprehend the *EnvironmentalNode*, which hosts temperature, humidity, atmospheric pressure, noise, and luminosity sensors, and the *PollutionNode* which hosts the CO, CO_2, NO_2, and O_3 sensors.

The Data Model of the Smart Street Cosenza. By instantiating the SEM data metamodel introduced in Sect. 2 we obtained a set of SSC data models related to different functionalities producing data. For the sake of simplicity, only a subset of them is here provided. In particular, we provide the description of all the data sources related to the noise information gathered in the SSC.

Figure 4 shows the *NoiseSource* data source which is produced by the *Noise-Measure* sensing functionality. From the diagram it emerges that this data source produces a stream of float data that requires to be made persistent. It is located in a specific place identified by the *StreetAddress* location indicating where the noise sensor is placed. Since we are in a city context, the noise detected can be generated by a set of *NoiseProducers* identified as *Vehicles, People, StreetWorks,* or produced by the occurrence of *SecurityThreats* (e.g., roars or screams).

It's worth noting that, a noise sensor can have neighbor noise sensors so that its produced measures are correlated to those measured in its neighborhood. If, during data collection, this constraint is not verified, a possible failure in one sensor can be identified. This constraint is modeled in the figure by the *NeighborNoiseCorrelation* related to other NoiseSources.

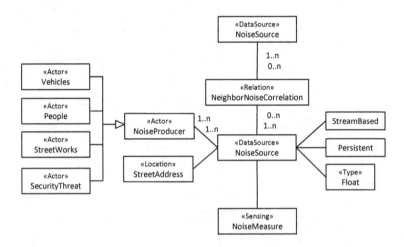

Fig. 4. An instantiation of the data metamodel for the *NoiseSource* in the Smart Street Cosenza.

Figure 5 models the abstract *NoiseStats* data source which is related to the *Noise* aggregation monitoring functionality. *Average* and *Variance* data sources extend *NoiseStats* thus meaning that the *Noise* functionality produces aggregated data related to average and variance of sensed noise. The *NoiseStats* data source produces stream based and persistent float values. The location *Street* here means that the statistical data are evaluated by considering the whole SSC. The *StreetNoiseSources* relation shows that the *NoiseStats* depend on all the *NoiseSources* existing in the SSC. Since the *NoiseProducers* shown in Fig. 4 affect the sensed noise data, they are considered also as affecting the statistics on such data. As a consequence, both *NoiseStats* and *NoiseSource* data sources share the same actors.

Figure 6 models the *AnomalySource* data source which is produced by the *AnomalyDetection* recognition functionality. This data source is event based and persistent. The type of data created by this source is *AnomalyEvent* and carries a set of fields that let understand about the gravity of the anomaly detected and how long the anomaly lasted. An anomaly event can happen in a specific place identified by the *StreetAddress* location, which indicates where the noise sensor detecting the specific anomaly is. The *StreetNoiseSources* relation models that the *AnomalySource* depends on the *NoiseSources, Average* and *Variance*

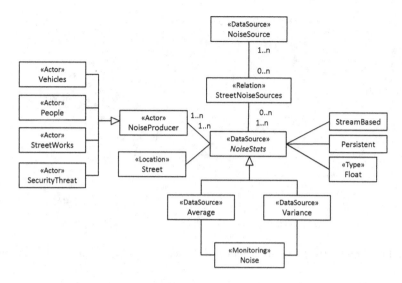

Fig. 5. An instantiation of the data metamodel for the *NoiseStats* in the Smart Street Cosenza.

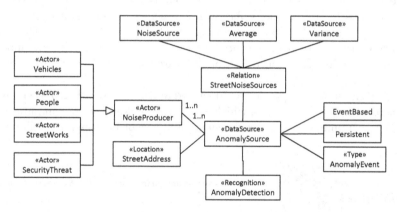

Fig. 6. An instantiation of the data metamodel for the *AnomalySource* in the Smart Street Cosenza.

data sources in the SSC. As in Fig. 4 and in Fig. 5, the *NoiseProducer*s here comprehend vehicles, people, street works, and security threats.

3.3   Implementation and Deployment of the Smart Street Cosenza

The SSC, here designed through SEM, has been realized by exploiting the iSapiens platform [6], which is an agent-based IoT-platform suited for the creation of edge-based and distributed SEs.

The current deployment of the SSC is depicted in Fig. 7. The SSC consists of a set of thirteen computational nodes, and about seventy sensor nodes directly

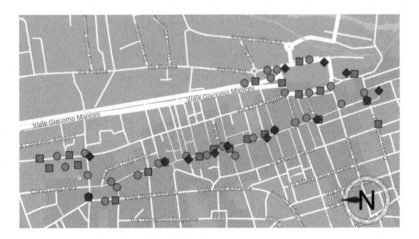

Fig. 7. The Smart Street Cosenza, deployed devices: ◊ computational node, □ and ○ sensor nodes.

deployed on the streets of the city. Each computational node is a Raspberry Pi 2 mod.B hosting the iSapiens platform. The sensor nodes (both *Environmen-talNodes* and *PollutionNodes*) are made up of Libelium Waspmotes Plug&Sense, customized with the relevant sensors (see Fig. 8. The deployed devices and the Smart Street Server are connected through a wireless network covering the whole SSC area.

All the functionalities previously identified and modeled in Fig. 3 are realized by implementing specific agents, which run in the deployed set of computational nodes. The communication between agents and sensor devices are mediated by

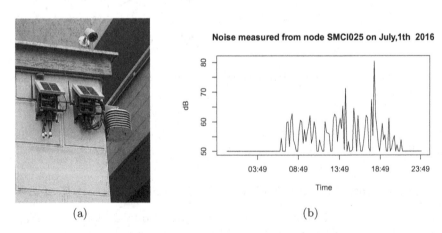

Fig. 8. Deployed sensor nodes (a) and the noise measures (dB) gathered by node SMCI025 on July, 1st. 2016 (b).

exploiting the *Virtual Objects* device abstraction, which is a feature provided by the iSapiens platform. Further details on the SSC implementation can be found in [6].

4   Conclusion

This paper has shown the SEM framework and its application for modeling real large smart environment scenarios. In particular, the Smart Street Cosenza has been presented as a case study. The Smart Street Cosenza is a Smart City application developed and deployed in the city of Cosenza, Italy. The exploitation of the SEM framework has proven to be effective in designing the target scenario, by capturing its functional and data requirements. Moreover, it results also effective as a useful tool for both reasoning about and analyzing functional and data dependencies. The models obtained by using SEM have been subsequently exploited for the real implementation of the Smart Street Cosenza. As enabling technology, the iSapiens agent-based IoT platform has been used.

On-going and future works are devoted to: (i) exploit SEM for improving and extending the existing Smart Street Cosenza with other functionalities (e.g., for traffic control and parking management); (ii) extend the SEM metamodel, e.g., by adding further concepts for explicitly model behavioral and temporal requirements of the algorithms involved in the modeled functionalities.

Acknowledgment. This work has been partially supported by "Smart platform for monitoring and management of in-home security and safety of people and structures" project, DOMUS District, funded by the Italian Government (PON03PE_00050_1).

References

1. Jin, J., Gubbi, J., Marusic, S., Palaniswami, M.: An information framework for creating a smart city through internet of things. IEEE Internet Things J. **1**(2), 112–121 (2014)
2. Kunzmann, K.R.: Smart cities: a new paradigm of urban development. Crios **4**(1), 9–20 (2014)
3. Rashidi, P., Cook, D.J.: COM: a method for mining and monitoring human activity patterns in home-based health monitoring systems. ACM Trans. Intell. Syst. Technol. **4**(4), 64:1–64:20 (2013)
4. Roalter, L., Kranz, M., Möller, A.: A middleware for intelligent environments and the internet of things. In: Yu, Z., Liscano, R., Chen, G., Zhang, D., Zhou, X. (eds.) UIC 2010. LNCS, vol. 6406, pp. 267–281. Springer, Heidelberg (2010). https://doi.org/10.1007/978-3-642-16355-5_23
5. Giordano, A., Spezzano, G., Vinci, A.: Smart agents and fog computing for smart city applications. In: Alba, E., Chicano, F., Luque, G. (eds.) Smart-CT 2016. LNCS, vol. 9704, pp. 137–146. Springer, Cham (2016). https://doi.org/10.1007/978-3-319-39595-1_14
6. Cicirelli, F., Guerrieri, A., Spezzano, G., Vinci, A.: An edge-based platform for dynamic smart city applications. Future Gener. Comput. Syst. **76**(Suppl. C), 106–118 (2017)

7. Cicirelli, F., Fortino, G., Guerrieri, A., Spezzano, G., Vinci, A.: Metamodeling of smart environments: from design to implementation. Adv. Eng. Inform. (ADVEI), **33**, 274–284 (2017). Special Issue on Collaborative Systems

8. Zanella, A., Bui, N., Castellani, A., Vangelista, L., Zorzi, M.: Internet of things for smart cities. IEEE Internet Things J. **1**(1), 22–32 (2014)

9. Atzori, L., Iera, A., Morabito, G.: The internet of things: a survey. Comput. Netw. **54**(15), 2787–2805 (2010)

10. Gil-Castineira, F., Costa-Montenegro, E., Gonzalez-Castano, F., Lpez-Bravo, C., Ojala, T., Bose, R.: Experiences inside the ubiquitous Oulu smart city. Computer **44**(6), 48–55 (2011)

11. Murty, R.N., Mainland, G., Rose, I., Chowdhury, A.R., Gosain, A., Bers, J., Welsh, M.: CitySense: an urban-scale wireless sensor network and testbed. In: 2008 IEEE Conference on Technologies for Homeland Security, pp. 583–588, May 2008

12. Sanchez, L., Muñoz, L., Galache, J.A., Sotres, P., Santana, J.R., Gutierrez, V., Ramdhany, R., Gluhak, A., Krco, S., Theodoridis, E., et al.: SmartSantander: IoT experimentation over a smart city testbed. Comput. Netw. **61**, 217–238 (2014)

13. Evangelatos, O., Samarasinghe, K., Rolim, J.: Syndesi: a framework for creating personalized smart environments using wireless sensor networks. In: Proceedings of the 2013 IEEE International Conference on Distributed Computing in Sensor Systems, DCOSS 2013, Washington, DC, USA, pp. 325–330. IEEE Computer Society (2013)

14. Fortino, G., Guerrieri, A., Russo, W., Savaglio, C.: Towards a development methodology for smart object-oriented IoT systems: a metamodel approach. In: 2015 IEEE International Conference on Systems, Man, and Cybernetics (SMC), Kowloon Tong, Hong Kong, pp. 1297–1302, October 2015

15. Booch, G., Rumbaugh, J., Jacobson, I.: Unified Modeling Language User Guide. Addison-Wesley Object Technology Series, 2nd edn. Addison-Wesley Professional, Reading (2005)

16. UML®: Unified Modeling Language®. http://www.omg.org/spec/UML/ (2017) Accessed 15 Oct 2017

Quality Monitoring of Products
for the Production Plant of a Snack Company

Johanna Alejandra Villalobos Camacho[1],
Octavio José Salcedo Parra[1,2(✉)], and William Muñoz Prieto[2]

[1] Universidad Nacional de Colombia, Bogotá D.C., Colombia
{joavillalobosca, ojsalcedop}@unal.edu.co,
ccosalcedo@udistrital.edu.co
[2] Faculty of Engineering - Universidad Distrital
"Francisco José de Caldas", Bogotá D.C., Colombia
wmunozp@udistrital.edu.co

Abstract. The quality control of processed products is a constant and fundamental practice in any company. In the food industry this control focuses on the final result of the product being handled. Once this has gone through the different stages that are required for its elaboration, measurements are usually made to evaluate the final properties and verify that the required standards are met to be distributed. There are many parameters that are evaluated, some related to the appearance of the Product and others related to texture and taste. The work that will be done will be directed to present a proposal to improve the efficiency in the quality control of products of a food company, in which different types of snacks are processed, packaged and distributed. Automate for evaluate parameters of weight of the packaged product, volume of air inside the packages and verification of the taste. These evaluations are currently carried out manually by the company's employees, which requires time and is prone to frequent errors, to automate these processes, facilitate the growth and development of the company and guarantee better results for the products being handled.

Keywords: Quality control · Manufacturing processes · Product parameters
Arduino · Android · Remote connection · Sensors

1 Introduction

In the processed food industry and packaging one of the biggest issues to take into account is product quality control, especially when dealing with foods there are endless considerations to deal with, among which are the correct balance of ingredients, the quality of these ingredients and the way in which they ensure that the product arrives in the best conditions before the consumer. The correct balance of ingredients ensures that the consumer will be satisfied with the product because of its taste, generally these proportions are already standardized in each company, but there may be some variant that would change the flavor of the product, a monitoring of flavors would greatly facilitate flavor control in these industries. The quality of the ingredients is also fundamental, not only those that are a direct part of the product but those that are used for

© Springer Nature Switzerland AG 2018
G. Fortino et al. (Eds.): IDCS 2017, LNCS 10794, pp. 107–115, 2018.
https://doi.org/10.1007/978-3-319-97795-9_10

its processing, such as the oil used to fry food, if this oil is in poor condition, the final result of the product will be poor quality, that is why companies usually check the state in which these substances are samples taken and analyzed, making this process more automatic would speed up quality control. Finally, a product comes out in prefect conditions of flavor and texture at the end of the production process, this would be of no use if there were no ways to protect the product until it reaches the consumer, this is why there are parameters that must be respected when packing products and monitoring these parameters consistently would guarantee excellent results.

2 Background

For the analysis of the way in which it could possibly develop, the part of control of weight of the project one has references of works like:

In [1], the work aims to show the development of an automated system of statistical quality control for weight control in products manufactured in a laboratory. For this purpose they use an electronic balance and develop a graphical interface to facilitate the analysis of data. It may be useful to use the operating principle of the balances, i.e. the load cells.

The article talks about an iLoad Series® load cell [2, 3] which has a USB connection, which allows you to connect to the computer and establish a connection for sending data.

For the case of data collection of weights, a sequence is proposed, where the intervention of each team is shown to interact [1]. The solution given for the data record provided by the balance [1], is based on the modification of some found examples of a LabVIEW® development environment [3, 4].

The communication between the data reading platform and the program for processing information, Microsoft Access®, is done by a procedure detailed in article [1].

The decision to make the application for the control based on the Android operating system is strengthened by analyzing the results shown in [2–4], which shows the increase in recent years that has the use of this operating system, among other features [2–4]. In addition, an illustrative example of the design and implementation of an Android application for remote control of electronic devices [2–4] is shown.

The research oriented towards the solution of the monitoring of the flavor led to the analysis of the article which presents an analysis of the functioning of the gustatory system of human beings, to make an analogue of the way in which a machine could do something similar.

By making a similarity between the sense of taste, its neural relationships and its behavior towards different substances, it is possible to approach the necessary tools for an electronic implementation. In the article consulted, an electrode is used, which has the capacity to interact with the chemical components of the evaluated foods, this idea would facilitate the monitoring of flavor, although it should be evaluated in which state of the food can be used electrode, the work consulted refers only to foods in liquid state.

Another source was an article published in the New York Times "A robot with the very fine palate" where the implementation of an electronic language developed in

Thailand is presented with the help of engineers, food experts and cooks. It can be concluded from here that such an implementation requires knowledge of different areas, such as electronics, computer systems, chemistry, cooking and human body behavior.

The article "A step closer to the Electronic Capture of Flavors", talks about the NC & T device capable of identifying the total sweetness of natural and artificial sweet substances with 100% accuracy, in addition it can be implemented to identify the sweeteners used in solid foods. It is possible to visualize with this the reliability to which the control mechanism can arrive, in this case they are able to cite with an accuracy of up to 100% how sweet is determined products, based on a predefined scale. In this way a clearer way of identifying the flavors could be had, for our case a scale of salinity could be generated, which is the most predominant flavor of the products that are handled in the company, although also would be useful scales of spice, or of the more specific flavors that are handled in the production plant.

One of the most frequent analogies found in articles related to taste recognition is that of the cells of the ton "Impressive flavor machine" of the digital magazine "digital brain" talks about an instrument capable of measuring the flavors, artificially recreating the "flavor cells" of the tongue, making an analogue with the chemical reactions of the human language. This would be an opportunity to understand the biological functioning of the human gustatory system and to be able to implement it more reliably and easily to an artificial system capable of fulfilling the same functions.gue with electronic elements, as well in the article.

3 Methodology

Initially a study of the current situation of the company will be carried out, the way in which the control of parameters of weight, volume and flavor of the finished products is handled. The existing equipment in the company will be identified and any improvements that can be made will be analyzed. This in order to finalize the work can be made a contrast between the two methods of quality control, waiting for the automated method to reflect great advantages over the current control system.

We will analyze the data collection that is handled in the process plant, the importance of each of these values and the way in which they are processed for analysis. After understanding the objectives of the company to perform these measurements will propose a novel system of measurement of each parameter. In which efficiency, reliability and continuity are guaranteed in the measurements that are made.

Finally, the best way to process the data will be identified and an information collection and treatment system will be implemented for each problem and a joint transmission form for the general visualization of the parameters.

The use of different electronic elements, including sensors and electronic cards, will be taken into account, it will be taken into account that the products are transported on conveyor belts that operate on average at speeds of 0.20 m/s and that can be located after the product packaging process.

For the case of the volume control it is necessary a sensor capable of generating the distance data from one point to another, for this case an ultrasonic type (See Table 1).

Table 1. Technical specifications of the ultrasonic sensor Hc-sr04

Sensor HC-SR04	
Model	HC-SR04
Input Voltage	5 V
Sensor angle	<15°
Precision	0.3 cm
Size	5.4 cm × 2 cm × 1.3 cm

For the weight control it is necessary a sensor that handles this type of parameters, the load cells are the most simple and reliable method for these measurements, the one that is intended to be used is a load cell types as described in Table 2.

Table 2. Technical specifications of the load cell

Nominal load	1 kg
Voltage	3–12 V
Size	3.15 × 0.5 × 0.5″
Weight	30 g

The connection between a computer and the data transmission is generated by an electronic board (Intel Edison Kit for Arduino - eMMC) which has an integrated one that allows a bluetooth connection.

The compatibility of all these devices makes it necessary for the operating system of the host computer to be Windows, a specific version is not necessary (See Table 3).

Table 3. Electrode technical specifications

Measuring range	1 ms/cm–20 ms/cm
Voltage	3–12 V
Temperature	5–40 °C
Compatible	Arduino

It is also important to highlight what types of products are those that are intended to be evaluated in order to be clear to the circumstances (Table 4). The sensing system should be exposed, initially selecting one of the product lines that are handled in the company in one of its most common sizes, of this is important the dimensions that the product presents (See Fig. 1).

- Product Type: potato in size 30 g.
- Dimensions: 17 × 10 cm.

Table 4. I OTN layer information

	Atlanta network	NSFNet	EON
Number nodes	15	14	18
Number of links	44	42	66
Number of demands	210	182	306
Number of demands multicast	15	14	18
Number of routes	224	486	306
Number multicast trees	15	14	18
Number segments with protection	224	486	306

Fig. 1. Products evaluated

4 Control Systems Design

4.1 Package Size Control

Checking the amount of air left in the package is important because it is the way to protect the product. If you have a data of the width of the package that should be had for a good protection, if that measure is very low would run the risk of damage of the product, on the contrary if it is very high the value would have problems for the packaging of the product.

The proposal to monitor this value consists of the use of an ultrasonic sensor to detect the height of the product.

An ultrasonic sensor works by measuring the sending time and receiving a sound pulse. For the particular case of this application will be made use of an Hc-sr04 sensor, compatible with Arduino.

The technical specifications of this sensor can be seen in Table 1.

Based on this, the height of the package can be determined by reference to the conveyor belt on which the product is mounted.

$$D1 - D2 = High$$

D1: Distance between sensor and band
D2: Distance measured by the sensor

Taking into account that the range of the selected sensor is 15°, the sensor should be located in the middle of the conveyor belt at a distance of no more than 30 cm in height from the floor of the belt. This data is fundamental for the final calculation of the height of the package, because the sensor measurement is associated with this distance to calculate the data you want: *Distance from sensor to belt:* 30 cm.

For data analysis, an Arduino card is used, which will allow the pulse to be sent to the sensor so that it is activated, to store the data that the sensor throws (time units) and to do the time conversion at a distance.

For this conversion it is necessary to make the following considerations:

- Sound velocity is 343 m/s under ambient temperature conditions 20 °C, atmospheric pressure at sea level.
- The height control register of the package is handled in cm.

Making the necessary conversion you have to:

$$343\,\frac{m}{s}\,100\,\frac{cm}{s}\,\frac{1}{1000000}\,\frac{s}{\mu s} = \frac{1}{29.2}\,\frac{cm}{\mu s}$$

With this you have that the sound takes 29.2 μs to go a centimeter.

Thus we have the distance from the time of the emission and the reception of the pulse can be determined by (taking into account that is taken to and from the wave):

$$Distance\,(cm) = \frac{time\,(\mu s)}{(29.2)(2)}$$

Thus making the relevant connections can be controlled and stored with the help of the Arduino.

4.2   Package Weight Control

The weight control for the packages is important for the company and for the consumer, on the one hand it guarantees that the consumer acquires products with the content that is offered, and on the other hand it diminishes the losses that can be generated in the production of the company.

To monitor this parameter it is proposed to make use of load cells installed in a base to which the packages would arrive after being verified its volume.

A load cell is a transducer that converts the force applied to it into a measurable electrical signal. Structurally they are composed of an area designed to be deformed when a load or force is applied. This area contains an extensiometric gauge (electrical resistance) that deforms, this deformation is converted into electrical signal.

The arrangement of this mechanism would be serious at the end of the conveyor belt that is part of the volume measurement process.

Fig. 2. Package arrangement for weight control. Source: Authors

Its configuration would be a top surface that receives the packages, the loading syringe correctly oriented and a holding base, as shown in Fig. 2.

Due to the packet sequence, an eject mechanism must be installed to move the packages out of the weighing system.

4.3 Product Flavor Monitoring

As for the design for the monitoring of the flavor of products, it was considered in the first stay the functioning of the human body system related to the sense of taste.

In order to make an artificial model for the analysis of the taste, one must first understand how the human language works, it offers different sensitivities in different regions: the tip of the tongue is more sensitive to sweetness and salinity, the acidity sensation is best detected on the lateral sides of the tongue and the maximum sensitivity to bitterness appears on the back of the tongue.

In the case of the flavor monitoring system, the set of sensors (representing the language) would conform to different detection elements. Each would be a sensor with capabilities to detect a particular flavor. This would be achieved by using different materials/composition for each sensor as well, with the different reactions that would occur upon contacting the flavor compounds analyzed and the sensor, A change of electrical properties would be generated in the sensor material, altering the received detection signal and thus giving a way to differentiate them. After the signals are processed by a computer that stores the converted signals, this system would be a very important part of the flavor monitoring system, since each of the various sensor elements of the system will generate a response that would be complicated because several components could be involved. Therefore, a large capacity multidimensional data processing unit is required.

4.4 Control and Processing of Data

For the control and storage of data of both measurement steps, an Arduino card will be used, the necessary connections and codes will be described below.

- Volume control
  The connection diagram would be as shown in the Fig. 3.

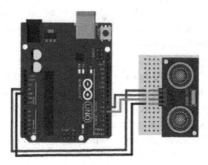

Fig. 3. Settings for the volume control circuit. Source: Authors.

This configuration allows to generate the electric pulse that drives the sensor and read the time it takes to return to the sensor, in addition can be implemented in the code the corresponding equation to make the necessary conversions.

– Weight control

For the case of the weight an additional component is added.

This module is an interface between the load cells and the microcontroller, allowing you to read the weight easily (internally is responsible for reading the wheatstone bridge formed by the load cell), here the analogue reading is converted into digital, since it has an internal 24-bit A/D converter.

To obtain an adequate reading of the data, the calibration of the system is fundamental, for it is implemented a part of code that performs this function.

The fundamental idea of calibration is to find the value of the scale to be used, i.e. find the conversion factor to convert reading value to a value with units of weight. This requires the actual value of the series of packets to be measured or some similar reference.

Finally the data reading is generated with the second part of the code, it makes use of the scale defined in the calibration.

4.5   Simulations

Assuming a continuous production, where the packages pass on the band at a speed of 20 m/s, with an average bag length of 15 cm, it is estimated that a package will pass under the ultrasonic sensor every 5 s, therefore the Arduino Program with a delay of 5 s. Simulating this, measurements of the air cushion are obtained

5   Analysis of Results

The treatment of statistical data that can be generated by having the record of the information that is taken with an automated system is of great importance for the company's production analyzes, although there is the possibility of accessing them with new technologies such as load cells with an integrated USB system (Loadstar Sensors [2]), in the development of this project there is a more economical option, which is the connection of a basic load cell with an electronic card, which fulfills the same function. Although it should be noted that the idea of a load cell with these types of connections (USB) could bring advantages such as simplicity of connection and saving in terms of programming time required by the electronic card system, making the connection without intermediaries with the computer. The simulations were based on reflecting the results by means of a display, because it was not possible to represent the computer as such, if the methodology used in the article "Application for the Quality Control by Weight applied to an Automated System of Quality Control Integrated to Cim del Ctai in the Pontificia Universidad Javeriana" (Van Vianen [1]).

The complete analysis could be made available since the export of the data comes directly to the Microsoft Access® program, where data processing is greatly facilitated.

Similarly, the creation of an interface for the reception of information becomes fundamental, as mentioned in (Van Vianen [1], p. 50), since it allows a greater understanding of the analysis that is carried out.

For the taste analysis, the use of an electrode as a sensor (Rajibur 2016, p. 4), for the distinction of the chemical substances present in the evaluated samples, has great existence when it comes to liquid substances, as it is easier for the sensor to interact with the desired molecules, in terms of solid samples as the current work would be necessary to evaluate the response to contact between the electrode and the food and depending on it to evaluate a different alternative both for the presentation of the sample and for the type of sensor used. And considering that the production of average packets is 90 units per minute, it could be said that the control is not very significant, therefore this situation does not rule out 100% the possibility of finding low weights in the packages. The implementation of the system raised could give total guarantees on this parameter, ensuring 100% that a product is delivered as promised.

6 Conclusions

With the implementation of an automated control system for the volume and measurement of the air mattress could increase the number of packages that can be verified. With the method that is currently managed on average can be verified 8 packets per minute, but taking into account the characteristics with which the measurement system was designed, a total of 20 packets per minute could be reached, that is to increase the number of controls by 60% more than the one currently in use.

The verification of the net weight of finished products is important for production, not only for regulatory purposes (the company could be fined if its products do not offer the quantity indicated in the packages) but this control would generate savings in product waste that could be presented without constant control, currently this verification is performed randomly only with a small number of units (10 packs per minute).

References

1. Van Vianen, W.: Aplicativo para el Control de Calidad por Peso Aplicado a un Sistema Automatizado de Control de Calidad Integrado al CIM del CTAI en la Pontificia Universidad Javeriana. Trabajo de Grado (2011)
2. Loadstar Sensors Inc.: Loadstar introduces iLoad load sensor. Rcuperado de http://www.automation.com/content/loadstar-introduces-iload-load-sensor
3. National Instruments: Qué es NI Labview. Recuperado de http://www.ni.com/labview/whatis/esa/
4. Lozano, M.: Desarrollo de una Aplicación Móvil Android Para Control Remoto de un Servicio Web. Trabajo Fin De Grado - Grado En Ingeniería De Sistemas Audiovisuales (2012)

A Quantitative System of Sedentary Condition Based on Wireless Body Area Network

Xiaogang Li, Yanhong Ge, Wenfeng Li$^{(\boxtimes)}$, and Congcong Ma

School of Logistics Engineering, Wuhan University of Technology,
Wuhan, People's Republic of China
{lixg,liwf,macc}@whut.edu.cn, 115060274@qq.com

Abstract. Most of the current methods to identify sedentary take time as a major parameter, this methods are too simple and cannot make people intuitively understand their sedentary situation. A number of studies have shown that standing up and doing some activity can have a good effect on relieving the sedentary condition, and changing sitting postures also do the same work, and even mildly movement can be beneficial for relieving sedentary condition. This paper propose a quantitative system of sedentary condition based on wireless body area network. In the process of identifying the sedentary condition, we consider not only the sedentary time, but also the time they are not on chairs, the number of times they leave chairs and the change amount of sitting postures. Then we also grade the sedentary level by the above parameters. Finally we display the data of the sedentary time, the time they are not on chairs, the number of times they leave chairs, the change amount of sitting postures and the sedentary level. So it can make people intuitively understand of their sedentary condition. Experiment results show that the algorithm is reasonable and it can identify people's sedentary condition effectively.

Keywords: Wireless body area network · Sedentary level · Pressure sensor
Sedentary condition quantification

1 Introduction

With the maturity of sensor technology and the development of wireless communication technology, the application of Wireless body area network (WBAN) gradually get into people's daily life. Take remote medical for example, wireless wearable medical-care system has become possible. According to people's needs, user can form the WBAN structure through a variety of sensors placed in various parts of the body, then we can acquire the information of human health and other conditions.

At present, more and more attention is paid to the study of sedentary behavior in the world. Researchers also conducted a large amount of experimental research in sedentary pathology. Srinivasan points out that taking 2 min per hour to stand up helps to reverse the negative effects of sedentary, Tom Greene, a veteran researcher at the University of Utah School of Medicine, believes there is a limit to the amount of physical activity, and his new findings suggest that even brief and mild exercise can be beneficial for relieving sedentary condition [1]. A study in the American Journal of

© Springer Nature Switzerland AG 2018
G. Fortino et al. (Eds.): IDCS 2017, LNCS 10794, pp. 116–127, 2018.
https://doi.org/10.1007/978-3-319-97795-9_11

Physiology pointed out that "restlessness" can break the hazard of sedentary [2],the research team in the University of Missouri invited 11 healthy people to participate in the experiment, the experiments sit on the chair, with one leg not moving, and lightly lift the other side of the leg for 1 min, then put down the leg to rest for 4 min, 3 h later, the researchers measured leg's vascular function and found that the moving leg's blood flow increased significantly. Alan Hedge's research showed that the harm of sedentary can be reduced by changing sitting postures and getting up to do activity [3]. The researchers also found that if you insist on physical activity for at least 1 h a day, the harm of sitting for 8 h can be eliminated [4].

2 Related Work

In the sedentary behavior recognition, in the sedentary behavior recognition, Rakesh Kumar uses pressure sensors to detect sedentary behavior and time is the only parameter. This method is relatively simple and cannot accurately identify the sedentary behavior [5]; when Yan detects the sedentary behavior, her principle is that people take less than 100 steps per minute, the principle is simply, and the relationship between the number of steps and the amount of physical activity is not clear, so it can't accurately identify the person's sedentary behavior [6]. In order to detect whether a person is sedentary, Rosenger, Y. E. Shin, Gowtham Kumar and Chelsea Dobbins put three-axis accelerometer on the corresponding part of human body to estimate the activity of the human body. This method take the human activity into account, but it only recognizes a large activity and does not consider the mild activity, it is not accurate in discriminating sedentary behavior and may be overestimated or underestimated, so it can not accurately recognize sedentary behavior [7–10].

In summary, the present methods are simple, the identify model is not meticulous and the factors that take into account is not enough. And in the sedentary behavior research process, they just simply identify the sedentary behavior, and did not identify the sedentary condition, so it cannot intuitively let people know their sedentary condition.

Therefore, when recognizing the sedentary condition of a person, we comprehensively consider the influential factors of sedentary. It not only divides the time into sedentary time and the time of leaving the chair, but also adds the factors of standing up and the amount of changing postures. In the sedentary recognition, we not only identify the occurrence of sedentary behavior, but also quantify the sedentary condition, So it can make people intuitively understand their sedentary condition. The quantitative indicators include sedentary time, the time they are not on the chair, the amount of times they leave chair and the change amount of sitting postures.

3 Hardware Design

With thin pressure sensor, we can identify whether people is on the smart cushion and the sitting posture. After data processing, we can quantify the indicators of the sedentary condition, so it can make people intuitively understand of their sedentary condition. Referring to some stress map of people's sitting posture, and find the most sensitive point when people sit on the chair, then we put pressure sensors on these four points. Through the micro-controller we can read the analog value of pressure (Fig. 1).

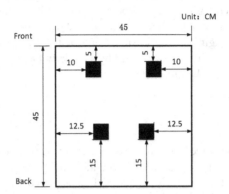

Fig. 1. Location of the pressure sensor

The hardware design of the system is based on wireless sensor network technology. The core of the system is FSR406 pressure sensor, and it also includes data processing module and Bluetooth module, so it realizes the function of wireless transmission. We collect the data from pressure sensor by microprocessor, and then the results will transfer to the phone. The system is packaged into a smart cushion, and it can be directly put on the user's common seat without wearing (Fig. 2).

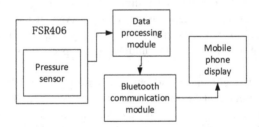

Fig. 2. The block diagram of the hardware system

4 Algorithm Design

A. Parameters extraction

Sedentary time is the time which people sit on the smart cushion, it requires a long time to identify sedentary time. When all the pressure sensor data is not zero, it means that the person is sitting on the chair, and the time is counted as sedentary time. The eigenvalue1 is f_{ci}:

$$f_{ci} = \sqrt{f_1^2 + f_2^2 + f_3^2 + f_4^2} \tag{1}$$

f = (f1, f2, f3, f4) represent the values of four pressure collected by the sensors.

Parameter1: T1 represents sedentary time, when people sit on the seat, f_{ci} will increase, and the time is counted as sedentary time. And we should set threshold of f_{ci} to accurately identify whether the person is on the chair or not. Then the system will record the time that the person is on the Chair, and that is sedentary time, so we get our first parameter.

Parameter2: Q_t means the number of times people getting up and leave the seat. Scientific research shows that, the most useful way to ease sedentary is to get up and leave the seat. When recognizing the level of sedentary, we should set Q_t as the second parameter. We also use f_{ci} as eigenvalue. When the threshold is less than the selected threshold and the duration time is more than or equal to ten seconds, we say that the person has left the seat once and Q_t will increases one. When duration time is less than 10 s, we say that person's sitting posture changes once.

Parameter3: T_2 means the time they are not on the chair. When fci is less than the threshold and the duration time is more than or equal to ten seconds, which showing the person have left the seat, we record the leaving time and set T_2 as the third parameter.

Parameter4: Z_g means the change amount of sitting posture. When person's sitting posture changes a lot, it is useful for easing sedentary. In order to accurately identify the level of sedentary, we set Z_g as the fourth parameter. For the purpose of measuring the amount of posture changes, we designed a algorithm.

The eigenvalues2 f_{pi} is used to identify whether persons' sitting posture has changed a lot, to do this, we analysis the change of pressure sensor, and define the following formula:

$$f_{pi} = \sqrt{\sum_{i=1}^{4} [f_i - p_i]^2} \tag{2}$$

f_i represents the real-time pressure values of each pressure sensor;

p_i represents the pressure values of each pressure sensor when the person are in normal sitting posture;

When people's sitting posture changes, the pressure value that collected by each sensor will change. So when the pressure value change a lot, it means that the person's sitting posture has a big change, and then the change amount will increase one.

B. The identification of sedentary level

Above of all, we can see that the eigenvalue1 can extract the sedentary time and the time they are not on the chair. Eigenvalue1 can also know whether the person leaves the seat and records the number of times they leave the seat. The eigenvalue2 can identify whether the sitting posture has changed largely, and then we record the times of posture changes.

Then we do the work to identify the level of sedentary. At first we extract the sedentary time in an hour, then we collect the data of the pressure sensor and set suitable threshold f_c of the eigenvalue1 f_{ci}, when $f_{ci} > f_c$, we record the time,by doing so we get the sedentary time T_1. When the data are less than fci and the duration time is longer than ten seconds, we say that the person has left the seat once and record the amount of the times in an hour as Q_t, and we also record the time that they are not on the chair as T_2.

Then we extract the changes amount of sitting posture within one hour, and set suitable threshold f_p of the eigenvalue2 f_{pi}, when $f_{pi} > f_p$, it means that the person's sitting posture has changed a lot. When posture changes, the amount will increase one and we record the amount in a hour.

After extracting the above data, we need to do the data fusion. Because the effect of each parameter on sedentary mitigation is different, so it needs to give the corresponding contribution ratio for each parameter.

When we do the data fusion, parameters need to be integrated. Because the different parameters have different degrees to relief sedentary, so we choose the weighted fusion method to do the data processing. The following is its theoretical formula:

$$\begin{cases} \sum_{j=1}^{n} W_j = 1 \\ Y = \sum_{j=1}^{n} W_j Y_j \end{cases} \tag{3}$$

W_j represents weighted index, Y_j represents the amount of each parameter, Y is the amount of fusion.

We divide the parameters into two categories, one is time parameter, the other is the amount of times parameter. For the time parameter, the study shows that when we leave the seat for two minutes during an hour, it will do good for relieving the sedentary, because sedentary time has side effect to ease the sedentary, the weight index should be negative, the amount of fusion is as follows:

$$Y = \left(-\frac{1}{30}\right) \times T_1 + \frac{29}{30} \times T_2 \tag{4}$$

For the number of times parameter, referring to the definition of metabolic equivalence of nephrology activities, the metabolic equivalent for leaving chair is between 3-6 [METs], and with an average of 4.5 [METs]. The metabolic equivalence of sitting posture changing is between 1.5-3 [METs], and with a average of 2.25 [METs]. So the weight index of leaving chair is 2 times than sitting posture changes. And the amount of fusion is as follows:

$$Y' = \frac{2}{3} \times Q_t + \frac{1}{3} \times Z_g \tag{5}$$

For the integrated fusion of time parameters and the amount of times parameters, National Health and Nutrition Examination Survey (NHANES) divides the sedentary behavior scientifically into dangerous sedentary state, general sedentary state and not sedentary state. Dangerous sedentary state means one people keeps a posture unchanging and even without mild activities in an hour. General sedentary state means people do mild activity for 1 to 5 min in one hour. Not sedentary state means people do mild activity for more than 5 min in one hour. The algorithm to identify sedentary level is as follows (Fig. 3):

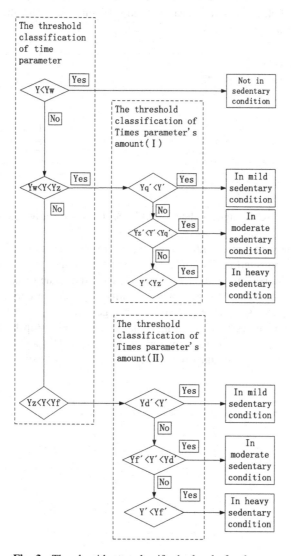

Fig. 3. The algorithm to classify the level of sedentary

5   Experimental Verification

5.1   Threshold Extraction of Parameters

Experimental condition: we select 8 experimenters who are always in sedentary condition, four male and four female, and we do our experiment on a normal seat.

The experimenters sat on the smart cushion for one minute, then the experimenters get up and left the smart cushion for one minute, finally the experimenters sat on the smart cushion for one minute again, and we record the sensors' data. Then we do the experiment reversely. Through the comparison of two pair of the sensor's data, we can set the appropriate threshold to accurately distinguish whether the person is on the seat or not. As shown below, the red line can be a good distinction, so the threshold is set as $f_c = 200$ (Figs. 4 and 5).

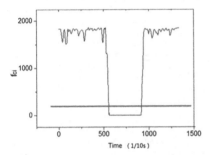 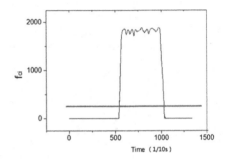

Fig. 4. Sit–leave–sit (Color figure online)   **Fig. 5.** Leave–sit – leave (Color figure online)

For the change amount of sitting posture, the experimenters continue to changes their gestures on the smart cushion in 10 min, and record the sensor's data. As shown in Fig. 6, when the person's sitting position changes, the value of f_{pi} will have a big change, so the eigenvalue2 can accurately identify whether the person's gesture has changed a lot. Figure 7 shows the value of f_{pi} when gesture changes in 10 min, Fig. 9 is the summary graph of Eigenvalue2, Fig. 8 shows the relationship between accuracy and the value of f_{pi}, the standard deviation of the data is 244, and it is efficiency to identify whether people's gesture has changed a lot, so the estimated threshold is $f_p = 244$.

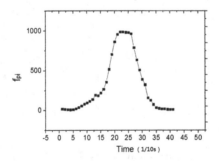

Fig. 6. The value of f_{pi} when gesture changes once

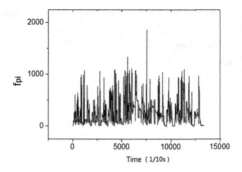

Fig. 7. The value of f_{pi} when gesture changes in 10 min

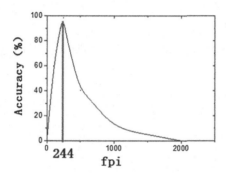

Fig. 8. The relationship between accuracy and the value of f_{pi}

5.2 Threshold Extraction of Data Fusion

According to the research by National Health and Nutrition Examination Survey (NHANES), for the time parameter, we get the following threshold:

$$\begin{cases} Y_w = 180(s) \\ Y_z = -60(s) \\ Y_f = -120(s) \end{cases} \qquad (6)$$

Threshold Y_w: In this condition, people are not in sedentary condition, we set the leave time to 5 min.

Threshold Y_z: In this condition, people are in general sedentary condition, we set the leave time to 1 min.

Threshold Y_f: When people are in an extremely sedentary state, we set the leave time to zero minute.

For the amount of times parameter, the experiment process is as follows, at first, experimenters sit on the smart cushion, the experimenters need to artificial simulate the sedentary condition, which include not in sedentary condition, in mild sedentary condition, in moderate sedentary condition, in heavy sedentary condition. Then we can get the different kind of sedentary data. We get 8 experimenters, each one do experiment for 5 h, and each hour form a set of data. Finally, we calculate the mean of the data, and get the following Figs. 10, 11 and 12.

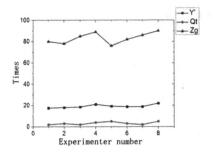

Fig. 9. Not in sedentary condition

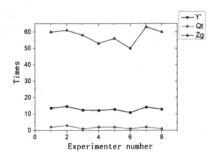

Fig. 10. In mildly sedentary condition

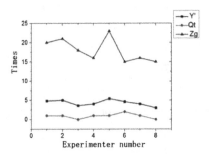

Fig. 11. In moderate sedentary condition

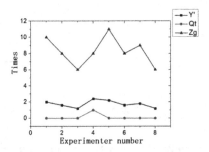

Fig. 12. In heavy sedentary condition

In order to obtain the threshold of the number of times, we need to extract the data from the above data, and then we can determine the threshold of the amount of times. After processing the data, we get the following Fig. 13:

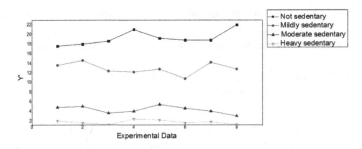

Fig. 13. The analysis chart of Y'

When we identify whether people are in general sedentary state, we need to get the threshold of the amount of times. So we analysis the mean value of the 8 experimenters, by analysis the chart of Y' value, we can get the threshold of mild sedentary Y'_q, the threshold of the moderate sedentary is Y'_z, just as follows:

$$\begin{cases} Y'_q = 12.9 \\ Y'_z = 4.3 \end{cases} \tag{7}$$

When we identify whether people are in dangerous sedentary state, we also need to get the threshold of the amount of times. Taking into account in dangerous sedentary state, the threshold should increase appropriately. In dangerous sedentary states, the metabolic equivalents ranged from 1.0 to 1.3 [METs], with an average of 1.15 [METs]; in the general sedentary state the metabolic equivalent was between 1.5 and 3 [METs], with an average of 2.25 [METs]. So the metabolic equivalent ratio should increase 1.8 times, we get the threshold of mild sedentary Y'_d, the threshold of moderate sedentary Y'_f:

$$\begin{cases} Y'_d = 1.8Y'_q \\ Y'_f = 1.8Y'_z \end{cases} \tag{8}$$

By identifying the sedentary time, the time not on the chair, the number of times they leave chairs and the change amount of sitting posture, the level of sedentary, and then we sent the data to the phone through Bluetooth, and achieve the purpose to make people intuitively understand of their sedentary condition.

Then we do experiments to verify the accuracy of the algorithm. For sedentary time, experimenters sit on the smart cushion for forty minutes, we record the time by our system. For the time not on the chair, experimenters leave the seat forty minutes, and we record the time by our system. For the amount of times they leave the seat, experimenters leave the seat for 100 times, we record the amount the system count. For the changes amount of sitting posture, experimenters sit on the seat and change their posture for 200 times, we record the amount that the system count. For the level of sedentary condition, Experimenters simulate the different conditions of sedentary according to the algorithm, and simulate not in sedentary condition, mild sedentary condition, moderate sedentary condition and heavy sedentary condition for 5 times respectively, and record the accurate amount that the system record. Then we get the data as in Table 1:

Table 1. Experimental data

Number	Experimental data			
	Parameters	Total amount	Accurate amount	Accuracy
1	Sedentary time	40 min	40 min	100%
2	The time not on the seat	40 min	40 min	100%
3	Amount of times they leave seat	100	100	100%
4	Change amount of sitting posture	200	182	91%
5	Level of sedentary condition	20	16	80%

6   Conclusion

We put forward the method to quantify the sedentary condition based on WBAN, and elaborate the algorithm and method. We also do a lot of experiments, and extracts the sedentary time, the time not on the chair, the number of times of leaving chair and the change amount of sitting posture, the level of sedentary. By analysis the data we get, we can achieve the purpose to make people intuitively understand of their sedentary condition. The experimental results show that the algorithm is reasonable and can accurately reflect the sedentary condition of the human body.

Acknowledgment. At first, i want to take this chance to thanks to my tutor Wenfeng Li. In the process of composing this paper, he gives me much academic and constructive advice, and helps me to correct my paper. My great gratitude also goes to some of my friends and classmates who have selfless and generously helped me with my paper.

References

1. Beddhu, S., Wei, G., Marcus, R.L., Chonchol, M., Greene, T.: Light-intensity physical activities and mortality in the united states general population and CKD subpopulation. Clin. J. Am. Soc. Nephrol. (2015)
2. McAllister, R.M., Delp, M.D., Thayer, K.A., Laughlin, M.H.: Muscle blood flow during exercise in sedentary and trained hypothyroid rats. Am. J. Physiol. Heart Circ. Physiol. **269** (6), H1949–H1954 (1995)
3. Li, X.: Sedentary cause heart disease and Japanese media to teach you to reduce the risk of sedentary. Chin. J. Food **7**, 109–110 (2014)
4. Jin, J.: One hour daily activities will eliminate the hazards of sedentary. Jiangsu Health Care **2**, 53–54 (2017)
5. Kumar, R., Bayliff, A., De, D., Evans, A., Das, S.K., Makos, M.: Care-chair: sedentary activities and behavior assessment with smart sensing on chair backrest. In: 2016 IEEE International Conference on Smart Computing (SMARTCOMP), pp. 1–8 (2016)
6. Rosenger: A user-centred approach to reducing sedentary behaviour. In: 2014 IEEE 11th Consumer Communications and Networking Conference (CCNC), pp. 1–6 (2014)
7. Shin, Y.E., Choi, W.H.: Physical activity recognition based on rotated acceleration data using quaternion in sedentary behavior: a preliminary study. In: 2014 36th Annual International Conference of the IEEE Engineering in Medicine and Biology Society, pp. 4976–4978 (2014)
8. Golla, G.K., Carlson, J.A., Huan, J., Kerr, J., Mitchell, T., Borner, K.: Developing novel machine learning algorithms to improve sedentary assessment for youth health enhancement. In: 2016 IEEE International Conference on Healthcare Informatics (ICHI), pp. 375–379 (2016)
9. Dobbins, C., Merabti, M., Fergus, P., Llewellyn-Jones, D.: A user-centred approach to reducing sedentary behaviour. In: 2014 IEEE 11th Consumer Communications and Networking Conference (CCNC), pp. 1–6 (2014)
10. Chau, J.Y., Van Derploeg, H., Dumn, S., et al.: A tool for measuring workers' sitting time by domain the Workforce Sitting Questionnaire. Br. J. Sports Med. **4**(15), 1216–1222 (2011)

11. He, Q.: Towards sedentary lifestyle prevention: an auto-regressive model for predicting sedentary behaviors. In: 2016 10th International Symposium on Medical Information and Communication Technology (ISMICT), pp. 1–5 (2016)
12. Siirtola, P., et al.: Detecting and profiling sedentary young men using machine learning algorithms. In: 2014 IEEE Symposium on Computational Intelligence and Data Mining (CIDM), pp. 296 – 303 (2014)

Private Comparison Protocol and Its Application to Range Queries

Tushar Kanti Saha[1(✉)], Mayank[2], Deevashwer[2], and Takeshi Koshiba[3]

[1] Division of Mathematics, Electronics, and Informatics,
Graduate School of Science and Engineering, Saitama University, Saitama, Japan
`saha.t.k.512@ms.saitama-u.ac.jp`
[2] Department of Computer Science and Engineering,
Indian Institute of Technology (Banaras Hindu University), Varanasi, India
`{mayank.cse14,deevashwer.student.cse15}@iitbhu.ac.in`
[3] Faculty of Education and Integrated Arts and Sciences, Waseda University,
Tokyo, Japan
`tkoshiba@waseda.jp`

Abstract. We consider the problem of private comparison protocol and its application to private range queries for accessing a private database. Very recently, Saha and Koshiba (NBiS 2017) proposed an efficient privacy-preserving comparison protocol using ring-LWE based somewhat homomorphic encryption (SwHE) in the semi-honest model. The protocol took 124 ms (resp., 125 ms) for comparing two 16-bit (resp., 32-bit) integers. But this protocol is not efficient enough to process range queries to a large database where several thousand comparisons are required. In this paper, we propose an efficient parity-based private comparison protocol and show its application to private range queries with a modified packing method. Here the security of the protocol is also ensured by ring-LWE based SwHE in the same semi-honest model. Our practical experiments show that our comparison protocol enables us to do a single comparison in 84 ms (resp., 85 ms) for 16-bit (resp., 32-bit) integers which is more efficient than Saha et al.'s protocol. Besides, it takes about 0.499 s (resp., 2.247 s) to process a 3-out-of-11 range query in a database of 100 records (resp., 1000 records) including 11 attributes, which outperform state of the art.

Keywords: Comparison protocol · Range query · Batch technique
Somewhat homomorphic encryption

1 Introduction

Since Yao addressed the two millionaires' problem in 1982 [23], the private comparison protocol plays a vital role in large cryptographic problems in data mining, machine learning, private database queries, and so on. Furthermore, private access to database records is now very important for maintaining the privacy of its users and their queries. In addition, a private range query is crucial when the

© Springer Nature Switzerland AG 2018
G. Fortino et al. (Eds.): IDCS 2017, LNCS 10794, pp. 128–141, 2018.
https://doi.org/10.1007/978-3-319-97795-9_12

users need to find some records within a certain range for some attributes in a database. For example, a health researcher of a research organization wants to count the number of middle-aged (31–50 years) patients with high sugar level admitted in a hospital. Here neither the health researcher can reveal his query to the hospital nor the hospital can reveal its database records to the research organization. In this case, a third party like the cloud can help in this computation, but it is hard to find such a fully trusted cloud service provider.

On the contrary, cloud computation is becoming popular gradually all over the world since its evolution over the Internet. People are using the Internet not only for sending mail and documents and searching for required information over the Internet but also outsourcing their data in the cloud. Besides, cloud service providers are now giving several services like IaaS, PaaS, and SaaS to their customers with a low cost [15]. Now business and research organizations, institutes, and IT companies are interested to store their data in the cloud. Here they want to secure their data by applying some encryption schemes. At the same time, they like to access data by engaging some queries and apply some statistics, machine learning, and data mining algorithms on encrypted outsourced data. Therefore, there should have some approaches which allow computation on encrypted data.

In this respect, homomorphic encryption (HE) can be a solution to the above problem which allows both addition and multiplication over encrypted data. Homomorphic encryption has come forward after the seminal work of Gentry in 2009 [8]. Moreover, there exists three types of homomorphic encryption namely: partial homomorphic, fully homomorphic, and somewhat homomorphic encryption (SwHE). Among these types, SwHE is more acceptable due to supporting any number of additions and few multiplications with a comparatively high speed than others. In this paper, we use the SwHE scheme of Lauter et al. [13] which is a variant of SwHE scheme proposed by Brakerski and Vaikuntanathan [4]. In addition, from the above-mentioned applications, we concentrate on the problem of private access to the database by employing range queries [2,11,12,22]. For processing a range query, many comparisons are required between a given value in the predicate of an attribute and each value of the database records for the corresponding attribute. Here, an efficient private comparison protocol with SwHE is indispensable to evaluate the problem of private range queries for accessing records from a table in a large database.

1.1 Related Work

In this section, we review some recent problems related to private comparison protocol using homomorphic encryption. In 2008, Damgård et al. [7] proposed an efficient comparison protocol for on-line auction utilizing an additively homomorphic encryption scheme in the semi-honest model. But it took about 280 ms for only one comparison between two 16-bit integers running on 6 otherwise idle machines including dual processors. Recently, Saha and Koshiba [20] improved their technique by proposing another efficient privacy-preserving comparison protocol engaging ring-LWE based SwHE along with some packing methods. But their protocol is not practical enough to address range queries where several thousand comparisons are required to access a large database. Also, we review the problems of private range queries for accessing a secure database. In 2013, Boneh et al. [2] proposed a technique of processing range queries only by applying SwHE scheme along with conjunctive, disjunctive, and update queries. But their performance of query processing is time-consuming in a practical sense. In 2016, Kim et al. [12] engaged the security scheme of Brakerski-Gentry-Vaikuntanathan (BGV) in [3] to describe another protocol for processing conjunctive, disjunctive, and range queries over encrypted data in the cloud. They showed the implementation of their protocols in another paper [11] and it took about 160 ms to access each record including 11 attributes of 40-bit values to achieve a security level of 125-bit. Furthermore, they required a multiplicative depth of $\lceil \log l \rceil + 2\lceil \log(1 + \rho) \rceil$ for their range query on l-bit message with ρ attributes. Later on, to provide security to both function and data in the predicate of a query, Kim et al. [11] also showed another method for processing these same types of queries. By keeping the same database settings and security level, it took about 200 ms per record to reply a threshold query with three conditions. Here they used a high depth multiplication circuit for computing the comparison for range queries. Very recently, Xue et al. [22] presented a two-cloud architecture for a secure access to a database with the Paillier cryptosystem [14] that provides privacy preservation to various numeric-related range queries. But their model stores the private key to one of the clouds. But it is difficult to find such a trusted cloud in reality.

1.2   Motivation

As discussed in the previous section, existing comparison protocols are not efficient enough for the computation of a range query where many comparisons are required to process that query in a large database. We also observed that the cost of range query computation increases due to high depth multiplication circuit. The main motivation behind this work is that if we would have a low depth circuit for comparison computation then we can reduce the computation cost. The another motivation is the vast applications of private comparison protocol including e-commerce [7], data mining [10], machine learning [9], database query processing [6,11,12,22], and so on. Besides, outsourced private computation is now popular due to providing security to the queries and data of the individuals or some organizations.

1.3   Our Contribution

Our contribution in this paper is twofold.

- Firstly, Saha et al. [20] proposed an efficient privacy-preserving comparison protocol in the semi-honest model which took 124 ms (resp., 125 ms) for comparing two integers of 16-bit (resp., 32-bit). But the protocol is not efficient enough to address a range query to the large database where several thousand comparisons are required to be performed to process that query.

Here they used binary encoding for their Hamming distance based computation to compare two integers, which required a large lattice dimension. Therefore, we propose an efficient private comparison protocol by employing a base-β encoding which outperforms Saha et al.'s protocol of integer comparison in the same semi-honest model. In addition, our practical implementation shows that our protocol consumes 84 ms (milliseconds) (resp., 85 ms) for a single comparison of 16-bit (resp., 32-bit) integers.

- Finally, Kim et al. [11] presented a protocol for processing conjunctive, disjunctive, and range queries over encrypted data in the cloud. But it took about 200 s to process a range query from a database 1000 records of 11 attributes with 40-bit values. Here we extend the comparison protocol to compute private range queries over encrypted data in the cloud where many comparisons are required in a single computation. To do this, we modify the data packing method in [16] to support batch computation of the comparisons required for range queries. Besides, it took 0.499 s (resp., 2.247 s) for a range query with three conditions in its predicate using database of 100 records (resp., 1000 records).

For the above two cases, we achieve a security level of at least 140-bit.

2 Preliminaries

We describe some basic notations and terms that we use for the rest of the paper.

2.1 Notations

Let R be a polynomial ring such that $R = \mathbb{Z}[x]/(x^n + 1)$ where $\mathbb{Z}$ is the ring of integers and n is the lattice dimension for the ring-LWE based SwHE scheme in [17]. In addition, $\mathbb{Z}^\theta$ defines a θ-dimensional integer vector space. For a prime number q, the field of integer modulo q is denoted by $\mathbb{Z}_q$ called ciphertext space. Similarly, t is the largest prime less than $2^{\lceil \log_2 t \rceil}$ which defines plaintext space R_t. Furthermore, δ defines the standard deviation used to define discrete Gaussian error distribution $\chi = D_{\mathbb{Z}^n, \delta}$ in [17]. Moreover, the function $Enc_{pk}(m) = ct(m)$ defines the encryption of a message m using the public key pk to produce the ciphertext $ct(m)$. For the database, τ and α denote the total number of records and attributes respectively. Besides, k denotes the number of conditions in the predicate of a range query and σ denotes the batch size for a large set of records.

2.2 Private Comparison

The private comparison is a technique of comparing two numbers securely when their owners do not want to disclose their information to each other. Here the comparison result may be required by the data owners or any other third party who is interested in this computation. For example, a financial magazine wants to rank between two rich persons who do not want to disclose their assets either to one another or to the magazine company.

2.3   Private Range Queries

A threshold query is a query in which the predicate contains an attribute greater than or less than a threshold value. For instance, find those patients from a hospital database whose fasting plasma glucose >7.0 mmol/L (126 mg/dL). In addition, a range query in a database means a query containing predicate consisting comparison condition within a range ($<, >$). For example, find the patients in a hospital whose ages are between 31 to 50. Here we can say that a range query is a conjunctive combination of two threshold queries. Sometimes, range queries and threshold queries are used synonymously in database query processing. In this paper, we consider the private range queries to access a private database. Consider a patient table of a hospital database contains τ records with α attributes. Since a range query requires to compare the value of an attribute in the predicate with all the values appeared in the corresponding attribute of the patient table, many comparisons are needed here. Here, we can engage a private comparison protocol for the range query computations.

2.4   Base-β Data Encoding

Data encoding is a technique of representing data (letters, numbers, punctuation, and certain symbols) into a specialized format (such as binary, decimal, octal, and so on) for the efficient transmission or storage [19]. This stored data can be processed further for getting some results. Moreover, the encoded data can be decoded (reverse of encoding) to get its original form. Very recently, Saha and Koshiba [19] showed the base-β ($\beta \in \mathbb{Z}$) fixed length encoding which is a kind of special encoding to represent the data over the alphabets $\{0, 1, \ldots, \beta-1\}^d$ where d is the length of a number in the base-β form. Generally, data are represented in binary form $\{0, 1\}^l$ for most of the digital storages. Saha et al. [20] used the binary encoding to represent an l-bit number that we call base-2 encoding where alphabet set is $\{0, (2-1)\}^l = \{0, 1\}^l$. For representing a decimal number z with a binary encoding, it requires $l = \lfloor \log_\beta(z) \rfloor + 1$ digits where $\beta = 2$ for binary case. In addition, Saha et al. [20] used an l-bit binary conversion algorithm for any integer of $l = 16 \sim 32$-bit used in their comparison protocol. If we use base-β encoding rather than binary encoding, we can achieve a vector size reduction of $d = \lceil l/\log_2(\beta) \rceil$ where l is the length of a number in binary form. For example, if we convert the decimal number $(248)_{10}$ into a binary vector then it can be represented as $(1, 1, 1, 1, 1, 0, 0, 0)_2$. But we can convert the same number to base-8 vector as $(3, 7, 0)_8$. In this paper, we use base-β fixed length encoding ($\beta > 2$) instead of binary encoding to reduce the vector size for handling range queries efficiently.

3   Our Protocol

In this section, we elaborate our private comparison protocol and show its application to private range queries to a large database.

3.1 Private Comparison Protocol

To describe our private comparison protocol, let us consider two billionaires ranking problem which includes four parties: Alice, Bob, Charlie, and Dev. Only two parties (Alice and Dev) in our setting are needed to be online during the protocol execution. Consider that Alice is financial magazine owner who wants to rank between two billionaires named Bob and Charlie. Besides, Bob and Charlie do not want to disclose their wealth either to each other or to Alice. To do this ranking, we apply a private comparison protocol. To facilitate the private comparison, we need an unbiased intermediary party like Dev in the cloud to perform all the computations needed to decide the comparison result. Here consider that the amount of wealth belonging to Bob and Charlie can be represented by the l-bit integers a and b which can be converted to integer vectors as $a = (a_0, \ldots, a_{d-1})$ and $b = (b_0, \ldots, b_{d-1})$ using base-β fixed length encoding such that a_i or b_i is the i-th digit in the base-β representation with $0 \leq i \leq d-1$. Now the computation of parity-based comparison between two vectors a and b can be realized by following arithmetic equation.

$$c = 2(a - b) \bmod t \tag{1}$$

where t is the largest prime less than $2^{\lceil \log_2 t \rceil}$. We map out comparison result c into mutually exclusive class even or odd within an integer ring $\mathbb{Z}_t$. Here if the parity of first non-zero element of c is 1 then $a < b$; otherwise, $a > b$. Besides, Alice and Dev also add some random masks to hide actual result from each other for security. Assume that Dev is an honest-but-curious party. Firstly, Alice generates a random number $r \in \mathbb{Z}_t^*$ and sends it to Dev in the cloud. She also generates a valid public key and secret key pair (pk, sk) and sends the public key pk to Bob, Charlie, and Dev via a secure channel. At this point, Bob encrypts his vector a using the public key pk and sends $Enc_{pk}(a)$ to Dev. In addition, Charlie encrypts his vector b by employing the same public key pk and sends $Enc_{pk}(b)$ to Dev. Now Bob and Charlie go offline for the rest of the protocol operating among Alice and Dev as follows.

1. First, Dev computes $2 \cdot \left(Enc_{pk}(a) \boxplus (-Enc_{pk}(b))\right)$ and a homomorphic multiplication $Enc_{pk}(r) \boxtimes 2 \cdot Enc_{pk}(a - b)$ is then performed.
2. To obfuscate the result from Alice, Dev generates a random integer vector $r_1 \in \mathbb{Z}_t^d$ and homomorphically adds this to $Enc_{pk}(2 \cdot r \cdot (a - b))$ to get $Enc_{pk}(2 \cdot r \cdot (a - b) \boxplus r_1)$, which is then sent to Alice for decryption.
3. Alice decrypts $Enc_{pk}(2 \cdot r \cdot (a - b) \boxplus r_1)$ to get $2 \cdot r \cdot (a - b) + r_1$ using her secret key sk and sends the decrypted result back to Dev.
4. Then Dev produces $2 \cdot r \cdot (a - b)$ by subtracting r_1. Since the result of $(a - b)$ is obfuscated here, Dev is unaware of the result of the computation.
5. Now Dev traverses through the vector and selects the first non-zero value ϕ found at position p with $\phi = 2 \cdot r \cdot (a_p - b_p)$ where a_p (resp., b_p) denotes the value at the p-th position in the vector a (resp., b).
6. Then Dev sends only $\phi \cdot r_2$ to Alice where r_2 is a random mask in $\mathbb{Z}_{\lfloor t/2\beta \rfloor}^*$. Here the random mask is multiplied to obfuscate the main result from Alice.

7. After receiving $\phi \cdot r_2$ from Dev, Alice computes $\gamma = \phi \cdot r_2 \cdot r^{-1}$ in the group $\mathbb{Z}_t^*$ (since t is prime, all the elements of $\mathbb{Z}_t - \{0\}$ are invertible).
8. Finally, Alice publishes the comparison result by checking the parity of γ. A parity bit of 1 implies that $a < b$; otherwise, $a > b$.

Remark 1. Here we achieve a passive security for our protocol under the assumption that Dev is semi-honest. In other words, Dev follows the protocol but tries to learn information from the protocol. Furthermore, we use the same ring-LWE based SwHE scheme used in Saha et al. [17] for ensuring the security of our protocol in the semi-honest model. At this point, we skip its review due to the page limitation.

3.2 Use of Comparison Protocol to Private Range Queries

As discussed in Sect. 2.3, we can say that private comparison protocol can be employed to private range queries computation. Our comparison protocol can be used for only one comparison of two integers whereas a private range query requires many comparisons. To illustrate, consider the patient table in a hospital database containing τ records with α attributes. Here, a health researcher of a research organization wants to count the number of middle-aged (31–50 years) patients admitted with type-2 diabetics from a hospital database. We also consider these computations among four parties where a database expert (Bob) is sending a query to the cloud (Dev) on behalf of the health researcher (Alice). Here neither Bob wants to reveal his query to the hospital (Charlie) nor Charlie wants to reveal its information to Bob. In addition, the corresponding SQL statement can be written as *select count(PID) from patient where age > 30 ∧ age < 51 ∧ fastingPlasmaGlucose > 7*. Furthermore, the predicate of the query contains $k = 3$ conditional statements. Now Alice can process this query by taking intersection three separate threshold queries with one condition as *select PID from patient where age > 30 ∧ select PID from patient age < 51 ∧ select PID from patient fastingPlasmaGlucose > 7*. Finally, she counts the number PIDs appeared in the intersection result. To evaluate the query, τ comparisons are required between the given value of an attribute in the predicate and each value of the records of the corresponding attribute. If we use our comparison protocol to process this query, it is required to run comparison protocol a total of 3τ times between Bob and Dev, which is time-consuming. To process this range query efficiently, some other techniques are indispensable.

3.3 Batch Technique

The batch technique is a process of executing a single instruction on multiple data. This means that the batch technique allows us to perform a single-instruction-multiple-data (SIMD) type operations on data. To process the range query mentioned in the previous section along with the same database settings, we need 3τ comparisons. If we use comparison protocol in Sect. 3.1, we will be required to run the protocol 3τ times which is inefficient along with communication cost. Can we do the range query computation in an efficient way other than this? In 2016, Saha et al. [16] used the batch technique for the private batch equality test (PriBET) protocol to compare a single integer with a set of integers for finding equalities. Here we can also use the same batch technique for processing private range queries where many comparisons are needed to perform for getting the query results from the private database. To apply this batch technique in our computation, we need to use some packing methods as in [13,16,17,24].

3.4 Packing Methods

Packing method refers to the process of encoding many messages in a single polynomial. In [13], Lauter et al. used a packing method to efficiently encode the binary representation of an integer within a polynomial to support efficient arithmetic operations. Now we use Lauter et al.'s packing method for the arithmetic computation of our comparison protocol described in Sect. 3.1.

To describe the packing method, let a be an l-bit integer which can be presented by the base-β integer vectors as $\mathbf{A} = (a_0, a_1, \ldots, a_d) \in R_t$ of size $d = \lceil l/\log_2 \beta \rceil$. Here a_i represents the i-th digit of an integer a in its base-β representation. For $d \leq n$, we encode the integer vector $\mathbf{A}$ in the base ring $R = \mathbb{Z}[x]/(x^n + 1)$ by the Lauter et al.'s packing method as

$$Poly_1(\mathbf{A}) = \sum_{i=0}^{d-1} a_i x^i \in R_t. \tag{2}$$

Moreover, we also modify the packing method of Saha et al. [16] for processing range queries mentioned in Sect. 3.2. Furthermore, we use polynomial ring-LWE based SwHE for the security of our protocol where every computation is performed within the same lattice dimension n. From the table I in [16], we observed that computation cost of our encryption scheme used mostly depends on the lattice dimension n. Our private comparison protocol also requires the lattice dimension of n to compare two integers of length d in the base-β representation. For the practical case, we need to set $n = 2048$ at least to get a security level of 140-bit [16]. On the other hand, to represent an integer of 40-bit, it requires a vector size of $d = 10$ in the base-16 representation. Here, d is very small as compared to n for a single comparison. Now there exist many unused spaces (for example, $n - d = 2048 - 10 = 2038$ in this case) for a single comparison. But our range query computation requires many comparisons. If we can encode many integers within this lattice dimension for the computation of many comparisons simultaneously, then we will be able to reduce the computational cost. Furthermore, we encode $\sigma = \lfloor n/d \rfloor$ integers within the lattice dimension n to support batch computation of many comparisons. Specifically, we encode σ integers in a single polynomial. Let $\{c_1, \ldots, c_\sigma\}$ be a set of σ integers of l-bits. We generate another base-β integer vector $\mathbf{C} = (c_{1,0}, \ldots, c_{1,d-1}, \ldots, c_{\sigma,0}, \ldots, c_{\sigma,d-1}) \in R_t$ of length $d \cdot \sigma$ where $c_{i,j}$ represents the j-th digit of integer c_i in its base-β representation.

For $d \cdot \sigma \leq n$, the vector $\mathbf{C}$ is encoded in the same base ring $R = \mathbb{Z}[x]/(x^n + 1)$ by modifying the packing method in Saha et al. [16] as follows:

$$Poly_2(\mathbf{C}) = \sum_{i=1}^{\sigma} \sum_{j=0}^{d-1} b_{i,j} x^{(i-1) \cdot d + j} \in R_t. \tag{3}$$

According to the SwHE in Sect. 2 of [17], the packed ciphertexts for $Poly_i(\mathbf{P}) \in R$, for instance, $\mathbf{P}$ can be replaced by $\mathbf{A}$ and $\mathbf{C}$ as in Eqs. (2) and (3) respectively, are defined for some $i \in \{1, 2\}$ using the public key pk as

$$ct_i(\mathbf{P}) = Enc_{pk}(Poly_i(\mathbf{P})) \in (R_q)^2. \tag{4}$$

In addition, the following propositions are needed to hold for the multiplication required for the comparison circuit.

Proposition 1. *Let $\mathbf{A} = (a_0, a_1, \ldots, a_{d-1}) \in R_t$ be an integer vector and $\mathbf{M} = (r, 0, \ldots, 0) \in R_t$ be another random integer vector where $|\mathbf{A}| = |\mathbf{M}| = d$. If the ciphertext of $\mathbf{A}$ and $\mathbf{M}$ can be represented by $ct_1(\mathbf{A})$ and $ct_1(\mathbf{M})$ respectively by Eq. (4) then under the condition of Lemma 1 (see Sect. 2.3 in [17] for details), the decryption of homomorphic multiplication $ct_1(\mathbf{A}) \boxtimes ct_1(\mathbf{M}) \in (R_q)^3$ will produce a polynomial of R_t without any change in the polynomial degree.*

Proposition 2. *Let $\mathbf{C} = (c_{1,0}, \ldots, c_{1,d-1}, \ldots, c_{\sigma,0}, \ldots, c_{\sigma,d-1}) \in R_t$ be an integer vector of size $d \cdot \sigma$ produced from set of σ integers $\{c_1, \ldots, c_\sigma\}$. In addition, $\mathbf{N} = (r, 0, \ldots, 0)$ be another random integer vector where $|\mathbf{N}| = d \cdot \sigma$. Whenever the ciphertext of $\mathbf{B}$ and $\mathbf{N}$ are represented by $ct_2(\mathbf{B})$ and $ct_2(\mathbf{N})$ respectively by Eq. (4), under the condition of Lemma 1 (see Sect. 2.3 in [17] for details), decryption of homomorphic multiplication $ct_2(\mathbf{B}) \boxtimes ct_2(\mathbf{N}) \in (R_q)^3$ will produce a polynomial of R_t without any change in the polynomial degree.*

4   Secure Computations

In this section, we mention only the homomorphic operations needed for our comparison protocol along with its extension to compute private range queries.

4.1   Private Comparison Protocol

The homomorphic computation required in our private comparison protocol can be done efficiently by applying our packing method along with the encryption scheme. Let us consider the same base-β integer vectors a and b as $\mathbf{A}$ and $\mathbf{B}$ respectively for the private comparison. As discussed the comparison protocol in Sect. 3.1, Dev homomorphically computes the arithmetic in Eq. (1) by employing the packing method in Eq. (2) as $ct_1(c) = 2 \cdot (ct_1(\mathbf{A}) \boxplus (-ct_1(\mathbf{B})))$. According to Proposition 1, Dev also homomorphically multiplies a random mask $r \in \mathbb{Z}_t$ given by Alice as random integer vector $\mathbf{M} = (r, 0, \ldots, 0) \in R_t$ to $ct_1(c)$ to get $ct_1(c') = ct_1(c) \boxtimes ct_1(\mathbf{M})$. Besides, Dev generates another random mask $r_1 \in \mathbb{Z}_t^d$ that can be represented as another integer vector $\mathbf{M}' = (r_{1,0}, \ldots, r_{1,d-1}) \in R_t$ and adds the vector to $ct_1(c')$ to produce $ct_1(c'') = ct_1(c') \boxplus ct_1(\mathbf{M}')$.

4.2   Private Range Queries Computation

Since we apply our comparison protocol using the batch technique for the efficient computation of the private range queries, we need similar secure computations as discussed in the previous section. Here we employ the packing method in Eq. (3) along with Proposition 2. Let us consider an integer $a \in \mathbb{Z}_t^d$ of length d that is needed to compare with a set of τ integers $\{c_1, \cdots, c_\tau\}$ of the same length. Since we compute within the lattice dimension n, so we can process at most σ data at a time from the database records for batch comparison. Now we make a batch vector $\mathbf{C} = (c_{1,0}, \ldots, c_{1,d-1}, \ldots, c_{\sigma,0}, \ldots, c_{\sigma,d-1}) \in R_t$ of length $d \cdot \sigma$. By employing base-β encoding, we represent a as the base-β integer vector $\mathbf{A} = (a_0, \ldots, a_{d-1})$. We also form another base-β integer vector $\mathbf{D} = (a_0, \ldots, a_{d-1}, \ldots, a_0, \ldots, a_{d-1}) \in R_t$ by repeating integer a σ times where $|\mathbf{D}| = d \cdot \sigma$. According to comparison protocol in Sect. 3.1, Dev homomorphically computes the arithmetic in Eq. (1) by applying the packing method in Eq. (3) as $ct_2(g) = 2 \cdot (ct_2(\mathbf{C}) \boxplus (-ct_2(\mathbf{D})))$. According to Proposition 2, Dev also homomorphically multiplies a random mask $r \in \mathbb{Z}_t$ given by Alice as random integer vector $\mathbf{N} = (r, 0, \ldots, 0) \in R_t$ of length $d \cdot \sigma$ to $ct_2(g)$ for getting $ct_2(g') = ct_2(g) \boxtimes ct_2(\mathbf{N})$. Besides, Dev generates another random mask $r_1 \in \mathbb{Z}_t^{d \cdot \sigma}$ that can be represented as another integer vector $\mathbf{N}' = (r_{1,0}, \ldots, r_{1,d-1}) \in R_t$ and adds the vector to $ct_2(g')$ to produce $ct_2(g'') = ct_2(g') \boxplus ct_2(\mathbf{N}')$.

5   Evaluation

In this section, we show the implementation of private comparison protocol and its application to private range queries using the batch technique. Besides, we show the batch implementation of our comparison protocol separately to show its practicality towards big data processing. Here we show the parameter settings for our experiments and our experimental results. Also, we evaluate achieved security level at the end of this section.

Table 1. Performance comparison for private comparison protocol

Integer size (bits)	Security level		Total time (milliseconds)	
	Saha et al. [20]	Our method	Saha et al. [20]	Our method
16	140	140	124	84
32	140	140	125	85

5.1   Parameter Settings

Now we describe the parameters for the underlying SwHE scheme in [17] that we used for our protocol security. As mentioned in [17], we chose the values of (n, q, t, δ) appropriately to ensure a correct decryption. To get a security level of minimum 128-bit, we need to set the lattice dimension $n = 2048$, $t = 2048$, and $q = 61$-bit [16] where $q \geq 16n^2t^2\delta^4$ as discussed in Sect. 4.3 of [24]. Here we set $(n, q, t, \delta) = (2048, 61 \text{ bits}, 2039, 8)$ for our comparison protocol. In case of batch comparison, we set the batch size σ to 16384 (resp., 8192) for 16-bit (resp., 32-bit) integer which requires a lattice dimension of $n = 65536$ where $q \geq 16n^2t^2\delta^4 = 2^4 \cdot 2^{32} \cdot 2^{22} \cdot 2^{12} = 2^{70}$. Therefore, we fix $(n, q, t, \delta) = (65536, 71 \text{ bits}, 2039, 8)$ for our batch comparison. According to our packing methods in Sect. 3.4, considering 40-bit values and using base-16 encoding, we get a vector of size 10 for each integer value. At this moment, we can fit 200 values comfortably inside a lattice dimension of 2048. Following along, readers might argue using a smaller lattice dimension for the case of 100 records but we chose $n = 2048$ to get an acceptable level of security (≥ 128-bit). For the case of 1000 records, we required 5 blocks of $n = 2048$ each. We decide on q by fixing $n = 2048$, $t = 2039$ for records (and $t = 2048$ for attribute matching) and $\delta = 8$. Also, we set $q \geq 2^4 \cdot 2^{22} \cdot 2^{22} \cdot 2^{12} = 2^{60}$ for matching both attribute and value. Finally, we set the parameters $(n, q, t, \delta) = (2048, 61 \text{ bits}, 2048, 8)$ and $(n, q, t, \delta) = (2048, 61 \text{ bits}, 2039, 8)$ for matching both attribute and value respectively. For attribute name matching, we use the same procedure as used in [18].

Table 2. Performances of private comparison protocol with the batch technique

Integer size (bits)	Batch size (σ)	Parameters (n, t, q, δ)	Security level	Total time (Seconds)
16	16384	(65536, 2039, 71 bits, 8)	6744	4.087
32	8192			4.057

5.2   Performance Analysis

We implemented our comparison protocol and private range query in C++ programming language along with PARI C library (2.9.1 version) [21] and ran the program on a single machine configured with 3.6 GHz Intel Core-i5 processor equipped with 8 GB of RAM inside Linux environment. As shown in Table 1, our comparison protocol took 84 ms (resp., 85 ms) for a single comparison of both 16-bit (resp., 32-bit) integers. On the other hand, the protocol of Saha et al. [20] took 124 ms (resp., 125 ms) for comparing two integers of 16-bit (resp., 32-bit). Besides, we experimented our protocol for batch computation for 16-bit (resp., 32-bit integers) which took 4.087 s (resp., 4.057 s) for 16384 (resp., 8192) comparisons as shown in Table 2. On an average, the batch comparison is able to handle one million comparisons of 16-bit integers within 4.16 min which can be further minimized in a real distributed cloud environment involving many PCs at a time. Now we show the performance of our protocol using the batch technique for processing the private range queries over an encrypted database. We created our two databases with 11 attributes with 40-bit integer values, with

Table 3. Performance of our protocol in application to 3-out-of-11 range query with 40-bit data

τ (# of Record)	k (# of conditions)	Timing (seconds)		Security Level	
		Kim et al. [12]	Our Protocol	Kim et al. [12]	Our Protocol
100	3	16	$(0.219 + 0.280) = 0.499$	125	140
1000	3	160	$(1.967 + 0.280) = 2.247$	125	140

the first one having 100 records and the second one having 1000 records. Similar to [12], all the queries had 3 conditions in the range query. All the values of the database record were encoded by base-16 meaning that all the digits in the encoded vector taken from the alphabet set $\{0,1,2,\ldots,15\}$. We also encoded the attribute names using an 8-bit integer. As already mentioned in the previous section, the program segment for privately matching the attribute names was taken from the implementation of [18]. For the case of 100 records (resp., 1000 records), our 3-out-of-11 (3 range conditions out of 11 available attributes) range query took 0.219 s (resp., 1967 s) for value comparisons and 0.280 s for both cases of attribute matching as shown in Table 3. On the contrary, Kim et al. [12] needed 16 s for 100 records and 160 s for 1000 records case. It is obvious that our protocol performs a way faster than existing secure range query protocols as well as it is, in our knowledge, the fastest existing solution to private batch integer comparison. Moreover, Kim et al. required a multiplicative depth of $\lceil \log l \rceil + 2\lceil \log(1 + \rho) \rceil$ for their range query on l-bit message with ρ attributes. On the contrary, our method required two homomorphic multiplications of depth 0 due to using our packing method. Also, the communication complexity of our protocols is $\mathcal{O}(k \cdot \tau \cdot l \log q)$.

5.3 Security Level

In 2016, NIST [1] defined an acceptable security level as more than 128-bit for any security scheme that is valid beyond 2030. In addition, Chen and Nguyen [5] estimated in lattice-based cryptographic schemes that it is required to have the root Hermite factor $\pi < 1.0050$ to achieve an 80-bit security level. As discussed in [13], the running time t_{adv} is defined as $\lg(t_{adv}) = 1.8/\lg(\pi) - 110$ where the root Hermite factor π is expressed as $c \cdot q/\sigma = 2^{2\sqrt{n \cdot \lg(q) \cdot \lg(\pi)}}$. According to above discussion, we achieve a security level of 140-bit for our comparison protocol which is equal to that of Saha et al. [20]. On the contrary, we also achieve 140-bit security level for our range query case whereas Kim et al. [12] achieved 125-bit of security level. Due to using a higher lattice dimension of 65536, we also achieve a higher security level of 6744-bit in our batch comparison.

6   Conclusions

Throughout this paper, we discussed an efficient parity-based private comparison protocol using base-β fixed length encoding by employing ring-LWE based SwHE in the semi-honest model. In addition, our private comparison protocol was able to compare two integers of 16-bit (resp., 32-bit) consuming 84 ms (resp., 85 ms). Therefore, our comparison protocol works faster than Saha et al.'s protocol [20] for a single comparison. Furthermore, database implementation of our comparison protocol to evaluate a private range query also outperformed Kim et al.'s implementation [12] for 100 and 1000 records case along with security level. Besides, we believe that our batch comparison with the modified packing method enabled us to perform one million inequality comparisons for 16-bit integer within a few minutes which is a big step towards big data processing.

Acknowledgments. This work is supported in part by JSPS Grant-in-Aids for Scientific Research (A) JP16H01705 and for Scientific Research (B) JP17H01695.

References

1. Barker, E.: Recommendation for key management. In: NIST Special Publication 800–57 Part 1 Rev. 4, NIST (2016)
2. Boneh, D., Gentry, C., Halevi, S., Wang, F., Wu, D.J.: Private database queries using somewhat homomorphic encryption. In: Jacobson, M., Locasto, M., Mohassel, P., Safavi-Naini, R. (eds.) ACNS 2013. LNCS, vol. 7954, pp. 102–118. Springer, Heidelberg (2013). https://doi.org/10.1007/978-3-642-38980-1_7
3. Brakerski, Z., Gentry, C., Vaikuntanathan, V.: (Leveled) fully homomorphic encryption without bootstrapping. In: Proceedings of the 3rd Innovations in Theoretical Computer Science Conference, pp. 309–325. ACM (2012)
4. Brakerski, Z., Vaikuntanathan, V.: Fully homomorphic encryption from ring-LWE and security for key dependent messages. In: Rogaway, P. (ed.) CRYPTO 2011. LNCS, vol. 6841, pp. 505–524. Springer, Heidelberg (2011). https://doi.org/10.1007/978-3-642-22792-9_29
5. Chen, Y., Nguyen, P.Q.: BKZ 2.0: better lattice security estimates. In: Lee, D.H., Wang, X. (eds.) ASIACRYPT 2011. LNCS, vol. 7073, pp. 1–20. Springer, Heidelberg (2011). https://doi.org/10.1007/978-3-642-25385-0_1
6. Cheon, J.H., Kim, M., Kim, M.: Optimized search-and-compute circuits and their application to query evaluation on encrypted data. IEEE Trans. Inf. Forensics Secur. **11**(1), 188–199 (2016)
7. Damgård, I., Geisler, M., Krøigård, M.: Homomorphic encryption and secure comparison. Int. J. Appl. Crypt. **1**(1), 22–31 (2008)
8. Gentry, C.: Fully homomorphic encryption using ideal lattices. In: Symposium on Theory of Computing – STOC 2009, pp. 169–178. ACM, New York (2009)
9. Graepel, T., Lauter, K., Naehrig, M.: ML confidential: machine learning on encrypted data. In: Kwon, T., Lee, M.-K., Kwon, D. (eds.) ICISC 2012. LNCS, vol. 7839, pp. 1–21. Springer, Heidelberg (2013). https://doi.org/10.1007/978-3-642-37682-5_1

10. Kantarcioglu, M., Nix, R., Vaidya, J.: An efficient approximate protocol for privacy-preserving association rule mining. In: Theeramunkong, T., Kijsirikul, B., Cercone, N., Ho, T.-B. (eds.) PAKDD 2009. LNCS (LNAI), vol. 5476, pp. 515–524. Springer, Heidelberg (2009). https://doi.org/10.1007/978-3-642-01307-2_48

11. Kim, M., Lee, H.T., Ling, S., Ren, S.Q., Tan, B.H.M., Wang, H.: Better security for queries on encrypted databases. IACR Cryptology ePrint Archive, 2016/470 (2016)

12. Kim, M., Lee, H.T., Ling, S., Wang, H.: On the efficiency of FHE-based private queries. IEEE Trans. Dependable and Secure Comput. (to appear). https://doi.org/10.1109/TDSC.2016.2568182

13. Lauter, K., Naehrig, M., Vaikuntanathan, V.: Can homomorphic encryption be practical? In: ACM Workshop on Cloud Computing Security Workshop, CCSW 2011, pp. 113–124. ACM, New York (2011)

14. Paillier, P.: Public-key cryptosystems based on composite degree residuosity classes. In: Stern, J. (ed.) EUROCRYPT 1999. LNCS, vol. 1592, pp. 223–238. Springer, Heidelberg (1999). https://doi.org/10.1007/3-540-48910-X_16

15. Saha, T.K., Ali, A.B.M.S.: Storage cost minimizing in cloud - a proposed novel approach based on multiple key cryptography. In: 1st Asia-Pacific World Congress on Computer Science and Engineering (APWConCSE), pp. 1–9. IEEE (2014)

16. Saha, T.K., Koshiba, T.: Private equality test using ring-LWE somewhat homomorphic encryption, In: 3rd Asia-Pacific World Congress on Computer Science and Engineering (APWConCSE), pp. 1–9. IEEE (2016). https://doi.org/10.1109/APWC-on-CSE.2016.013

17. Saha, T.K., Koshiba, T.: Private conjunctive query over encrypted data. In: Joye, M., Nitaj, A. (eds.) AFRICACRYPT 2017. LNCS, vol. 10239, pp. 149–164. Springer, Cham (2017). https://doi.org/10.1007/978-3-319-57339-7_9

18. Saha, T.K., Mayank, Koshiba, T.: Efficient protocols for private database queries. In: Livraga, G., Zhu, S. (eds.) Data and Applications Security and Privacy XXXI. DBSec 2017. LNCS, vol. 10359, pp. 337–348. Springer, Cham (2017). https://doi.org/10.1007/978-3-319-61176-1_19

19. Saha, T.K., Koshiba, T.: Privacy-preserving equality test towards big data. In: Proceedings of the 10th International Symposium on Foundations & Practice of Security, FPS (2017)

20. Saha, T.K., Koshiba, T.: An efficient privacy-preserving comparison protocol. In: Barolli, L., Enokido, T., Takizawa, M. (eds.) NBiS 2017. LNDECT, vol. 7, pp. 553–565. Springer, Cham (2018). https://doi.org/10.1007/978-3-319-65521-5_48

21. The PARI∼Group, PARI/GP version 2.7.5, Bordeaux (2014). http://pari.math.u-bordeaux.fr/

22. Xue, K., Li, S., Hong, J., Xue, Y., Yu, N., Hong, P.: Two-cloud secure database for numeric-related SQL range queries with privacy preserving. IEEE Trans. Inf. Forensics Secur. **12**(7), 1596–1608 (2017)

23. Yao, A.C.: Protocols for secure computations. In: 23rd Annual Symposium on Foundations of Computer Science, pp. 160–164. IEEE (1982)

24. Yasuda, M., Shimoyama, T., Kogure, J., Yokoyama, K., Koshiba, T.: Practical packing method in somewhat homomorphic encryption. In: Garcia-Alfaro, J., Lioudakis, G., Cuppens-Boulahia, N., Foley, S., Fitzgerald, W.M. (eds.) DPM/SETOP -2013. LNCS, vol. 8247, pp. 34–50. Springer, Heidelberg (2014). https://doi.org/10.1007/978-3-642-54568-9_3

Congestion Control in Lan-to-Lan Connections

Andrés Felipe Hernández Leon[1], Octavio José Salcedo Parra[1,2(✉)],
and Miguel José Espitia Rico[1]

[1] Internet Inteligente Research Group,
Universidad Distrital "Francisco José de Caldas", Bogotá D.C., Colombia
anfhernandezl@correo.udistrital.edu.co,
{osalcedo,mespitiar}@udistrital.edu.co,
ojsalcedop@unal.edu.co
[2] Universidad Nacional de Colombia, Bogotá D.C., Colombia

Abstract. The entire design and simulation process of an algorithm is presented to reduce congestion in networks from point to point. A state of the art recompilation is established in terms of current end-to-end networks and their weaknesses are discussed. The algorithm is designed as a series of steps that must be followed according to the metrics related to such networks. Using the same methodology, a testing framework is applied to the algorithm through variations of the resulting network with the ns2 software. The simulations are carried out over different scenarios and are compared to the results of real end-to-end network. Several recommendations and conclusions shown by the research are included as well as ideas regarding future work.

Keywords: ACK · Algorithm · Buffer · Congestion · Network interconnection
ns2 · Protocols · TCP

1 Introduction

Since the internet ceased to be used solely for military and academic purposes and began permeating the commercial sector [1], the number of users and traffic generated started to constantly grow which led to congestion in networks. This contributes to the generation of errors and other aspects that lower the quality of the service. Hence, there was a need to create congestion control algorithms. This work focuses in end-to-end networks beginning with the identification of the causes of the congestion in the current internet followed by an analysis of the failures of various algorithms. Then, the algorithm's development process is shown and finally the simulations and results are discussed.

2 Background

Through the first revision of the state of the art, an article called [2] was found. The authors propose a mechanism to reduce the congestion control by establishing totally symmetrical and bidirectional links between the networks' ends. They also give priority to the ACK using software tools over LINUX. With these propositions, the authors managed to improve the network's performance by 90%.

© Springer Nature Switzerland AG 2018
G. Fortino et al. (Eds.): IDCS 2017, LNCS 10794, pp. 142–151, 2018.
https://doi.org/10.1007/978-3-319-97795-9_13

Another work called [3] discusses congestion in LAN (short distance) networks. The authors propose in this case to assign a fixed bandwidth when the networks are very close to a critical point of congestion. This bandwidth is lower than necessary which makes it a viable solution over short timespans. The same procedure is carried out with the buffer which is reduced with the Agile-SD.

Agile-SD showed slightly better results under normal conditions and significantly better results when the buffer and bandwidth were reduced for short timespans. This led to a low error rate in the transmission and an average improvement of 40%.

Another work called [4] deals with congestion in data centers. This is a network different from other types of networks since data centers require a decent latency and being in total capacity of avoiding collapses when traffic increases.

The authors propose a congestion algorithm for TCP called DC-Vegas which takes the advantages of the DCTCP algorithm and surpasses the conventional issues regarding delays. Agile-SD can accomplish in real time the minimum data transmission requirements in data centers and requires a slight modification. The simulations were performed with ns2 and attained an improvement of 80%.

Another work is named [5] where the focus lies in the buffer size from different routers where a package can go through. The main issues mentioned are three: the excessive bandwidth, the appearance of data bursts instead of data flows and the asynchronicity in the packages. Therefore, the authors define a congestion control algorithm called *desynchronized multichannel TCP* that creates data flow with several parallelized channels which are completely independent in terms of synchronization. This enables them to adapt to the router needs avoiding traffic problems mainly in the data bursts. The simulations revealed that there are still bottleneck issues with the multichannel strategy but such issues are 75% lower than in other congestion control algorithms in optical networks.

The article [6] shows the state of the art of the congestion control algorithm TCP VEGAS which has a lower performance than TC RENO by between 37% and 71% plus package losses of one fifth to up to half. Three techniques adopted by the TCP Vegas algorithm are mentioned and the results of their experiments are compared to real internet measurements.

Finally, they state that a new system of waiting periods must be included as well as a methodology that controls the number of additional buffers that occupy the network connection and a slow start modified mechanism.

3 Design of the Algorithm to Reduce Congestion in Lan-Wan-Lan Networks

According to the state of the art, five aspects where considered:

- How to relate the buffer's available capacity in every node with the number of packets that are handled by each one.
- How to determine the most appropriate size of the packets considering that the buffer's available memory varies in time.

- How to restrict the time slots where the ACK would behave correctly and where it would react to congestion
- How to know which type of traffic must be given priority and why in order to reduce the network congestion when it comes up
- How to determine the amount of time during which the model must change its characteristics with the purpose of adjusting as needed.

To establish the relation between these characteristics, the research was complemented with real infrastructure measurements which showed the actual behavior of a LAN-WAN-LAN network that handled different types of traffic and services. The number of nodes and buffers within a WAN network vary from one to another. Hence, the capacity of the buffer of each node must be considered [7]. Each packet passes through different routers or switches and each one of them has different capacities. Additionally, the point where a LAN network ends and a WAN network starts presents shifts in speeds and changes segments sizes and routers [8]. Therefore and according to the observations in the real network measurements, it was established that the buffer size [9] determines the maximum packet size by dividing the total capacity between the most used services in the network. A total of 6 divisions were taken since this is the number of most used services according to real measurements (Table 1).

Table 1. Available buffer ranges and classification

Free buffer percentage (%)	Classification
Between 100 and 90	Operating network
Between 89 and 70	Ideal
Between 69 and 50	Stable network
Between 49 and 30	
Between 29 and 10	Congested network
Between 9 and 1	

For the packet size it was considered that the maximum allowed size is 64 KB [9]. From the real network measurements, the simplest webpage that was tested was Google which showed sizes of up to 50 and 60 KB. During the days of measurement, it was observed that the percentage error was reduced if the packet size was also reduced. As the packets were smaller, the amount of transmission errors became smaller and the opposite effect was seen when packets were bigger.

The packet sizes do not have a constant behavior so it was decided to eliminate this feature by implementing a series of fixed sizes for the packets. This assured stability was maintained for the system. According to the observations on real network measurements, a value of 1 KB was chosen as minimum and 50 KB as maximum. This range was divided into 6 sections that correspond to the top 6 used services in the network (Table 2).

When the available buffer and the packet sizes have been classified, they are correlated to find an equilibrium that avoids the package losses and does not increase the amount of delay that each packet will have in the queue: The more buffer is

Table 2. Sizes of the packets to be transmitted within the range imposed by the model and their classification

Packet Size (KB)	Classification
1	Small
10	
20	Average
30	
40	Large
50	

available, the larger will the packet size be and the less buffer is available, the smaller will the packet size be. This relationship between both metrics translates as follows (Table 3):

Table 3. Sizes of the packets to be transmitted within the range imposed by the model and their classification

Free buffer percentage (%)	Packet size (KB)
Between 100 and 90	50
Between 89 and 70	40
Between 69 and 50	30
Between 49 and 30	20
Between 29 and 10	10
Between 9 and 1	1

The ACK time determines the speed in which the packets are being received and processed. To determine the ranges, the average of the average times of the real network was calculated which is mathematically known as the great average [10]. The network was supervised for five days.

The average ACK time for the LAN network was 1.5 ms and the WAN network was 5 ms. Those values were considered as the maximum values of the model. This value is then divided between the total of most used services in the real network (Table 4).

When the measured data was analyzed, it was decided to divide them into seven services: six that use TCP and one that uses UPD. The traffic generated by UDP cannot be ignored (Table 5).

When the metrics have been classified, it is indicated how the model works with the following steps:

1. Determine the amount of buffer dedicated to the network
2. Determine the average amount of concurrent users
3. Divide the amount of available buffer between the number of concurrent users
4. Divide the total buffer between the number of most used services

Table 4. Average concurrence percentages of the follow-ups made to the real LAN-WAN-LAN network services

Service	Port	Use (%)
FTP	20,21	
TelNet	23	
SMTP	25	
POP3	110	95%
DNS	53	
HTTP	80,8080	
UDP	69,161	
Remaining		5%
Total		100%

Table 5. Relationship between the service times and the ACK times for the LAN network

ACK times (s)	Enabled ports
Tack >= 1.5 ms	80,8080 (HTTP)
Tack < 1.5 ms and >= 1.29 ms	53 (DNS), 80,8080 (HTTP)
Tack < 1.29 ms and >= 1.08 ms	25 (SMTP), 110 (POP3), 53 (DNS), 80,8080 (HTTP)
Tack < 1.08 ms and >= 0.87 ms	20,21 (FTP), 25 (SMTP), 110 (POP3), 52 (DNS), 80,8080 (HTTP)
Tack < 0.87 ms and >= 0.66 ms	23 (Telnet), 20,21 (FTP), 25 (SMTP), 110 (POP3), 52 (DNS), 80,8080 (HTTP)
Tack < 0.66 ms and >= 0.45 ms	69,161 (UDP), 23 (Telnet), 20,21 (FTP), 25 (SMTP), 110 (POP3), 52 (DNS), 80,8080 (HTTP)
Tack < 0.45 ms	All ports

5. Determine the groups of most used services in the network and the priority each one has
6. Take as maximum value 50 KB and minimum 1 KB for the packet sizes and divide it between the total of most used services
7. Determine the average ACK time both in the LAN and WAN networks
8. Take the average as the maximum range of the times and divide such range between the total of most used services
9. Determine the average bandwidth per link for the WAN network
10. Divide such average and divide it between the total of most used services
11. Establish a relation between the data obtained in steps 4 and 6
12. Establish a relation between the data obtained in steps 8 and 10

4 Simulation of the Algorithm to Reduce Congestion in Lan-Wan-Lan Networks

The simulations were carried out with the ns2 software. The LAN network is on one end with the seven services that represent 95% of the traffic. The same schematic was used on the other end. Three nodes were used in the WAN network (8, 13 and 18) because in the real measurements each WAN link has 80 MB of bandwidth and every node has 20 MB assigned to itself (Fig. 1).

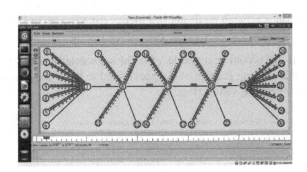

Fig. 1. Simulation of the real network in ns2

5 Simulation Analysis

In the scenarios where the amount of buffer diminished, the packet size diminished too. This led to packet loss. Only in 3 out of the 36 scenarios the packets were discarded due to no space in the buffers. In the 33 remaining scenarios, the number of packets rose but the error percentage was lower than the real values of the reference network. Implementing ranges with fixed values for the packet sizes according to the amount of available buffer is more effective than not doing so.

Packets with a fixed size of 50 KB compared to the real reference values were seen to be increasing in number by 113.60% with a 27.84% reduction of the transmission error. Packets with a fixed size of 40 KB compared to the real reference values were seen to be increasing in number by 126.33% with a 20.25% reduction of the transmission error. Packets with a fixed size of 30 KB compared to the real reference values were seen to be increasing in number by 144.42% with a 36.07% reduction of the transmission error (Fig. 2).

Packets with a fixed size of 10 KB compared to the real reference values were seen to be increasing in number by 228.54% with a 37.97% reduction of the transmission error. Packets with a fixed size of 1 KB compared to the real reference values were seen to be increasing in number by 908.33% with a 49.36% reduction of the transmission error.

It was observed that varying the packet sizes within fixed ranges is more effective when bandwidth is constant: if the bandwidth does not vary in time, it means that the network is restricted in terms of the number of services. This would increase the

Fig. 2. Relation between maximum size packets (64 KB) and 30 KB packets

number of packets that would be discarded. For the six scenarios with fixed bandwidth, it was observed that varying the size of the packets led to lower the transmission errors than those of the reference values (Fig. 3).

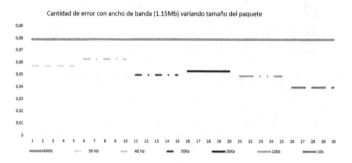

Fig. 3. Transmission error with bandwidth (1.15 Mb) while varying packet size

It was seen that when applying the algorithm, in 33 out of the 36 scenarios the simulated network was more efficient than the real one. The significant improvements are expressed as follows (Table 6):

Table 6. Comparison of the efficiency between the simulated network and the real one for each scenario

Real network (Control values)	Percentage error of reference transmission 0.079	Improvement percentage
Scenario 15	0.03	62.02
Scenario 16	0.028	64.55
Scenario 21	0.022	72.15
Scenario 22	0.021	73.41
Scenario 23	0.023	70.88
Scenario 27	0.032	59.49
Scenario 34	0.081	Worse by 2.5
Scenario 35	0.086	Worse by 8.86
Scenario 36	0.089	Worse by 12.65

Only in three scenarios the simulated network was less efficient than the real one with increases in error by 2.5% up to 12.65%. These cases have the highest congestion where the available buffer was the minimum and the packet size was 1 KB (Fig. 4).

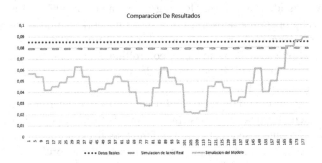

Fig. 4. Comparison of the efficiency between the simulated network and the real one for each scenario

6 Comparison with Other Works

The simulation results were compared to other projects with the purpose of determining the efficiency obtained from the algorithm (Table 7).

Table 7. Comparison of the improvements of the congestion from the present work with other projects carried out previously by other authors

Project	Congestion improvement
Unleashing Tor, Bit Torrent & Co How to Relieve TCP Deficiencies in Overlays	90%
Agile-SD: A Linux-based TCP congestion control algorithm for supporting high-speed and short-distance networks	40%
DC-Vegas: A delay-based TCP congestion control algorithm for datacenter applications	80%
Exploring parallelism and desynchronization of TCP over high speed networks with tiny buffers	75%
TCP Vegas: End to End Congestion Avoidance on a Global Internet	43%–73%

7 Conclusions

To achieve a reduction in the congestion of LAN-WAN-LAN networks it is important to know the main metrics that determine the quality of service and the relationship between them. For example, some metrics are the amount of buffer and the packet sizes or the ACK times under the available bandwidth. There must be some precaution when establishing the relationship between metrics basically because there are metrics that cannot relate to others or some metrics offer better results when they are specifically related to another metric.

The amount of available buffer will determine the packet size. The more the buffer is available, the larger will the receivable packets be without the risk of rejection. This relationship was divided into ranges leaving a maximum of 90% and a minimum of 70% for an ideally operating network. For a stable network, the range goes from 50% to 30% and for a congested operating network it goes from 10% to 1%. Giving fixed values for the packet sizes allows to easily controlling congestion since service-related random factors are eliminated. Hence, the model was set with a 50 KB maximum size and a minimum size of 1 KB.

ACK times are an important factor and it is the one that determines the amount of bandwidth. If there are fast responses, this means that the transmission medium can handle a larger amount of sent data from different services.

When the best balance between metrics is achieved, the algorithm and the network present their best performance. At this point of equilibrium, the packet size in the buffer queue cannot be too small but not too large either. The equilibrium point must be between 20 and 50 KB with a bandwidth between 2.29 MB/s and 2.86 MB/s for the LAN network. The packet size made the percentage error vary between 43.03% and 73.41%. These values were an improvement over the other scenarios.

References

1. Kurose, J.F., Ross, K.W.: Computer Networking: A Top-Down Approach, 7th edn. Pearson (2017)
2. Kim, J.-M., Lee, S.-Y., Kim, J.-H.: TCP congestion window tuning for satellite communication using cross-layer approach. In: 2016 Eighth International Conference on Ubiquitous and Future Networks (ICUFN) (2016)
3. Giambene, G.: Queuing Theory and Telecommunications Networks and Applications. Springer, Roma (2005). https://doi.org/10.1007/978-1-4614-4084-0
4. Zhang, X., Ding, M., Wan, R.: PFO: Priority-based flow scheduling for online social network datacenter. In: 2016 IEEE 11th Conference on Industrial Electronics and Applications (ICIEA) (2016)
5. Sait, S.Y., Murthy, H.A., Sivalingam, K.M.: Organization-level control of excessive internet downloads. In: 2016 IEEE 41st Conference on Local Computer Networks (LCN) (2016)
6. Aftab, A., Ghani, A., Abidi, Z.: Simulation based performance evaluation of TCP variants along with UDP flow analysis of throughput with respect to Simulation based performance evaluation of TCP variants along with UDP flow analysis of throughput with respect to delay, buffer size and time. In: 2016 International Conference on Open Source Systems & Technologies (ICOSST) (2016)
7. Marks, D., Tschorsch, F., Scheuermann, B.: Unleashing Tor, BitTorrent & Co.: how to relieve TCP deficiencies in overlays. In: 35th Annual IEEE Conference on Local Computer Networks, pp. 320–323 (2010)
8. Alrshah, M., Othman, M., Ali, B., Hanapi, Z.M.: Agile-SD: a Linux-based TCP congestion control algorithm for supporting high-speed and short-distance networks. J. Netw. Comput. Appl. **55**, 181–190 (2015)

9. Wang, J., Wen, J., Li, C., Xiong, Z., Han, Y.: DC-Vegas: a delay-based TCP congestion control algorithm for datacenter applications. J. Netw. Comput. Appl. **53**, 103–114 (2015)
10. Cui, C., Xue, L., Chiu, C.-H., Kondikoppa, P., Park, S.-J.: Exploring parallelism and desynchronization of TCP over high speed networks with tiny buffers. J. Netw. Comput. Appl. **69**, 60–68 (2014)

Implementing an Application that Automates Glaucoma Detection Through the Use of Image Processing and Fuzzy Logic

Santiago Silva Cartagena[1], Octavio José Salcedo Parra[1,2(✉)], and Rafael Antonio Acosta Rodríguez[1,2]

[1] Internet Inteligente Research Group,
Universidad Distrital "Francisco José de Caldas", Bogotá D.C., Colombia
{sansilvac, raacostar}@correo.udistrital.edu.co,
osalcedo@udistrital.edu.co
[2] Universidad Nacional de Colombia, Bogotá D.C., Colombia
ojsalcedop@unal.edu.co

Abstract. This article centers in providing a system for the optimization of recognizing different structures that constitutes the depth of the retina (retinal fundus images) to build a Glaucoma detection tool. This is achieved through the implementation of an application that uses the OpenCV library to process images and fuzzy logic to deliver an accurate diagnosis and hence control the evolution of the disease. When developing the app, several processing images techniques were implemented which will provide the information we need to determine the state of the disease and the fuzzy logic will aid in interpreting the obtained data. In this article, the combination of two different Glaucoma detection techniques is tested as well as the generation of a disease diagnosis, which offers results within a pre-established range. With the implementation of these techniques, it is stated that a higher refinement is necessary in the detection of Glaucoma starting from the image processing stage.

Keywords: Diagnosis · Fuzzy logic · Glaucoma · Image processing
Medicine · OpenCV · Optimization · Retinal fundus images

1 Introduction

Glaucoma is a state where there is damage in the optical nerve and the damage is caused gradually. This occurs when there is high pressure in the eyes and is often hereditary. It is detected mostly during the final stages of life [1]. For emergency doctors, patients with ophthalmological pathologies represent a real issue because they are the first to deal with the diagnosis and initial handling of such patients. Since Glaucoma is a common pathology in consultation, its diagnosis as well as its adequate treatment, must be fast and accurate to avoid irreversible side effects [2].

The diagnosis of Glaucoma is achieved via the examination of the optical nerve and its ability to transmit a visual message to the brain. This allows to establish if the optical nerve has been damaged or not and if it has, it can also be determined whether the state of the nerve is worsening. Different tools, techniques and instruments are used

G. Fortino et al. (Eds.): IDCS 2017, LNCS 10794, pp. 152–160, 2018.
https://doi.org/10.1007/978-3-319-97795-9_14

by the ophthalmologist to define the diagnosis. The optical nerve can be easily examined by using an instrument called the ophthalmoscope which offers a clear image of the retina, its color and the state of the nerve. These specific factors will give us a clue in determining the cause of vision loss.

Therefore, the present project is focused on giving an optimization of the Glaucoma detection tools through the implementation of an app that, along with the use of image processing and fuzzy logic, delivers a correct diagnosis and allows the supervision of this pathological disease.

2 Background

In [3] the segmentation method is obtained in two methods: Gray level discontinuity, which consist in segmenting the image based on big changes in the gray levels between pixels which is the base of the detection of edges, lines and isolated points, etc.

Gray level similarity which image divisions are grouped using pixels with similar features.

Ashish and Kishore Dutta published an adaptive algorithm for the detection of threshold called CDR which shows the progression of Glaucoma [4]. Segmentation is performed through the reprocessing of the image and using morphological operations for the detection of threshold within structures. The operations used for image processing are divided into four different types: Erosion, Dilatation, Opening and Closing. The described applications for each morphological operation focus on reducing noise in the reprocessing of a gray-scale image and object segmentation in an image to extract objects and competent information after applying morphological operations.

James Lowell (2004) published an article where the location and segmentation of the main optical nerve is established using low-intensity images of the retinal fundus [1]. A template is also proposed to relate the optical nerve with its identification. The method in this article identifies an optical disc in color images of the retinal fundus (retinographies) with a 96% precision according to the obtained results being validated by public repositories. An advantage of the method is stated where the user's intervention is not necessary. The results coincide by 97% with the area of the optical disc.

Clemencia de Vivero and Oscar Forero Moncaleano present in their book key aspects for treating acute Glaucoma by both general and emergency doctors [5]. Additionally, they show different aspects of the progression of Glaucoma and how to identify them, as well as the treatment and the consequences of not treating it adequately. If treatment is begun at an early stage, it is described that the most likely outcome is that it will not develop any changes in the optical nerve or vein occlusions in the retina, which are irreversible and could permanently affect the visual field and even damage the person's vision.

G.D. Joshi published in the IEEE magazine an article that presents how the disc and cup areas are segmented through the use of the image's retinal color [6]. This paper also discusses the detection of Glaucoma and also uses diverse geometric factors for the ocular disc, which is used to find the determining CDR factor for the identification of the Glaucoma's evolution.

S.E. Zohora presented an article where different classification techniques for spontaneous retinal images are reviewed. They are vital in the process of properly detecting Glaucoma [7]. An evaluation of the CDR (cup to disc ratio) is also included as well as several image processing methods.

Nicolas Varachiu presents a Glaucoma detection approach based on fuzzy logic, genetic algorithms and neural networks [8]. He also establishes the basis for developing a system for the diagnosis and prediction of Glaucoma with fuzzy logic where each feature that needs to be considered for diagnosis is described. The accuracy percentage of Glaucoma detection is increased through this alternative by performing an evaluation of the possible risks during the process. Additionally, the author describes how the evolution of computational intelligence enables advances on complex medical processes and increases the effectiveness of the method in the particular case of Glaucoma detection.

3   Methodology

The interior of the surface of the eye mainly consists of the internal parts of the retina. This inner layer contains the head of the optical nerve, blood vessels, the fovea, etc. In Fig. 1 of the retina, the disc region is known as the disc and cup area of the eye. The optical cup is considered as the brightest section in the image of the retina's deepest area and represents the visual portion of the eye. In terms of identifying Glaucoma, this region represents the progression of the disease where Glaucoma is determined if the optical cup is damaged.

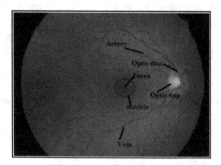

Fig. 1. Image from the retina's depth. Source: [4]

Glaucoma is calculated through the disc radius – optical cup ratio. If the patient presents a radius ratio of 0.3 or higher, he is suffering from the disease [9].

The automated classification of Glaucoma must not rely on segmentation measurements. Hence, we use features provided by several studies regarding the state of the retina in different Glaucoma stages.

Patterns and structures of interest are highlighted by applying different transforms and methods such as the Wavelet Transform and Steerable Gaussian Filters with the additional use of OpenCV (an image processing library) and NumPy arrays for storing diverse images along with their functionalities for creating pixel-wise processing kernels. The evolution of the disease is then isolated for its eventual analysis and, by adding fuzzy logic, quantifiers can be provided for inferences which will make for a more precise advancement of the disease for each isolated case.

3.1 Images of the Retinal Fundus

This stage considers images of the retinal fundus where the regular and irregular aspects are identified (Glaucoma is presented in different stages) taken from an open source dataset of the Ophthalmology Department of the Friedrich-Alexander University Erlangen-Nuremberg (Germany), along with a dataset provided by the Open Rotterdam Glaucoma Imaging Data Sets website. This allows the establishment of a set of 354 images that will serve as support for the study. These images include the same measurement standard since the machine that produces them generates them according to the size of the pupilometer.

3.2 Segmentation of Disc and Optical Cup

In the analysis of the retinal fundus image, the structures that are part of the optical nerve can be identified through different segmentation methods. The interest is centered in the disc-cup ratio which is converted to gray scale. Some additional pre-processing stages over the retinal fundus image allow the extraction of the optical disc and the cup area for their eventual analysis.

Basically, for the processing of the two structures of interest, the image will be divided into two different channels: green and red. The optical disc area will be identified over the red channel and the optical cup area over the green channel. This step is performed to eliminate any type of structure that does not interest us for the retinal image analysis. Afterwards, the segmentation (Fig. 2) is started to then proceed with the diagnosis.

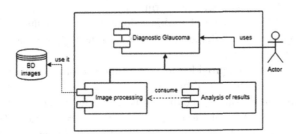

Fig. 2. Application structure. Source: Authors

Figure 2 shows a structural diagram as the application's development is proposed which is executed locally and the main access module is the diagnosis component that uses image segmentation and analysis.

4 Design

For the implementation of the tool, OpenCV3.2 will be used which is an open source library coded in Python2.7 designed for image and video processing, object detection, etc. It will enable all types of transformations over the image. Additionally, PyFuzzy will be used which is a framework coded in Python2.7 for working with fuzzy sets for the processing of fuzzy logic operations.

Use of OpenCV3.2: The OpenCV3.2 library provides different methods to process images. One in particular is the Wavelet Transform processing. Its use is crucial for the identification of structures within the image since it acts as a noise suppressor and compressing tool. This is relevant when dealing with big volumes of images for their posterior analysis.

Furthermore, this library can manipulate different types of kernels (exploration matrixes over the image) for the identification of specific figures within the image to be processed. The Gaussian filters make use of this type of kernels to enhance the image (augmenting the intensity variations where they are produced), detecting edges (pixels where there are abrupt changes in intensity).

Use of PyFuzzy: Due to PyFuzzy being a framework oriented to fuzzy logic, it adapts better to the real world and the appreciations that can be performed over the images of processed retina examples. A key point to study is how advanced the disease is; with fuzzy sets provided by the framework, we can establish a diagnosis depending on the damage found in the image of the retina and express it in natural terms. So clinical Glaucoma can be diagnoses when the optical nerve has an aperture ranging between 110 and 142.

Use of NumPy 1.13: NumPy is the fundamental package for scientific development with Python.

Creation of n-dimensional arrays.

Sophisticated functions of Broadcasting

C/C++ integration tools

Use of lineal algebra, Fourier Transform, etc.

NumPy will be used to control bi-dimensional kernels for the analysis of every image and the application of different transforms over them. NumPy is compatible with different OpenCV functionalities.

Finally, statistics will be provided to support the use of the tool and the accuracy percentage of the diagnosis (See Table 1).

The risk in the progression of the disease is chosen as system output so the output variable in the proposed fuzzy logic model is given in terms of [Low. Normal, High], according to medical records. The ophthalmologist's knowledge of the pertinent data regarding Glaucoma was compiled in a set of fuzzy rules shown hereby.

Table 1. Definition of variables for the diagnosis of disease

N	Variable	Terms	Fuzzy logic format	Measure
1	Age	Old age	(0,0) (40,0) (80,1) (100,1)	Years
2	Myopia	Level	(0,0) (4,0) (7,1) (20,1)	Yes, No
3	Last check-up	Time	(0,0) (2,0) (5,1) (10,1)	Years
4	Use of steroids	Time	(0,0) (0.5,0) (6,1) (12,1)	Months
5	Presence of diabetes	Time	(0,0) (5,0) (10,1) (100,1)	Years
6	Intraocular Pressure (IOP)	High	(0,0) (16.5,0) (22,1) (45,1)	Mm Hg
		Normal	(11,0) (16.5,1) (22,0)	
		Low	(0,1) (11,1) (16.5,0) (45,0)	
7	Daily pressure fluctuations (IOP)	Low	(0,1) (5,0) (10,0)	Mm Hg
		High	(0,0) (3,1) (10,1)	
8	Age	Old age	(0,0) (40,0) (80,1) (100,1)	Years
9	Myopia	Level	(0,0) (4,0) (7,1) (20,1)	Yes, No
10	Last check-up	Time	(0,0) (2,0) (5,1) (10,1)	Years

5 Application

In first place, to develop the application the Python2.7 programming language was used which is highly useful with the correct use of libraries. The corresponding libraries were imported to develop our structure recognition script.

Afterwards, we proceed with the algorithm that segments each structure of interest, which correspond to the disc and cup of the cornea fundus.

Figure 3 shows the followed procedure to identify and separate the structures of interest in the cornea fundus image taken as an example. It is converted to HSV format to highlight the clearer area to be then converted into a gray scale image as shown in Figs. 4 and 5 where one represents a healthy retina and one shows a retina with Glaucoma.

```
hsv = cv2.cvtColor(image, cv2.COLOR_BGR2HSV)
cr_max = np.array([130,250,250])
cr_min = np.array([110,100,50])
mascara = cv2.inRange(hsv, cr_min, cr_max)
erosion = cv2.erode(mascara, kernel, iterations = 1)
dilatacion = cv2.dilate(mascara, kernel, iterations = 1)
apertura = cv2.dilate(erosion, kernel, iterations = 1)
aux = copy.deepcopy(apertura)
(cnts, _) = cv2.findContours(aux, cv2.RETR_TREE, cv2.CHAIN_APPROX_SIMPLE)
cnts = sorted(cnts, key = cv2.contourArea, reverse = True)[:10]
```

Fig. 3. Code used for structure identification over images. Source: Authors

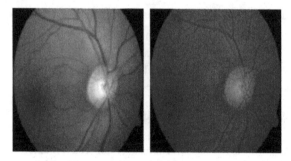

Fig. 4. Example image of the retina fundus in a healthy state (color and gray scale). Source: Authors

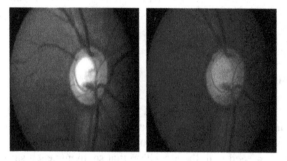

Fig. 5. Example image of the retina fundus with Glaucoma symptoms (color and gray scale). Source: Authors

When comparing the gray scale images, the structures of the retina can be identified as well as the changes from a retina in good condition to one with Glaucoma symptoms.

Then, more transforms are applied to the obtained gray scale images. The result is a binary image establishing a threshold where all image pixels over 125 are set as 250 or 1 and those under that threshold are set as 0 which leads to the binary image for the following cleaning and edge detection stages.

Over the new image, erosion is applied which intends to eliminate the noise. Afterwards, dilation is used to avoid the loss of erosion and then the opening operation fills the holes within the identified structure.

6   Discussion of the Results

Firstly, the 354-image dataset was evaluated where all types of images were mixed with early Glaucoma symptoms, advanced Glaucoma symptoms and no symptoms.

In these images where the different stages of the disease are shown the optical cup and radius disc areas were identified to develop an assessment of the state of the retinal fundus.

When identifying the radius portion between the two structures of the image, it was detected which ones had Glaucoma symptoms, which had not and which had advanced Glaucoma. The Table 2 indicates how the use of the Wavelet Transform over OpenCV leads to acceptable results in terms of the identification of Glaucoma in images where the disease is advanced and where there is no symptom. This contrasts with the images with early Glaucoma where the processing tool shows a percentage well below the expected value.

Table 2. Sampling of obtained results when applying image processing over the dataset

No. of total images	Images with early Glaucoma	Images with advanced Glaucoma	Images without Glaucoma
354	100	144	110
Results	39.32%	88.273%	67.89%

After the analysis with only the image processing stage, the fuzzy logic was added for each patient's medical record along with the addition of the risk value. All of this combined can determine how likely is the person to have Glaucoma based only on his medical record.

After implementing fuzzy logic over each medical record related to the dataset images for the study, it was identified that in terms of images with advanced Glaucoma there was a reduction of 4.8166% approximately. The images without Glaucoma symptoms as well as the images with early Glaucoma raised their accuracy percentage of diagnosis.

Contrasts were identified with the authors of referenced articles. On one hand, there is a clear difference between the tools used to identify the different structures that are part of the retina. Tulasigeri and Irulappan develop validations of their results with MATLAB, Xilinx and Spartan6, FPGA [4]. In our case, OpenCV was used to develop image processing with a validation in Python and adding PyFuzzy to increase the probability of an accurate diagnosis based on the patient's medical history. On the other hand, Nicolas Varachiu develops a rule system to interpret clinical history and study an image set through an incremental model which can be refined with the establishment of rules and different iterations [7]. In spite of offering a useful set of rules to perform the corresponding study over the patient's medical track, he does not offer results to corroborate their effectiveness.

7   Conclusions

In this article, the combination of two Glaucoma detection techniques is tested with the purpose of delivering a diagnosis of the disease which offers results within the expected ranges. With the implementation of these techniques, it is identified that a higher refinement in the automation of Glaucoma detection is necessary starting from image processing.

With the use of image processing, along with the implementation of rules based on the patient's medical records and fuzzy logic, the results were all within expected ranges where certain flaws were detected in early Glaucoma images with 59.36% accuracy. However, when performing the study over images that did not present any symptom of the disease, there was an increase in accuracy going from 77.89% to 88.22% and a decrease in the advanced Glaucoma diagnosis since it went from 98.27% to 93.45%.

A variation was found in the accuracy percentage of the data when implementing different methods in the image processing phase. In this article, the Wavelet Transform tool integrated in OpenCV was used. Using another tool such as the Steerable Gaussian filters could vary significantly the results obtained as well as adding or removing rules from the rule system based on the medical records.

References

1. Lowell, J., Hunter, A., Steel, D., Basu, A., Ryder, R.: Optic Nerve Head Segmentation, vol. 23. IEEE (2009)
2. Issac, A., Parthasarthi, M., Dutta, M.K: An Adaptive Threshold Based Algorithm for Optic Disc and Cup Segmentation in Fundus Images. IEEE (2015)
3. Raju, P.D.R., Neelima, G.: Image Segmentation by Using Histogram Thresholding (2012)
4. Tulasigeri, C., Irulappan, M.: An advanced thresholding algorithm for diagnosis of glaucoma in fundus images. In: IEEE International Conference on Recent Trends in Electronics Information Communication Technology, p. 5 (2016)
5. Vivero, C.d., Forero, M.O.: Claves para el diagnóstico y manejo del glaucoma agudo para médicos generales y de urgencias. Pontificia Universidad Javeriana, Bogotá (2013)
6. Joshi, G.D., Sivaswamy, J., Karan, K.: Optic Disk and Cup Boundary Detection Using Regional Information. IEEE (2010)
7. Zohora, S.E., Chakraborty, S., Khan, A.M., Dey, N.: Glaucomatous Image Classification: A Review. IEEE (2016)
8. Varachiu, N., Karanicolas, C., Ulieru, M.: Computational Intelligence for Medical Knowledge Acquisition With Application to Glaucoma. IEEE (2002)
9. Rao, D.P.V., Gayathri, R., Sunitha, R.: Novel approach for design and analysis of diabetic retinopathy glaucoma detection using cup to disc ratio and ANN. In: 2nd International Conference on Nanomaterials and Technologies (2014)

Risk Driving Behaviors Detection Using Pressure Cushion

Zhenhai Yang[1], Meng Yu[1($\boxtimes$)], Wenfeng Li[1], Congcong Ma[1],
Raffaele Gravina[2], and Giancarlo Fortino[2]

[1] School of Logistics Engineering,
Wuhan University of Technology, Wuhan, China
{yangzhenhai,liwf,macc}@whut.edu.cn, ymmona@126.com
[2] Department of Informatics, Modeling, Electronics and Systems,
University of Calabria, Rende, Italy
r.gravina@dimes.unical.it, g.fortino@unical.it

Abstract. With the increasing frequency of traffic accidents, traffic safety has attracted attention of the researchers. Most of the traffic accidents are related to the driver's risky behavior or some improper driving habits, such as leaning against the window/door, picking up things, or looking backwards when driving at high speed. In this paper, to detect such risky behaviors, we propose a decision tree for classification that recognizes four kinds of driving behaviors: normal driving, looking backwards, leaning against the window and picking up things. A time series of pressure data were measured from a mat with 2×2 pressure sensors which are distributed on the driver seat. Regarding the pre-processing phase, a digital filter is used for noise reduction. Results show that our method can achieve an average recognition rate of 88.25%.

Keywords: Risk driving · Behavior recognition · Posture detection
Smart cushion · Pressure sensor

1 Introduction

The increase of car numbers has brought convenience to our life, but at the same time it is cause of several issues. Traffic safety is obviously one of them. According to the latest global status report on road safety from World Health Organization [1], about 1.25 million people die in car accidents each year around the world. The traffic safety problems have become the main issues to be addressed for Intelligent Transportation (IT), which has become unprecedentedly urgent due to the increasing number of the vehicles and drivers. In most cases, the traffic accidents are caused by drivers themselves, e.g. due to improper driving behavior or careless driving.

With the purpose of reminding the driver not to take dangerous actions, we propose to monitor their posture while they are driving. The current un-obstructive sensing technology makes it possible to obtain the driver's posture in the vehicle. Seat-cushion is one of the most attractive devices to be considered in the vehicle design process, regarding not only degree of comfort but also good non-invasive features for drivers and it almost have no negative effects on driving which can foster its promotion in

© Springer Nature Switzerland AG 2018
G. Fortino et al. (Eds.): IDCS 2017, LNCS 10794, pp. 161–172, 2018.
https://doi.org/10.1007/978-3-319-97795-9_15

vehicle manufacturing. However, most of previous related work on cushion-based approaches are used to assess drivers' degree of comfort [2–4], which might not essentially solve the risky driving problem. As an important interface between driver and cab environment, the cushion is playing an important role not only in improving seating comfort but also in obtaining drivers' body information, which can provide very useful information in recognizing postures of cushion users.

This paper presents an integrated method using Decision Tree (DT) algorithm and gravity-center model for recognizing four risk driving behaviors based on the obtained interface pressures. The contents of this paper are summarized as follows. Section 2 discusses current related works of the seated-cushion and drivers' posture detection system. Section 3 describes the designed cushion for risk driving posture detection. Section 4 represents the proposed method, the feature extraction, sitting posture model and diagnosis of sitting posture. Finally, concluding remarks of our study and the potential ideas on future research are given in Sect. 5.

2 Related Work

2.1 Driving Posture Detection

Most of the former researches on posture detection for vehicle occupants are based on the video or other wearable sensors.

Yan et al. presents a novel system which applies image processing method to detect driving state [5]. It uses convolutional neural network to automatically learn and predict pre-defined driving postures. Yamada et al. presents an Advanced Driver Assistance System (ADAS) which can monitor driving posture [6]. This system uses a camera to get joint positions of drivers. Yan proposed a vision-based solution to recognize the driver's unsafe behavior [7]. The proposed methods on the Driving-posture Dataset could achieve mean Average Precision (mAP) of 97.76% on the dataset.

Wang et al. proposed a Brain Computer Interface (BCI) system based on electroencephalography (EEG) for distracted driving [8]. Independent component analysis and self-organizing map were used to achieve the goal. Ling et al. [9] take driving behaviors, such as acceleration, braking, shifting and steering as recognition features to evaluate driving fatigue. Lee et al. proposed a drowsy driving detection based on the driver's physiological signals [10]. Eye activity measures, inclination of the driver's head, sagging posture, heart beat rate, skin electric potential, and EEG activities were detected in this system.

Cameras and other physiological sensors bring a high accuracy but at the same time show several drawbacks. Taking the visual method as an example, it has many limitations, the installation space is limited, the cost is very high when compared with other solutions, and it is source of privacy related issues. Other physiological detection methods may bring wearing difficulties, cumbersome detection, highly invasive, poor user experience and other related issues.

2.2 The Overview of the Functionalities of Current Cushion

A single chair or a seat is said to be sensory deprived because it cannot sense the actions of its occupant and therefore cannot interpret the user's intentions. But a smart cushion enables a chair to sense and interpret its occupant's actions. These works aim at enriching cushion functionalities from all aspects. In many studies, cushion is an approach for activity detection and sitting posture diagnosis. Huang et al. developed a smart chair based on a sensor array to recognize sitting postures [11]. The application of artificial neural network (ANN) was used to classify eight different patterns of pressure distribution. This system can also predict subsequent activities for individual users. Xu et al. proposed a textile-based sensing system, called Smart Cushion which can analyze the sitting posture of human being [12]. Dynamic time warping was used to classify the postures. Suzuki et al. proposed a low-cost, sensor based system to capture sitting postures [13]. A hidden Markov model approach was used to establish the recognition model. Ma et al. proposed a cushion-based posture recognition system to process pressure sensor signals for the detection of wheelchair user's posture [14, 15]. Pressure data can be useful to infer whether a subject is suffering fatigue [16]. A cloud-based wheelchair assist system was proposed for supporting user mobility of impaired people. Accelerometer, pressure data, and GPS signals were detected to monitor wheelchair status [17].

3 Hardware Design

The overall hardware design is shown in Fig. 1.

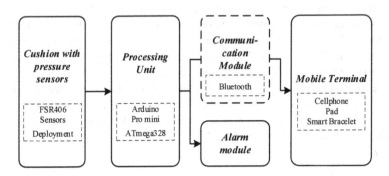

Fig. 1. Simplified hardware architecture of the proposed system

The system is composed of three main modules:

- *Cushion*: we chose a medium thick mat which can ensure users' comfort and avoid sensor deformation.
- *Processing unit*: Implemented with Arduino Pro Mini, a microcontroller-board based on the ATmega328. With a small size and powerful processing ability, the Pro Mini is very suitable for our cushion.

- *Communication module*: In the limited space in vehicle, Bluetooth is undoubtedly the best choice; it also features low power consumption and easy networking characteristics.

3.1   Pressure Sensors

Force Sensing Resistor (FSR406) [18] from Interlink Electronics company is chosen to accomplish our system. FSR406 is a light weight, small size, high precision, and ultra-thin resistive pressure sensor. This pressure sensor converts the pressure applied to the area of the FSR sensor film into a change in the resistance value to obtain pressure information. Table 1 presents the main parameters of the sensor.

Table 1. Pressure sensor mat specifications

Parameter name	Value
Pressure mat area	45 × 45 [cm]
Force sensitivity range	< 100 [g] to > 10 [kg]
Number of sensors	4 (2 × 2)
Sensing area	4.45 × 3.8 cm
Sensor size	Max = 51 × 61 [cm] Min = 0.5 × 0.5 [cm]

3.2   Distribution of the Sensors

Considering the need to reduce the cost and confirm accuracy, the sensor distribution is carried out according to the human anatomy. Aissaoui et al. [19] presented a pressure distribution of the body-seat interface based on image data at the body. Generally, the distribution of the body-seat interface can be divided into 4 parts, these four parts are two ischial tuberosities (IT) [20–22] regions and two thigh regions. The pressure at the IT regions is the highest, and gradually decrease around IT regions, the IT regions can symbolize the human focus. The pressure in the thigh regions is most sensitive to thigh pressure. These 4 regions are taken as sensitive area for the recognition. If the sitting posture changes, obvious changes will take place in the pressure values of these four areas. The distribution is shown in Fig. 2.

4   Proposed Method

The system is capable of recognizing four kinds of driving behaviors: Normal driving, leaning on the door, turning around and picking up things.

4.1   Preprocessing

Due to individual differences of drivers' body and the noise generated by the car bumps and some small body action, the raw signals need to be preprocessed before being analyzed. For this purpose, Finite Impulse Response (FIR) filter [23, 24] is chosen to

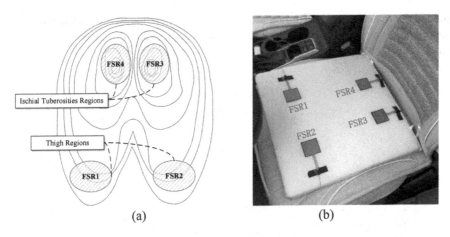

Fig. 2. Pressure distribution of human body (a) and sensor deployment (b)

filter raw signals; samples from Sliding Time Windows are then taken as training sample set.

The difference equation of the FIR filter is defined as

$$y(n) = \sum_{m=0}^{N-1} h(m)x(n-m) = h(n) \otimes x(n) \tag{1}$$

Where N is the length of the form of the filter, and $h(m)$ is the specific pulse filter system, the input and output signal are $x(n)$ and $y(n)$, the filtering system is obtained by the following equation

$$h(n) = w_N(n)h_d(n) \tag{2}$$

Where $h_d(n)$ is ideal filter and $w_N(n)$ is form function. In this article, the Hanning window function is used as

$$w_N(n) = \begin{cases} 0.5 - 0.5\cos\frac{2\pi n}{N-1} & 0 \leq n \leq N-1 \\ 0 \end{cases} \tag{3}$$

During the data processing, the sampling frequency of the pressure sensor is set to 125 Hz, with 4 s as a detection period, 500 data samples for each group, $N = 64$ for the filter form length.

4.2 Feature Extraction

First, how correct driving posture is present in a feature space is investigated. To do this, four postures (Normal driving (N), Lean on the door (L), Pick up things (P), and look backwards (LB)) are taken as examples. At each sampling time (every 0.2 s), 4 (= 2 × 2) pressure values are measured. Since the two sensors value of F_2 and F_3

attained the main feature of Turning around, the corresponding two values are used for looking backwards evaluation. In Fig. 3 four postures are displayed in the two-dimensional axis.

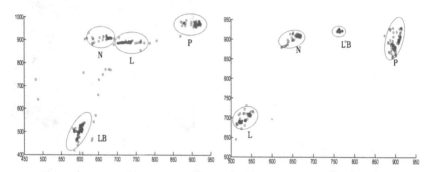

Fig. 3. Four driving postures of B (Look backward), L (Leaning on the door) and P (Picking up things) and normal posture (N) presented in two features [F_2–F_3(left)/F_1–F_4(right)].

The y axis represents the pressure analog value. In order to distinguish and identify these four actions, the following valid information can be extracted from the two graphs:

- Figure 3 shows that LB posture is represented as a distribution of small size area that is a little bit distant from the origins of other postures. LB posture has a smaller value in F_2 and F_3, but it has larger value in F_1 and F_4. Because when the drivers look backwards, he needs to turn his body to the right and use the right ischial tuberosities as a fulcrum to lift the left side of the body to complete this movement. When drivers take the LB posture, they tend to put their center of gravity on the right side to look back, then the distribution tends to be located in the lower right corner in the Fig. 3(a).

LB is not a typical center of gravity-related posture, while the other three postures occur because of the changes which is caused by the human torso or hip displacement. We observed that, the L, N and P have a close connection to the change of barycenter of human body. To distinguish the LB posture, the Decision Tree (DT) algorithm [25, 26] is used to determine the LB threshold and to classify LB and other postures (Fig. 4).

4.3   Model of Sitting Posture

According to the data we obtained, the P (picking up things) is the only posture whose F_1 and F_2 value increase simultaneously. Considering the limited driving space, if F_1 and F_2 increase at the same time by a certain degree, the driver is very likely to pick up or to sink down, and considering the characteristics ischial tuberosity is a human hip support point, value in F_3 and F_4 show only a slight reduction. The changes of F_1 and

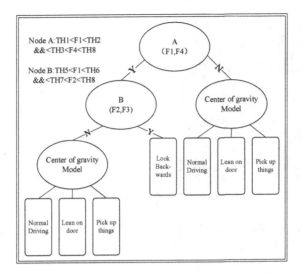

Fig. 4. The Decision Tree classification for driving postures

F_2 can be used to determine the value of the center of gravity of the y axis. The same procedure can be used in x axis.

$$\begin{cases} A = F_{1n} - F_{10} \\ B = F_{2n} - F_{20} \\ C = F_{3n} - F_{30} \\ D = F_{4n} - F_{40} \end{cases} \quad \begin{cases} X = (A-B) + (C-D) \\ Y = A+B \end{cases} \tag{4}$$

At the beginning of driving (t = t_0 to t = T_1), normal driving data are obtained as learning samples. We define the value of average value of normal driving as the initial state as $\alpha = [F_{10}, F_{20}, F_{30}, F_{40}]$. Real-time values are collected and recorded in an array as $\beta = [F_{1n}, F_{2n}, F_{3n}, F_{4n}]$. X, Y represents the vertical and horizontal coordinates of the postures' center of gravity. In Fig. 5, visual plane models are reported to show the body pressure distribution more intuitively (Fig. 5).

According to this model, a classification algorithm is proposed (see Fig. 6). The algorithm consists of two steps: Learning of normal driving and analysis of sitting posture.

During the learning of normal driving (t = 0 to t = t_0), the value of sensors in normal driving are collected to build a training samples, test drivers are asked to drive in a correct and normal way. Formally, we estimate α during this time period.

In the following time (t_0 to the end of the process), the threshold for (F_1, F_4) and (F_2, F_3) are determined by the decision tree algorithm, X, Y are then calculated to determine which area current position belongs to.

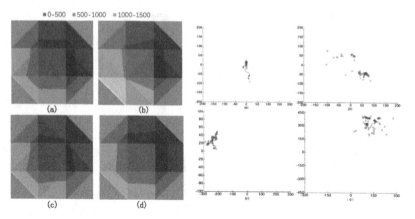

Fig. 5. Pressure distribution (left) and barycenter position (right) of four driving postures N (a), LB (b), L (c) and P(d).

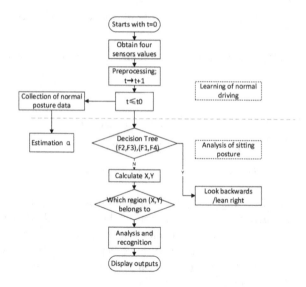

Fig. 6. Flow chart of proposed classification method

5   Experiments

5.1   Experiment Procedures

To verify the proposed approach on driver behavior recognition, we built a dataset obtained from twenty volunteer drivers (10 males, 10 females, mean age 25 ± 5 years, mean driving age 2–15 years). The participants are not required to drive in a way according to the description of the posture. To obtain a ground-truth, the driver's state are recorded through the human eye of the assistant seated in the car aside the driver and also supported by video recordings. When they appear to perform postures which can be diagnosed with one of the aforementioned postures, the corresponding label is recorded along with the current pressure data.

The volunteers were asked to drive in a straight road with no sharp brakes and turns. Test speed is about 30–40 km/h which can provide a safe environment for our experiment. According to the hardware designed in Sect. 3.1, the cushion was used to record the pressure data. We labeled the driver's current posture and collected the corresponding pressure signals. 100 experimental samples were collected for each posture, and every driver performed 10 sessions to ensure the accuracy of the data. Through the procedures discussed above, we built the dataset containing the four postures. From the dataset, we extracted four main postures which were closely related to the interface pressure. The experiments were done separately and the was terminated around three hours in total. The description of the four postures are as follows:

- Normal driving: Drive in a natural way with no particular actions.
- Leaning on the door: The elbow stretches out the window or the body leaning against the door.
- Picking up things: Lean over and pick up something under the seat or the steering wheel.
- Look backwards: Turn around and look backwards e.g. to talk with passengers in the backseat.

5.2   Results

Performance Results
After the model is established, we carried out an empirical performance evaluation of our posture recognition method on a new experiment and the experimental results are shown in Table 2.

Table 2. Each posture recognition result

Actual posture	Recognized posture			
	Normal driving	Lean on the door	Look backwards	Pick up things
Normal driving	88	0	10	2
Lean on the door	5	93	2	0
Look backwards	13	0	76	11
Pick up things	4	0	0	96

The results in Table 2 show that, Normal driving recognition accuracy is about 88%, Lean on the door recognition accuracy achieves 93%, Look backwards and Pick up things is around 76% and 96%. The results show that Look backwards posture is in a low accuracy. By recalling the details of the experiment, the behavior varies from drivers to drivers, and the how the action behaved is not the same. When the drivers appeared to perform LB posture, some of them just turn his head slightly while others turn the torso to look backwards, it leads to that the some look backwards postures are misrecognized. Lean on the door and pick up things have a obvious change in center of gravity, the recognition rate is high as the results show.

The recognition accuracy and identification of species may not be as good as camera-based algorithms or other methods, because the visual methods can collect the upper limb movement signal, while pressure cushion is only sensitive to the body hips and torso. On the other hand, camera-based recognition is inconvenient and strict in use conditions.

Comparison with Related Research

In order to verify the reliability of our method, we carried out a comparison with a literature study whose identification postures are very similar to ours, but based on computer vision.

According to ADAS system in [6], slumping over to the right (left), slumping forward with face down, and sinking down into the seat can be detected. They evaluated false detection of normal posture and mistakes in detection of abnormal posture, with "Strictness" to 40, 37, and 35. When the "Strictness = 35", the postures cannot be fully detected. Our system is able to solve this problem, besides, the postures we detected have similarities with the posture mentioned above. Slumping over to the left and leaning on the door are both torso tilted to the left. Similarly sinking down into the seat and picking up things. When the "Strictness = 35", the accuracy of similar postures are shown in Fig. 7.

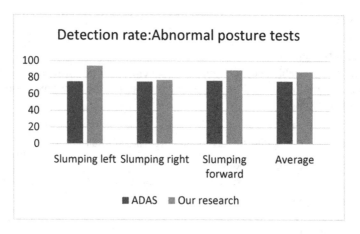

Fig. 7. Comparison results of similar posture

The ADAS system uses a visual algorithm, so it is very sensitive to the movement of the head, if the position of the head or torso is not fixed in the center of the camera, the accuracy of the to the detection cannot be ensured. As the result shows in Fig. 7, when the "Strictness = 35", the recognition accuracy is not ideal. But our research is sensitive to the movement of the torso which is closely related to the center of gravity. We can conclude that ADAS recognition accuracy is not better than what we obtained with the proposed method.

6 Conclusions

In view of the several dangerous driving behaviors in driving process, a classification algorithm and model was proposed in this paper. In this system, the recognition target is four postures, lean to the window/door, picking up things, or looking backwards, the sensor distribution deployment is designed based on the physiological characteristics of the human body. The data gathered from the sensors are preprocessed for noise reduction. Afterwards, the key features are extracted and recognition model is built. Finally, four driving postures can be distinguished, which can help redress the risky driving posture.

Driving behavior monitoring is still an open research challenge, and the use of smart cushions brings, in our vision, a new perspective to address this problem. As a smart device in car, its convenience and alarm function for drivers are meaningful in traffic safety field. Although our results are still preliminary, this intelligent, convenient, and no-invasive method can provide reference for future studies. Future research will be concentrated in enriching the types of postures and improving hardware. More experiments are needed and additional sensors could be considered to complete the identification function combined with our system.

Acknowledgements. This paper has been funded by the National Natural Science Foundation of China (No.71672137, 61571336) and China-Italy S&T Cooperation project "Smart Personal Mobility Systems for Human Disabilities in Future Smart Cities" (China-side Project ID: 2015DFG12210). This work has been also carried out under the framework of INTER-IoT, Research and Innovation action - Horizon 2020 European Project, Grant Agreement #687283, financed by the EU.

References

1. Global status report on road safety: World Health Organization. http://www.who.int/violence_injury_prevention/road_safety_status/2015/en/
2. Sun, S., Wu, Q., Chai, C., et al.: A driving posture prediction method based on driver comfort. In: International Conference on Computer-Aided Industrial Design and Conceptual Design, pp. 1–5. IEEE (2006)
3. Kim, D.Y., Bang, J.H., Lee, C.A., et al.: Numerical evaluation of time-dependent sagging for low density polyurethane foams to apply the long-term driving comfort on the seat cushion design. Int. J. Ind. Ergon. **64**, 178–187 (2017)
4. Su, C., Chu, Z.: Research on driving posture comfort based on relation between drivers' joint angles and joint torques. SAE Int. J. Commercial Veh. **7**, 45–49 (2014). (2014-01-0460)
5. Yan, C., Coenen, F., Zhang, B.: Driving posture recognition by convolutional neural networks. IET Comput. Vis. **10**(2), 103–114 (2016)
6. Yamada, T., Irie, H., Sakai, S.: High-accuracy joint position estimation and posture detection system for driving. In: Adjunct Proceedings of the 13th International Conference on Mobile and Ubiquitous Systems: Computing Networking and Services, pp. 219–224. ACM (2016)
7. Yan, S., Teng, Y., Smith, J.S., et al.: Driver behavior recognition based on deep convolutional neural networks. In: International Conference on Natural Computation, Fuzzy Systems and Knowledge Discovery, pp. 636–641. IEEE (2016)

8. Wang, Y.K., Chen, S.A., Lin, C.T.: An EEG-based brain–computer interface for dual task driving detection. Neurocomputing **129**, 85–93 (2014)

9. Ling, Z., Lu, X., Wang, Y., Zhou, Y., Wang, G., Li, J.: Local sparse representation for driver drowsiness expression recognition. In: Chinese Automation Congress (CAC) 2013, pp. 733–737 (2013)

10. Lee, B.-G., Chung, W.-Y.: Wearable glove-type driver stress detection using a motion sensor. In: IEEE Transactions on Intelligent Transportation Systems, vol. 18, pp. 1835–1844 (2017). ISSN 1524-9050

11. Huang, M., Gibson, I., Yang, R.: Smart chair for monitoring of sitting behavior. KnE Eng. **2**(2), 274–280 (2017)

12. Xu, W., Huang, M.C., Amini, N., et al.: ecushion: A textile pressure sensor array design and calibration for sitting posture analysis. IEEE Sens. J. **13**(10), 3926–3934 (2013)

13. Suzuki, S., Kudo, M., Nakamura, A.: Sitting posture diagnosis using a pressure sensor mat. In: IEEE International Conference on Identity, Security and Behavior Analysis (ISBA), 2016, pp. 1–6. IEEE (2016)

14. Ma, C., Li, W., Gravina, R., et al.: Posture detection based on smart cushion for wheelchair users. Sensors **17**(4), 719 (2017)

15. Ma, C., Li, W., Gravina, R., et al.: Activity recognition and monitoring for smart wheelchair users. In: IEEE, International Conference on Computer Supported Cooperative Work in Design, pp. 664–669. IEEE (2016)

16. Ma, C., Li, W., Cao, J., Wang, S., Wu, L.: A fatigue detect system based on activity recognition. In: Fortino, G., Di Fatta, G., Li, W., Ochoa, S., Cuzzocrea, A., Pathan, M. (eds.) IDCS 2014. LNCS, vol. 8729, pp. 303–311. Springer, Cham (2014). https://doi.org/10.1007/978-3-319-11692-1_26

17. Ma, C., Li, W., Cao, J., Gravina, R., Fortino, G.: Cloud-based wheelchair assist system for mobility impaired individuals. In: Li, W., et al. (eds.) IDCS 2016. LNCS, vol. 9864, pp. 107–118. Springer, Cham (2016). https://doi.org/10.1007/978-3-319-45940-0_10

18. Fsr406 Website. http://www.interlinkelectronics.com/force.php

19. Aissaoui, R., Kauffmann, C., Dansereau, J., et al.: Analysis of pressure distribution at the body–seat interface in able-bodied and paraplegic subjects using a deformable active contour algorithm. Med. Eng. Phys. **23**(6), 359–367 (2001)

20. Fisher, S.V., Patterson, P.: Long term pressure recordings under the ischial tuberosities of tetraplegics. Spinal Cord **21**(2), 99–106 (1983)

21. Bush, C.A.: Study of pressures on skin under ischial tuberosities and thighs during sitting. Arch. Phys. Med. Rehabil. **50**(4), 207–213 (1969)

22. Liu, C., Qiu, Y., Griffin, M.J.: Dynamic forces over the interface between a seated human body and a rigid seat during vertical whole-body vibration. J. Biomech. (2017)

23. Chen, K.H., Chiueh, T.D.: A low-power digit-based reconfigurable FIR filter. IEEE Trans. Cir. Syst. II Express Briefs **53**(8), 617–621 (2006)

24. Mohanty, B.K., Meher, P.K.: A high-performance FIR filter architecture for fixed and reconfigurable applications. IEEE Trans. Very Large Scale Integr. (VLSI) Syst. **24**(2), 444–452 (2016)

25. Estrada, J.E., Vea, L.A.: Real-time human sitting posture detection using mobile devices. In: Region 10 Symposium (TENSYMP), 2016 IEEE, pp. 140–144. IEEE (2016)

26. Heyer, P., Herrera-Vega, J., Rosado, D.-E.N.V., Enrique Sucar, L., Orihuela-Espina, F.: Posture based detection of attention in human computer interaction. In: Klette, R., Rivera, M., Satoh, S. (eds.) PSIVT 2013. LNCS, vol. 8333, pp. 220–229. Springer, Heidelberg (2014). https://doi.org/10.1007/978-3-642-53842-1_19

Robust Epidemic Aggregation Under Churn

Mosab M. Ayiad$^{(\boxtimes)}$ and Giuseppe Di Fatta

Department of Computer Science, University of Reading,
Whiteknights, Reading, Berkshire RG6 6AY, UK
m.m.ayiad@pgr.reading.ac.uk, g.difatta@reading.ac.uk

Abstract. In large-scale distributed systems data aggregation is a fundamental task that provides a global synopsis over a distributed set of data values. Epidemic protocols are based on a randomised communication paradigm inspired by biological systems and have been proposed to provide decentralised, scalable and fault-tolerant solutions to the data aggregation problem. However, in epidemic aggregation, nodes failure and churn have a detrimental effect on the accuracy of the local estimates of the global aggregation target. In this paper, a novel approach, the Robust Epidemic Aggregation Protocol (*REAP*), is proposed to provide robustness in the presence of churn by detecting three distinct phases in the aggregation process. An analysis of the impact of each phase over the estimation accuracy is provided. In particular, a novel mechanism is introduced to improve the phase that is most critical for the protocol accuracy. *REAP* is validated by means of simulations and is shown to achieve convergence with a good level of accuracy for a reasonable range of node churn rates.

Keywords: Distributed aggregation · Epidemic protocols
Gossip-based protocols · Mass recovery · Node churn

1 Introduction

In large-scale distributed systems, data aggregation is a fundamental task that is used to provide wide range of services, from the estimation of global system properties, such as resource capacity, average load and average uptime [1] to more complex network applications, such as failure detection [2], distributed data mining [3] and global attribute computation in Wireless Sensor Networks (*WSN*) [4]. Network protocols for aggregation typically compute a synopsis function such as (*sum, average, sample*, etc.) over a set of distributed data values with the purpose of providing global information about a network or a system. In large networks, centralised aggregation approaches limit the system scalability and can be subject to single points of failure and to bottlenecks [4]. Therefore, decentralised and fault-tolerance paradigms need to be utilised for an effective data aggregation solution. For instance, epidemic aggregation protocols are considered applicable and resilient to faults in large-scale distributed systems [5].

© Springer Nature Switzerland AG 2018
G. Fortino et al. (Eds.): IDCS 2017, LNCS 10794, pp. 173–185, 2018.
https://doi.org/10.1007/978-3-319-97795-9_16

Epidemic (a.k.a. Gossip-based) protocols enable scalable, fault-tolerant, and fully decentralised solutions for various distributed problems, such as information dissemination and data aggregation [6]. In epidemic data aggregation, computation and communication are uniformly distributed among nodes using a randomised communication strategy. The random pairwise communication approach provides stochastic guarantees that nodes in the system ultimately converge to a common state in logarithmic time w.r.t. the system size [1]. The convergence to a target value is expected under static network conditions. In realistic conditions e.g. existence of node churn, the accuracy of local estimation value cannot be guaranteed and the result at convergence may significantly differ from the correct target value. This limitation is a consequence of the violation of the mass conservation invariant in a distributed system [7]. The mass conservation invariant refers to the ideal aggregation of the initial states of all nodes in the system. During the aggregation process, nodes exchange their states and distribute the mass among nodes. The convergence is achieved when the mass is distributed equally over all nodes. The failure and unreported departure of nodes determine a loss of the mass stored in these nodes, hence violating the conservation invariant and may lead to an estimation error of the target result that depends on the local state at the nodes departing the system.

This paper investigates the epidemic data aggregation process and identifies three distinct phases. It is shown that node churn at each phase have different effect on the estimation error. In particular, one of the three phases is critical for producing accurate results and is further investigated, resulting in a novel mechanism to address the mass conservation invariant problem. In this paper, the Robust Epidemic Aggregation Protocol (REAP) is proposed: REAP adopts a distributed failure detection and mass restoration mechanism. At each node, REAP uses stochastic and heuristic methods to detect phases during the convergence process. The protocol implements a decentralised (PUSH-REPUSH) mechanism to detect failed and departed nodes and uses the timeout technique to trigger the mass restoration procedure. REAP is evaluated and validated by means of simulations. The experimental results show the ability of the protocol to produce a good accuracy with a moderate rate of churn. REAP achieves estimation error smaller than 1% in average at a churn rate less than or equal to 10%.

The term *churn* in this paper refers to nodes failure and unreported departure. Nodes fail and stop and do not restart. On another hand, an underlying reliable communication is assumed e.g. usage of *TCP* protocol, and hence communication failure and message loss are not examined. The churn of joining nodes is conveyed to future work due to limited space in the paper. A general approach to capture joining nodes is to implement a restart mechanism that repeats the aggregation operation with a fresh setting and encloses states of new nodes [1].

The paper is organised as follows. In Sect. 2, the analysis of the epidemic data aggregation process is explained. REAP is described in Sect. 3. Simulations and experimental results are discussed in Sect. 4. Some related work are listed in Sect. 5. Future work and conclusions are drawn in Sect. 6.

2   Epidemic Data Aggregation Process

Epidemic data aggregation is a global operation comprised of iterative distributed processes. Processes communicate in a randomised fashion and exchange their local information. Each process performs a designated algorithm (a.k.a *protocol*) on the local information to compute some global property or parameter. The output of the epidemic aggregation protocol at each node is a local estimation of the global function. Local estimations converge exponentially fast towards a target value. The distributed convergence corresponds to a reduction in the variance of the local approximation results. Eventually, all processes will converge to a target value with some tolerated error [1,6,7].

For the sake of this work, the Symmetric-Push-Sum Protocol (*SPSP*) [7] is used for the analysis of the aggregation process. *SPSP* is a proactive, decentralised and asynchronous aggregation algorithm that combines accuracy and stability of *Push-Sum* algorithms and efficiency and rapidity of *Push-Pull* algorithms. Each instance of *SPSP* periodically contacts a randomly chosen peer. For this purpose a simple Node Cache Protocol (*NCP*) [7] is used for sampling peers with an approximation of the uniform probability distribution and a k-regular random graph initialisation.

Let us consider a system of N nodes, each node i locally holds a numeric value x_i that represents a parameter or a local property in the node context. The aggregation is performed over a global set of local values, $f(x_i)$ $(0 < i \le N)$. In *SPSP*, each node i maintains an aggregation pair $\langle v_i, w_i \rangle$, where v_i is the aggregation value and w_i is the aggregation weight. The aggregation value is initialised with the local value, $v_i = x_i$, and the initialisation of the weight is determined by the required aggregation function [7]. At each time step t (*cycle*), the node i halves the values of the local pair $\langle \frac{v_{i,t}}{2}, \frac{w_{i,t}}{2} \rangle$ and sends it (PUSH) to a random peer. When node i receives a PUSH message from node j, node i halves its local value and weight, sends the pair to j (PULL) and updates the local pair $\langle v_i + v_j, w_i + w_j \rangle$. The local aggregation estimate $e_{i,t}$ at the time t is computed by $e_{i,t} = \frac{v_{i,t}}{w_{i,t}}$. After sufficient number of cycles, each aggregation pair $\langle v_i, w_i \rangle$ is evenly distributed to all nodes in the system, and thus the variation among local estimates quickly decreases and estimates converge to the target value.

Without loss of generality, in the remainder of this work the problem of estimating the system size, corresponding to the aggregation function *count*, is chosen to study the aggregation process. In distributed systems, the correct estimation of the size is an essential task since it can be used for many other purposes e.g. assessing resource availability [8], parameter setting and network monitoring [4]. The protocol in [9] requires size estimation as an input parameter to achieve consensus.

In *SPSP*, the aggregation function *count* requires a particular initial setting of the aggregation pair $\langle v_i, w_i \rangle$: the value is set to a unit count, i.e. $v_{i,t_0} = 1$ $(0 < i \le N)$, and the weight is set to $w_{\hat{i},t_0} = 1$ at a single *seed* node $\hat{i}$ whilst $w_{i,t_0} = 0$ $(0 < i \le N, i \ne \hat{i})$, where t_0 is the system starting time and the seed node $\hat{i}$ is an arbitrary node, which can be selected randomly or with a leader election method. During the aggregation process, the pairs $\langle v_i, w_i \rangle$ are periodically exchanged and mixed, distributing and equalising the values over all nodes. With a correct convergence and after some time t_c ($t_c > t_0$) the aggregation pair at each node i converges with a high probability [6] to $\langle 1, \frac{1}{N} \rangle$ and the local estimate e_i converges to a global target value n with a relative estimation error ϵ. On another hand and in a static network with ideal conditions, the total mass $\mathcal{M}$ is time invariant and is formulated as follows:

$$\mathcal{M}_v(\{v_i\}) = \sum_{i=1}^{N} v_i = N, \qquad \mathcal{M}_w(\{w_i\}) = \sum_{i=1}^{N} w_i = 1, \qquad (1)$$

and the local estimate e_i in the epidemic aggregation process converges as follows:

$$e_i \to n = \frac{\frac{\mathcal{M}_v}{N}}{\frac{\mathcal{M}_w}{N}} = \frac{\sum_{i=1}^{N} v_i}{\sum_{i=1}^{N} w_i} = N. \qquad (2)$$

As shown in the formula (2), $n = N$ when the mass conservation invariant holds and the local estimate e_i converges to the correct value N for $t \geq t_c$, also the estimation error ϵ_i converges to a very small value. However, the estimation error can be tolerated to some extent [6]. For some applications, a quick estimation might be more appropriate than a more accurate one which would take longer to compute. In the rest of the paper the symbol ε refers to the error threshold that is tolerated and determined by the application and the symbol ϵ represents the relative estimation error in local estimates during the aggregation process. The estimation error ϵ_i at each node i at any time $t \geq t_0$ is defined as:

$$\epsilon_i(t) = \frac{|e_i(t) - N|}{N}. \qquad (3)$$

A typical aggregation process in *SPSP* is shown in Fig. 1. The percentage of nodes converged to the true system size is illustrated in Fig. 1(a) for various system sizes. Figure 1(b) shows the average of local estimates in the system converging to the correct value N and Fig. 1(c) illustrates the average estimation error in ideal and dynamic network conditions.

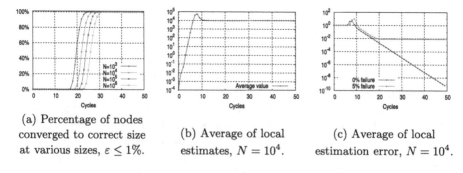

(a) Percentage of nodes converged to correct size at various sizes, $\varepsilon \leq 1\%$.

(b) Average of local estimates, $N = 10^4$.

(c) Average of local estimation error, $N = 10^4$.

Fig. 1. Size estimation in *SPSP*, $k = 30$

In dynamic networks, nodes can suddenly fail or leave the system, and hence there are two issues that need to be addressed. First, the target value (i.e. system size) is a time variant function $n(t)$. Although the protocol could be repeated periodically to follow the changes in the system size, a single global target value must be defined in each aggregation operation in order to achieve convergence. Secondly, the mass conservation invariant does not hold and node churn affect the accuracy of the estimates and may even prevent the convergence. In the next section, we show that partitioning the aggregation process at each node into phases helps to address these issues.

2.1   Phases of the Aggregation Process

Size estimation (global function *count*) is achieved with an aggregation process starting at t_0 and initiated at the seed node $\hat{\imath}$, which holds the weight $w_{\hat{\imath},t_0} = 1$. The seed node initiates an exponential diffusion process of the non-null weight. The computation at a generic node with the weight $w_{i,t_0} = 0$ are ineffective to the aggregation process until the node joins the diffusion propagation of the non-null weight $(w_i > 0)$ either by a PUSH or a PULL message. The convergence is achieved at time t_c when each node i holds a similar fraction of the initial weight $w_{i,t_c} = \frac{w_{i,t_0}}{N} = \frac{1}{N}$. At a time $t \geq t_c$, although the exchange of the aggregation pair among nodes and the computation in each node continue, the local estimate at every node holds to same approximation result. This is the consequence of the equal distribution of the system mass among nodes. In general, during the aggregation process a node i can be in one of the following three phases:

1. INITIAL, if $w_i = 0$,
2. PROPAGATION, if $w_i > 0$ and local convergence is not yet achieved, and
3. CONVERGENCE, if local convergence is detected.

To analyse the impact of node churn on the accuracy of local estimates during each phase, let us consider that node i is in the INITIAL phase. At each time $t > t_0$, the local estimate e_i is not available due to the null weight value. Message exchanges with other nodes in the same phase do not contribute nor modify the estimate values, either local or remote. A message exchange with a node in the PROPAGATION phase determines a local phase transition. Although, the failure of a node i in the INITIAL phase does alter the system mass $\mathcal{M}_v$, it has no impact over the convergence process and over the accuracy of the approximation results because the more critical system mass $\mathcal{M}_w$ is preserved. As a consequence, the unexpected departure of a node i in the INITIAL phase only effects the target value $n(t)$ from N to $N-1$, as if the node i was never part of the system. There is no need to address churn in the INITIAL phase, apart from redefining the target value: the target value we then refer to is the number of nodes which have entered the PROPAGATION phase $N_p(t) = N - f_{init}(t)$ where f_{init} is number of nodes in the INITIAL phase which have departed the system.

Likewise, churn in the CONVERGENCE phase have no impact on the accuracy of the estimations w.r.t. the redefined target value. This is due to the equal distribution of the initial mass $\mathcal{M}_v$ and $\mathcal{M}_w$ among existing nodes. The exchange of aggregation pair and the computation of the local estimate at each node in the CONVERGENCE phase always gives the approximation result which the system has converged to. This can be proven as follows, where for simplicity we assume ideal network conditions and that all nodes have entered the PROPAGATION phase ($N_p = N$). Considering the formula (2), the target value is $N = \frac{\sum_{i=1}^{N} v_{i,t_0}}{\sum_{i=1}^{N} w_{i,t_0}}$, and hence,

$$\sum_{i=1}^{N} v_{i,t_0} = N \sum_{i=1}^{N} w_{i,t_0}, \tag{4}$$

and the local estimate of each node i in the CONVERGENCE phase is a good approximation of the target value: $e_{i,t} = N \implies N = \frac{v_{i,t}}{w_{i,t}}$, hence the following relation holds:

$$v_{i,t} = N w_{i,t}. \tag{5}$$

Assume a node j in the CONVERGENCE phase has failed, the system mass is deprived of the pair $\langle v_j, w_j \rangle$. In this case, the target can be calculated as $n(t) = \frac{\sum_i v_{i,t_0} - v_{j,t}}{\sum_i w_{i,t_0} - w_{j,t}}$, and by using the formulas (4) and (5) we have:

$$n(t) = \frac{\sum_{i=1}^{N} v_{i,t_0} - v_{j,t}}{\sum_{i=1}^{N} w_{i,t_0} - w_{j,t}} = \frac{N \sum_{i=1}^{N} w_{i,t_0} - N w_{j,t}}{\sum_{i=1}^{N} w_{i,t_0} - w_{j,t}} = N. \tag{6}$$

This analysis shows that if a node departs the system after it has converged, the global target of the aggregation process does not change and the aggregation process remains stable. Any node still in the system maintains an asymptotic convergence to the same target value, which corresponds to the number of nodes which have entered the PROPAGATION phase (N_p). As a consequence, there is no need to address churn in the CONVERGENCE phase.

It is now clear that the PROPAGATION phase is the critical phase w.r.t. the convergence and the accuracy of the aggregation process. Unexpected departure of nodes in the PROPAGATION phase need to be addressed explicitly. Any node i in the PROPAGATION phase has weight $w_i > 0$ that is a portion of the total weight mass $\mathcal{M}_w$. Also, $w_i \neq \frac{\mathcal{M}_w}{N_p}$ as node i has not yet reached convergence. Nodes in this phase hold critical information needed for a correct convergence to the target value. At t_0, the seed node $\hat{i}$ is the first node in the PROPAGATION phase and the most critical node. For $t > t_0$ other nodes transit from the INITIAL phase to the PROPAGATION phase in the exponential diffusion process. Although the probability of losing weight mass is very small at t_0, it exponentially increases with the diffusion process. At the same time the portion of the weight mass held at nodes in the PROPAGATION phase decreases over time. Thus, the impact of losing some portions of the weight mass on the approximation results also decreases.

The loss of mass due to node churn causes an estimation error in the approximation results during the aggregation process as shown in the analysis. In order to provide robustness to the accuracy of the convergence in the presence of churn, the local state $\langle v, w \rangle$ needs to be protected while the node is in the PROPAGATION phase. One way to achieve that is by means of a failure detection to enable mass restoration from its local state. The next section describes the protocol *REAP* that adopts a specific mechanism to achieve this goal.

3 The Robust Epidemic Aggregation Protocol (REAP)

REAP adopts non-blocking and asynchronous communication scheme. The protocol implements a symmetric PUSH-PULL strategy similar to *SPSP* [7] and utilises a (PUSH-REPUSH) model that is exclusively used for the churn detection during the PROPAGATION phase. The protocol detects PUSH messages from nodes in the PROPAGATION phase and maintains temporary replicas of the aggregation pair $\langle v, w \rangle$ in these messages. *REAP* uses the temporary replicas in the mass restoration procedure that is triggered when a given timeout value is expired and a failed or departed node is detected. The protocol is illustrated in Algorithm 1

The detection of the PROPAGATION phase in *REAP* is performed as follows. A node i enters the PROPAGATION phase when receives a non-null weight ($w > 0$) and exits the phase when node i detects the convergence locally. The local detection of convergence is accomplished using a heuristic method [10] based on the computation of the moving average. Each node i in *REAP* maintains a fixed length queue $\mathcal{Q}$ to store the local estimate e_i and received estimate e_j from node j. Then after, node i computes the *Coefficient of Variance*, $\widehat{C_v} = \frac{s}{\bar{x}}$ for current elements in $\mathcal{Q}$ where s is the standard deviation and $\bar{x}$ is the arithmetic mean. The convergence is detected at node i when $\widehat{C_v}$ falls below a given error threshold ε for a number of consecutive cycles Υ. The error threshold ε controls the desired level of approximation accuracy and Υ is used to prevent precociously convergence detection during the convergence process.

In the PROPAGATION phase, each node i contacts a random node j twice: one time to perform a PUSH and a second time to perform a REPUSH. The two contact operations occur at two consecutive cycles, e.g. a node i sends the PUSH message to node j at time t and sends the REPUSH message at time $t + 1$. The PUSH and REPUSH messages carry the same information and hence *REAP* distinguishes the type of message by the order of reception. This manner enables the protocol to cope with asynchronous communication in which messages encounter different delays and a REPUSH message may be delivered before the corresponding PUSH message. Typically, the REPUSH message is used by the receiver node to detects the liveness of the sender node. A node i detects the failure or departure of node j when the REPUSH message from node j is not received within a predefined period $\mathcal{T}$ where $\mathcal{T}$ is the maximum timeout value.

REAP maintains a buffer of PUSH entries $\mathcal{P}$ to manage the PUSH-REPUSH operations. Each cycle the protocol inserts an entry $\mathbf{a}_p$ for the fresh PUSH information in $\mathcal{P}$. Each entry $\mathbf{a}_p$ holds the random peer's Id β, the contact time t, and the local values of the aggregation pair ($\mathbf{a}_p = \langle \beta, t, v, w \rangle$). In the subsequent

Algorithm 1. Robust Epidemic Aggregation Protocol

---

1 **Require:** $\mathcal{T}$, *maximum timeout value;* ε, *error threshold;* Υ, *cycles threshold;*

2 **Initialisation:** *each node i has:*
$v = 1$, $w = 0$, *except one seed node has* $w = 1$; *critical* PUSH *flag* $\rho = false$;
convergence flag $\hat{\rho} = false$;
a buffer for PUSH *entries* $\mathcal{P} = \{\mathbf{a}_p = \langle \beta, t, v, w \rangle, ...\}$, *where β is peer's id, t is current time, and v,w are aggregation pair;*
a recovery cache $\mathcal{R} = \{\mathbf{a}_r = \langle \alpha, \tau, v, w \rangle, ...\}$, *where α is sender id, τ is* REPUSH *receiving timeout, and v,w are replica pair;*
and has a fixed length queue $\mathcal{Q} = \{\}$;

---

3 **At each cycle c at node i:**

4 $\rho \longleftarrow w > 0$ **and** $\neg\hat{\rho}$ // Detect PROPAGATION phase

5 $j \longleftarrow getRandomPeer()$ // Perform PUSH

6 $v = \frac{v}{2}$; $w = \frac{w}{2}$

7 $send(j, v, w, \rho, reply = true)$

8 **if** ρ **then** $\mathcal{P} \longleftarrow \mathcal{P} \cup \{j, c, v, w\}$ // Insert critical PUSH in $\mathcal{P}$

9 **foreach** $\mathbf{a}_p \in \mathcal{P}$ **do**   // Perform REPUSH

10   **if** $\mathbf{a}_p.t < c$ **then**

11        $send(\mathbf{a}_p.\beta, \mathbf{a}_p.v, \mathbf{a}_p.w, \rho = true, reply = true)$

12        $\mathcal{P} \longleftarrow \mathcal{P} - \{\mathbf{a}_p\}$

---

13 **foreach** $\mathbf{a}_r \in \mathcal{R}$ **do**   // Perform churn detection and mass restoration

14     $\mathbf{a}_r.\tau \longleftarrow \mathbf{a}_r.\tau - 1$

15   **if** $\mathbf{a}_r.\tau == 0$ **then**   // Timeout value expired, restore mass

16        $v = v + \mathbf{a}_r.v$; $w = w + \mathbf{a}_r.w$

17        $\mathcal{R} \longleftarrow \mathcal{R} - \{\mathbf{a}_r\}$

---

18 **At event 'receive message m from j' at node i:**

19 **if** $m.reply$ **then**   // Distinguish a PUSH

20   **if** $\exists\mathbf{a}_r \in \mathcal{R}$ where $\mathbf{a}_r.\alpha == j$ **then**   // Distinguish a REPUSH

21        $\mathcal{R} \longleftarrow \mathcal{R} - \{\mathbf{a}_r\}$

22   go to line 18

23   **else**

24        $v = \frac{v}{2}$; $w = \frac{w}{2}$ // Perfrom PULL

25        $send(j, v, w, \rho = false, reply = false)$

26 $\mathcal{Q}.enqueue(\frac{v}{w}, \frac{m.v}{m.w})$ // Enqueue estimates

27 $v = v + m.v$; $w = w + m.w$ // Update aggregation pair

28 **if** $m.\rho$ **then** $\mathcal{R} \longleftarrow \mathcal{R} \cup \{\mathbf{a}_r = \langle j, \mathcal{T}, v, w \rangle\}$ // Replicate a critical pair

29 $\hat{\rho} \longleftarrow \widehat{C_v}(\mathcal{Q}) \leq \varepsilon$ for Υ cycles   // Detect convergence

---

cycle, the protocol performs a REPUSH operation using the information in the previous PUSH entry $\mathbf{a}_p$. After the REPUSH operation, the entry $\mathbf{a}_p$ is removed from $\mathcal{P}$ keeping the buffer size minimum.

Nodes in the PROPAGATION phase assign a flag to each PUSH message indicating that the message has a critical information for the aggregation process. On the reception of a critical PUSH message, the receiver node i updates local aggregation pair and then replicates the local pair and stores the replica in a local cache $\mathcal{R}$ using the entry $(\mathbf{a}_r = \langle \alpha, \tau, v, w \rangle)$ where α is sender's Id, τ is REPUSH receiving timeout and v, w are the replica's pair. In the subsequent cycle, node i receives a REPUSH message and deletes the corresponding entry in $\mathcal{R}$. In case the REPUSH message is not received within $\mathcal{T}$ cycles, the protocol assumes that the corresponding node has failed and the replicated pair in the entry $\mathbf{a}_r$ is used in the mass restoration process. The restored mass corrects the local aggregation pair values. The correction amount is then distributed among nodes through regular contact operations. The distribution of the restored mass produces a very small delay in the convergence speed but leads the convergence process to a lower estimation error of the target value.

As shown in Algorithm 1, at each cycle, the protocol detects the PROPAGATION phase and sets the PUSH flag in line 4. In lines 5–7 the protocol performs a PUSH operation. The protocol inserts fresh PUSH entry in $\mathcal{P}$ in line 8 and performs the REPUSH operation in lines 9–12. The detection of churn and the mass restoration procedure are performed in lines 13–17. The protocol distinguishes the PUSH and REPUSH messages in line 19 and line 20. The PULL message is formulated in lines 24 and 25. The protocol inserts local and received estimates in the queue $\mathcal{Q}$ in line 26. A critical aggregation pair is replicated and an entry $\mathbf{a}_r$ is stored in $\mathcal{R}$ cache in line 28. The local convergence is detected in line 29.

4   Simulations and Experimental Results

The protocol *REAP* is simulated using PEERSIM [11], a Java-based discrete-event P2P simulation tool. PEERSIM is flexible, configurable and scalable. The simulation model is fully Event-based and uses the event-driven engine in PEERSIM. Two events are used in the simulation: (i) The RUN EVENT is scheduled to trigger at every cycle and stops after a predefined number of cycles. At this event, a node performs contact operations, detects churn and performs the mass restoration. (ii) The MESSAGE RECEIVE EVENT occurs when a node receives a message. At this event, the incoming message is processed, the local aggregation pair is updated and the detection of convergence is performed.

Two protocols are examined in the simulations: *SPSP* and *REAP*. The performance and the accuracy of the protocols are monitored and recorded at each cycle using a dedicated external observer. The communication latency is adjusted for all messages to be delivered in the same global cycle. This adjustment is necessary to avoid transition of portions of the total mass $\mathcal{M}$ across cycles during the simulations. The adjustment is applied only for the sake of the simulations and can be relaxed in a realistic context. In each simulation run, a different random seed is applied to enforce randomisation and each experiment is repeated for tens of times to validate the setting and the results. The protocols are initialised by a peak data distribution whereas $v_i = 1$, $0 < i \leq N$; $w_0 = 1$ at seed node 0 and $w_i = 0$, $1 < i \leq N$. Protocols' parameters are carefully adjusted to certain values to meet practical applications requirements [9]: the timeout value is set to $\mathcal{T} = 3$ cycles, the tolerated error threshold is set to $\varepsilon = 1\%$, the minimum number of consecutive cycles is set to $\Upsilon = 5$ cycles, the length of the $\mathcal{Q}$ is set to 10 elements. On another hand, the protocol NCP is used as a peer sampling service and is configured to maintain a random k-regular overlay with $k = 30$.

The performance of $REAP$ is examined in a static network conditions. The Fig. 2(a) shows the smooth transition of nodes among phases and the correct computation of the entry and exit points of the PROPAGATION phase. In Fig. 2(b) the local estimate value of a randomly chosen node is illustrated for $SPSP$ and $REAP$ showing the performance similarity when no churn is encountered. The Fig. 2(c) shows the communication overhead of both protocols whereas $REAP$ produces only one extra message for a temporary period during the PROPAGATION phase.

To evaluate the protocol $REAP$, we examined the protocol against $SPSP$ at different churn rates: $\{0\%, 1\%, 5\%, 10\%, 20\%\}$. A number of random nodes are selected at each cycle from cycles $[0, 30[$ and removed from the system by an external actor during the aggregation process. In each case, the number of failing nodes is increased and distributed over the 30 cycles to ensure random selection of nodes from each phase of the aggregation process. The simulation experiment of each case is repeated for ten times and aggregation pair in each alive node is observed. During the simulations, the local estimation error is computed at each cycle by the external observer as $\epsilon_i = \frac{|e_i - N_p|}{N_p}$. The experiments results are averaged and overall results are illustrated in Figs. 3 and 4.

The Fig. 3 shows the total mass $\mathcal{M}_v$ and $\mathcal{M}_w$ during the aggregation process. Trends of lines in the figure show the correction in mass magnitude as a result of the mass restoration mechanism in $REAP$. The figure also shows that amount of correction in the comparison to $SPSP$. The improvement of accuracy in $REAP$ is shown in the Fig. 4. The figure illustrates the trend of estimation error in each case of the simulated churn. In the first case no churn is encountered and estimation error tends to a very small value indicating the correct convergence to the target value. In the rates less than 10%, the estimation error rises to

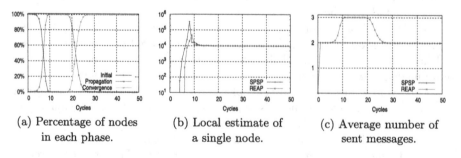

(a) Percentage of nodes in each phase.   (b) Local estimate of a single node.   (c) Average number of sent messages.

Fig. 2. Size estimation in $REAP$, $N = 10^4$, $\varepsilon = 1\%$, $\Upsilon = 5$, $k = 30$

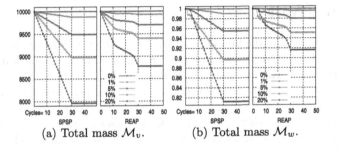

(a) Total mass $\mathcal{M}_v$.   (b) Total mass $\mathcal{M}_w$.

Fig. 3. Size estimation at various churn rates, $N = 10^4$, $\varepsilon = 1\%$, $\Upsilon = 5$, $k = 30$

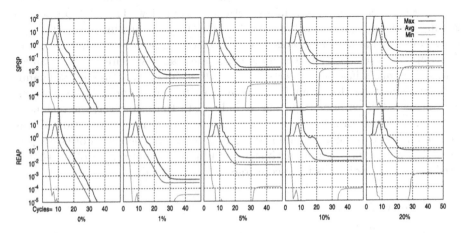

Fig. 4. Estimations error (ϵ) at various churn rates, $N = 10^4$, $\varepsilon = 1\%$, $\Upsilon = 5$, $k = 30$

1%, whilst the error exceeds 1% for higher rates. Generally, estimation error in *REAP* is lower than the error in *SPSP*. In the presence of churn, local estimates in *SPSP* converge to approximation result different from the target value as shown in Figs. 3 and 4.

The deficiency in the accuracy in *REAP* at higher rates of churn ($\geq 20\%$) is due to the increase in the *cascaded failure* event. Let us consider two nodes i and j, node i sends a PUSH message to node j and then fails. The node j requires Υ cycles before detecting the failure of node i. During this period node j fails too. In this case, the system mass deprives of aggregation pairs in node j and node i. Despite this limitation which can be a potential future research, the protocol *REAP* has enabled robust epidemic data aggregation for applications which can tolerate 1% of estimation error.

5   Related Work

The work in [10] proposed a number of heuristic methods to locally detect convergence in epidemic protocols, e.g. the calculation of standard deviation and root mean squared error over a number of buffered estimates are used as a criterion in the detection formulas. The work in [12] proposes a pessimistic approach and introduces a recovery mechanism which conserves the system mass in the presence of asynchrony and churn. This approach applies asynchrony to the work of [1] enabling loosely synchronised rounds. However, the round length is set long enough for messages to be delivered within the same round, i.e. out-of-round messages are ignored. The protocol computes some recovery shares in order to resolve the interference caused by asynchrony or churn. Authors in [13] studied the *Push-Pull* protocols from a practical point of view. The work proposes a gossip-based multi-pair asynchronous *Push-Pull* protocol and introduces the pair mass conservation as a mechanism to protect the mass conservation invariant. A gossip-based aggregation technique is proposed and evaluated in [14] namely *Flow Updating*. It has shown that *Flow Updating* can operate on faulty dynamic networks and that the technique is adaptable to churn, input value changes, and message loss without requiring periodic restarting. However, the technique is based on symmetric values exchange and hence a strong correlation among neighbour nodes is a core requirement. Also, the correct detection of nodes failure takes a certain amount of time in addition to a noticeable delay that is needed for local estimates to re-converge to a correct value.

6   Conclusions

In epidemic data aggregation, nodes failure and churn negatively affect the accuracy of the approximation results. In this paper, the aggregation process is analysed and three different phases are identified. The occurrence of node churn during each phase has a different impact on the accuracy of the approximation results. The second phase, namely the PROPAGATION phase, is identified as the most critical phase for the aggregation accuracy. The paper introduces a novel Robust Epidemic Aggregation Protocol (*REAP*) with an innovative PUSH-REPUSH communication technique to detect churn and restore the lost mass particularly for nodes in the PROPAGATION phase. *REAP* is validated by means of simulations and the experimental results have shown the ability of the protocol to attain robustness of the accuracy in the presence of churn. The average estimation error in *REAP* is less than 1% at churn rate up to 10%. This error falls within the tolerated threshold in epidemic applications. The future work includes studying the cascaded failure problem in *REAP* and may also address the aggregation process in a fully asynchronous system and lossy network scenarios.

Acknowledgements. The author Mosab M. Ayiad is supported for his PhD project by the Islamic Development Bank-Merit Scholarship Programme for High Technology (*MSP*), 2015-(600029531).

References

1. Jelasity, M., Montresor, A., Babaoglu, O.: Gossip-based aggregation in large dynamic networks. ACM Trans. Comput. Syst. **23**(3), 219–252 (2005). https://doi.org/10.1145/1082469.1082470
2. Katti, A., Fatta, G.D., Naughton, T., Engelmann, C.: Epidemic failure detection and consensus for extreme parallelism. Int. J. High Perform. Comput. Appl., 1094342017690910 (2017). https://doi.org/10.1177/1094342017690910
3. Fatta, G.D., Blasa, F., Cafiero, S., Fortino, G.: Fault tolerant decentralised K-Means clustering for asynchronous large-scale networks. J. Parallel Distrib. Comput. **73**, 317–329 (2012). https://doi.org/10.1016/j.jpdc.2012.09.009
4. Chitnis, L., Dobra, A., Ranka, S.: Aggregation methods for large-scale sensor networks. Trans. Sens. Netw. **4**(2), 9:1–9:36 (2008). https://doi.org/10.1145/1340771.1340775
5. Makhloufi, R., Bonnet, G., Doyen, G., Gaïti, D.: Decentralized aggregation protocols in peer-to-peer networks: a survey. In: Strassner, J.C., Ghamri-Doudane, Y.M. (eds.) MACE 2009. LNCS, vol. 5844, pp. 111–116. Springer, Heidelberg (2009). https://doi.org/10.1007/978-3-642-05006-0_10
6. Kempe, D., Dobra, A., Gehrke, J.: Gossip-based computation of aggregate information. In: 44th Annual IEEE Symposium on Foundations of Computer Science, Proceedings, pp. 482–491. IEEE (2003). https://doi.org/10.1109/SFCS.2003.1238221
7. Blasa, F., Cafiero, S., Fortino, G., Fatta, G.D.: Symmetric push-sum protocol for decentralised aggregation. In: Proceedings of International Conference on Advances in P2P Systems, pp. 27–32. IARIA (2011)
8. Kostoulas, D., Psaltoulis, D., Gupta, I., Birman, K., Demers, A.: Decentralized schemes for size estimation in large and dynamic groups. In: Fourth IEEE International Symposium on Network Computing and Applications, pp. 41–48. IEEE (2005). https://doi.org/10.1109/NCA.2005.15
9. Ayiad, M., Katti, A., Di Fatta, G.: Agreement in epidemic information dissemination. In: Li, W., et al. (eds.) IDCS 2016. LNCS, vol. 9864, pp. 95–106. Springer, Cham (2016). https://doi.org/10.1007/978-3-319-45940-0_9
10. Poonpakdee, P., Orhon, N.G., Di Fatta, G.: Convergence detection in epidemic aggregation. In: an Mey, D., et al. (eds.) Euro-Par 2013. LNCS, vol. 8374, pp. 292–300. Springer, Heidelberg (2014). https://doi.org/10.1007/978-3-642-54420-0_29
11. Montresor, A., Jelasity, M.: PeerSim: a scalable P2P simulator. In: Peer-to-Peer Computing, pp. 99–100. IEEE (2009). https://doi.org/10.1109/P2P.2009.5284506
12. Rao, I., Harwood, A., Karunasekera, S.: Gossip-based asynchronous and robust aggregation protocol - a pessimistic approach. In: Consumer Communications and Networking Conference, pp. 543–548. IEEE (2011). https://doi.org/10.1109/CCNC.2011.5766539
13. Roh, H.-G., Ignat, C.L.: Rapid and Round-free Multi-pair Asynchronous Push-Pull Aggregation. Technical report, INRIA (2012). https://hal.inria.fr/hal-00724232
14. Jesus, P., Baquero, C., Almeida, P.S.: Flow updating: fault-tolerant aggregation for dynamic networks. J. Parallel Distrib. Comput. **78**, 53–64 (2015). https://doi.org/10.1016/j.jpdc.2015.02.003

Author Index

Printed in the United States
By Bookmasters